Bürgergesellschaft und Demokratie

Herausgegeben von
A. Klein, Berlin, Germany
R. Kleinfeld, Osnabrück, Germany
H. Krimmer, Berlin, Germany
B. Rehder, Bochum, Germany
S. Teune, Berlin, Germany
H. Walk, Berlin, Germany
A. Zimmer, Münster, Germany

Die Buchreihe vereinigt qualitativ hochwertige Bände im Bereich der Forschung über Partizipation und Beteiligung sowie bürgerschaftliches Engagement. Ein besonderer Akzent gilt der politischen Soziologie des breiten zivilgesellschaftlichen Akteursspektrums (soziale Bewegungen, Bürgerinitiativen, Vereine, Verbände, Stiftungen, Genossenschaften, Netzwerke etc.). Die Buchreihe versteht sich als Publikationsort einer inter- und transdisziplinären Zivilgesellschaftsforschung.

Bürgergesellschaft und Demokratie schließt an die Buchreihe „Bürgerschaftliches Engagement und Non-Profit-Sektor" an. Sie wird unterstützt von Aktive Bürgerschaft e.V. (Berlin).

More information about this series at http://www.springer.com/series/12296

Ina Peters

Cohesion and Fragmentation in Social Movements

How Frames and Identities Shape the Belo Monte Conflict

Springer VS

Ina Peters
Hannover, Germany

Dissertation Universität Hamburg, 2016

Bürgergesellschaft und Demokratie
ISBN 978-3-658-19325-6 ISBN 978-3-658-19326-3 (eBook)
DOI 10.1007/978-3-658-19326-3

Library of Congress Control Number: 2017951202

Springer VS

Printed on acid-free paper

This Springer VS imprint is published by Springer Nature
The registered company is Springer Fachmedien Wiesbaden GmbH
The registered company address is: Abraham-Lincoln-Str. 46, 65189 Wiesbaden, Germany

Aos povos do Xingu

e a sua luta pela diversidade

Acknowledgments

This study would not have been possible without the material and moral support of a number of people and institutions. I am grateful to the GIGA German Institute of Global and Area Studies and the University of Hamburg for financial and institutional support. Special thanks go to Detlef Nolte and Kai-Uwe Schnapp as well as Stephanie Garling, Anja Jetschke, Robert Kappel, Dirk Nabers, Miriam Prys-Hansen, and Leslie Wehner.

I am sincerely grateful to my interview partners – scholars, professionals, and activists – who shared their stories and ideas with me. I have been asked to communicate my interviewees' gratitude for the kind and generous support granted by international nongovernmental organizations to civil society and church organizations in Altamira and Belém, and I am happy to do so.

My field research in Brazil was a wonderful experience that was facilitated by a number of people. I wish to thank Ricardo Filho and Mariana Carpes for helping me master the Portuguese language; Janet Chernela, Kathryn Hochstetler, Margaret Keck, and Lesley McAllister for valuable contacts and advice regarding field research; as well as Linde Nobre and Henyo Trindade Barretto Filho for background information and practical support in the field. Special thanks go to the Prelature of Xingu and to Padre Michael Rohde for hosting me during my fieldwork and for sharing their knowledge and experiences.

Throughout this study I have been lucky to rely on a wonderful team of colleagues and friends who have supported me with their professional advice and their friendship. I am grateful to Katrin Behrendt, Olaf Bock, Sara Braun, Alexandr Burilkov, Sonja Clasing, Riccarda Flemmer, Maren Koß, Judith Kreddig, Kamil Marcinkiewicz, Steffen Mohrenberg, Melanie Müller, Babette Never, Adrian Schaefer-Rolffs, Roland Willner, Stefanie Wodrig, and Dagmar Zanker.

Last but not least, I wish to thank my parents, my partner, my brother, and sister in law for their love, support, and encouragement.

Table of Content

List of Figures

List of Abbreviations

BNDES	Banco Nacional de Desenvolvimento Econômico e Social National Bank for Economic and Social Development
CCBM	Consórcio Construtor Belo Monte Belo Monte Construction Consortium
CEBs	Comunidades Eclesiais de Base Christian Base Communities
CEDI	Centro Ecumênico de Documentação e Informação Ecumenical Center of Documentation and Information
CGDEX	Comitê Gestor do Plano de Desenvolvimento Regional Sustentável do Xingu Management Committee of the Xingu Regional Sustainable Development Plan
CIMI	Conselho Indigenista Missionário Indigenous Missionary Council
CJP	Comissão Justiça e Paz Justice and Peace Commission
CNBB	Conferência Nacional dos Bispos do Brasil National Conference of Brazilian Bishops
CONAMA	Conselho Nacional do Meio Ambiente National Environmental Council
CPP	Conselho Pastoral dos Pescadores Pastoral Commission on Fishing
C.PP.S.	Congregatio Pretiosissimi Sanguinis Congregation of the Missionaries of the Most Precious Blood of Our Lord Jesus Christ
CPT	Comissão Pastoral da Terra Pastoral Land Commission

CSO	Civil Society Organization
DNAEE	Departamento Nacional de Águas e Energia Elétrica National Department of Water and Electrical Energy
EIA	Estudo de Impacto Ambiental Environmental Impact Assessment
EPE	Empresa de Pesquisa Energética Energy Research Company
FETAGRI	Federação dos Trabalhadores na Agricultura Federation of Agricultural Workers
FUNAI	Fundação Nacional do Índio National Indian Foundation
FVPP	Fundação Viver Produzir e Preservar Live, Produce, Preserve Foundation
GTM	Grounded Theory Methodology
IACHR	Inter-American Commission on Human Rights
IAMAS	Instituto Amazônia Solidária e Sustentável Solidarity-Based and Sustainable Amazon Institute
IBAMA	Instituto Brasileiro do Meio Ambiente e dos Recursos Naturais Renováveis Brazilian Institute of Environment and Renewable Natural Resources
IBGE	Instituto Brasileiro de Geografia e Estatística Brazilian Institute of Geography and Statistics
ILO	International Labour Organization
INPA	Instituto Nacional de Pesquisas da Amazônia National Institute for Research in the Amazon
IPAM	Instituto de Pesquisa Ambiental da Amazônia Amazon Environmental Research Institute
ISA	Instituto Socioambiental Socio-Environmental Institute

ISI	Import-substitution industrialization
MAB	Movimento dos Antingidos por Barragens Movement of Dam Affected People
MCT	Ministério da Ciência e Tecnologia Brazilian Ministry of Science and Technology
MDTX	Movimento pelo Desenvolvimento da Transamazônica e Xingu Movement for the Development at the Trans-Amazon Highway and Xingu
Metropolitan Committee	Comitê Metropolitano Xingu Vivo Para Sempre Metropolitan Committee Xingu Forever Alive
MJ	Ministério da Justiça Ministry of Justice
MPF	Ministério Público Federal Federal Public Ministry
MPST	Movimento para Sobrevivência na Transamazônica Movement for Survival on the Trans-Amazon Highway
MW	Megawatt
MXVPS	Movimento Xingu Vivo Para Sempre Xingu Forever Alive Movement
NDI	Núcleo de Direitos Indígenas Nucleus of Indigenous Rights
NGO	Nongovernmental Organization
PAC	Programa de Aceleração do Crescimento Growth Acceleration Program
PBA	Plano Básico Ambiental Basic Environmental Plan
PCTs	Povos e Comunidades Tradicionais Traditional Peoples and Communities
PDRS Xingu	Plano de Desenvolvimento Regional Sustentável do Xingu Xingu Regional Sustainable Development Plan

PIN	Plano de Integração Nacional National Integration Plan
PSB	Partido Socialista Brasileiro Brazilian Socialist Party
PT	Partido dos Trabalhadores Workers' Party
PV	Partido Verde Green Party
RIMA	Relatório de Impacto Ambiental Environmental Impact Report
SECTAM	Secretaria Executiva de Ciência, Tecnologia, e Meio Ambiente Executive Secretariat for Science, Technology, and the Environment
SEMA	Secretaria de Estado de Meio Ambiente State Secretariat of the Environment
SESAI	Special Secretariat for Indigenous Health Care Secretaria Especial de Saúde Indígena
SIASI	Sistema de Informação da Atenção à Saúde Indígena Health Information System for Indigenous Peoples
SMO	Social Movement Organization
SDDH	Sociedade Paraense de Defesa dos Direitos Humanos Pará Society for the Defense of Human Rights
TWh	Terawatt hour

1 Introduction

In February 2017 – only nine months after Brazil's then President Dilma Rousseff had inaugurated the infrastructure project – the Belo Monte Hydroelectric Power Plant at the Xingu River was put up for sale. The companies Neoenergia, Cemig, Light, Vale, Sinobras and J. Malucelli as well as the pension funds Petros and Funcef, which held 50.02% of the operating consortium Norte Energia S.A., instructed the investment bank of Bradesco to find potential investors for the still unfinished plant. After excessive cost increases, a series of disruptions, and allegations of involvement in the Lava Jatos corruption scandal, the companies concluded that the project was unprofitable (Portal Brasil 2016; Ordoñez and Fariello 2017; Scaramuzzo and Pereira 2017).

Activists and scholars have questioned the viability of a hydropower plant at the Xingu River ever since the Brazilian military regime presented its plans for the original project, called Kararaô Dam, in the 1970s. Back then, civil society organizations (CSO), indigenous communities, national and international nongovernmental organizations (NGO), and a large number of individuals established a social movement that was able to prevent the project in 1989.[1] However, the plan was revived and modified at the turn of the millennium and became one of the most controversial endeavors in Brazil's Growth Acceleration Program (Programa de Aceleração do Crescimento, PAC). The current project, called Belo Monte Dam, is located in the so-called Volta Grande (big bend) of the Xingu River near the city of Altamira and will be the third-largest hydropower plant in the world.[2] According to its supporters, the plant will fuel the country's electricity-intensive industrial sector, thus fostering Brazil's economic development. However, critics claim that the plant will impose substantial environmental, economic, and social costs on its surrounding area and the local population. As the caveats remain and the protest continues, the implementation of the project has raised questions about the domestic social, cultural, and environmental aspects of Brazil's emergence as a global power. Indeed, the country has shown

---

1 I use this term civil society organization to refer to the entire spectrum of nongovernmental, nonprofit voluntary organizations, including but not limited to social movements.

2 Throughout this study, Belo Monte Dam refers to the entire infrastructure project. However, it should be noted that there is a technical difference between a dam (a barrier to control the flow of water) and a hydroelectric power plant (an electric power generating station).

sustained economic growth and political development, and it has gained significant influence in the international political and economic arena; however, the fight against poverty and inequality as well as the struggle for a higher standard of living continue. Democratic principles have been implemented to a large extent, but they do not function completely in all areas of the vast Brazilian territory (De la Fontaine and Stehnken 2012a: 13–16).

What does the ongoing collective action against the Belo Monte Dam tell us about Brazil's development path? What can we learn from this case about the mobilization of social movements in rural areas and with respect to socio-environmental questions?[3] This study shows that the dispute over the advantages and disadvantages of the Belo Monte Dam is based on a deep disagreement over the underlying meaning of a hydropower project, and an array of social, political, economic, and environmental issues associated with its realization.

1.1 Research Question, Research Gap, and Aim of the Study

The collective action against the Belo Monte Dam is a fascinating empirical phenomenon because it has carried out a persistent and influential fight against a mega infrastructure project that is heavily promoted by the government and the construction industry. Although the Belo Monte project could not be prevented, movement participants have claimed success as they have hampered the construction works, demanded government reactions, contributed to a debate about development and the socioeconomic model in general, and generated international awareness. This success is by no means to be expected due to context conditions that are adverse to the mobilization and maintenance of collective action. First, the social and cultural heterogeneity of the local population is likely to result in different identities, cultures, interests, knowledge, and behavior, and may thus challenge the mobilization and cohesion of a social movement. Second, difficult socioeconomic conditions in the region, including geographical dispersion, and the remoteness and vastness of Amazonia hamper mobilization and collective action. And third, "asymmetrical and patrimonial power relations" as well as repression on the part of the project's proponents

3 Throughout this study, I use the term collective action in a broad sense to refer to any kind of joint activity performed by at least two individuals who pursue a common objective in the realm of contentious politics. The term social movement is used to refer to a specific form of collective action that is more organized and lasting, as defined in Chapter 2.

discourage the local population from raising their voice (Coy and Klingler 2011: 124).[4]

Against this background, how is it possible that the project's opponents have mobilized and sustained collective action over more than two decades? How do activists create cohesion between people with diverse social and cultural backgrounds, lifestyles, and interests? Focusing on the persistence of the collective action against the Belo Monte Dam, this study answers the following research question:

> **How have collective identities and collective action frames contributed to the persistence of the collective action and the maintenance of movement cohesion in the social movement against the Belo Monte Dam?**

This broad question can be broken down into a number of subordinate questions pertaining to two theoretical perspectives – namely, collective identities and collective action frames. How do movement participants seek to create a collective identity? And what are their motives and objectives? What meanings have activists attributed to the social conflict and their collective action? And how have they sought to create a collective action frame?

The in-depth analysis of these questions contributes to addressing theoretical and empirical research gaps. In empirical terms, the study improves our understanding of a specific phenomenon: the collective action against the Belo Monte Dam. Existing studies about the project either focus on technical and environmental issues, or they treat Belo Monte as merely one of several case studies. This study aims to provide insight into the identities, motives, and objectives of the opponents of Belo Monte and their understanding of the social conflict and their collective action. I argue that this type of knowledge is highly relevant from a policy point of view, as similar conflicts are emerging throughout Latin America due to an increasing state interest in the exploitation of natural resources.

Regarding theoretical research gaps, this study, first of all, improves our understanding of general dynamics in the processes of framing and identity construction. The analytical approach based on the grounded theory methodology (GTM) – which is discussed in detail in Chapter 3 – is particularly adequate for a detailed analysis of framing processes and identity work because it allows for

4 Repression is "any action by another group which raises the contender's cost of collective action" (Tilly 1978: 100, emphasis omitted). As "social control techniques" these actions may "rang[e] from police action to ridicule" (Mauss 1975: 60).

the emergence of concepts that adequately describe the interviewees' perception of the conflict and of their collective action. Moreover, the building of concepts from the empirical material – which is a constitutive element of the grounded theory methodology – makes it possible to compare the interviewees' understanding of a given situation to the theoretical concepts seeking to represent that situation. In this sense, the Belo Monte case study aims to contribute to the saturation of theoretical concepts in the collective identity approach and in the framing approach.

Second, the study contributes to our understanding of the regional context and its influence on political mobilization. By focusing on the level of the individual and his/her perception of the conflict and of the collective action, the study seeks to gain insight into the personalities of movement participants, their motivation for collective action, and the impact of these factors upon the persistence of the collective action and the maintenance of movement cohesion. The transfer of the results to other places – weather on the national or international level – is hampered by the unique circumstances of the Belo Monte conflict. Nonetheless, the study generates knowledge on social movements that act under specific context conditions, including the strong heterogeneity of the activists, complex socioeconomic conditions, and a sensitive ecosystem. Therefore, it will be informative for the analysis of similar occurrences of collective action in other countries, especially in democratic emerging powers that face similar challenges in terms of their economic, social, and political development.

Third, the study evaluates the applicability of Western social movement theories in non-Western case studies. Social movement scholars have called for more empirical research in general, and the study of non-Western social movements in particular. Polletta and Jasper argue that the study of non-Western social movements could yield interesting insights into the dynamics associated with identity formation, identity contestation, and the relationship between self and other (Polletta and Jasper 2001: 300). Hunt and Benford identify a need for empirical studies, as most of the literature on collective identity and related phenomena like solidarity and commitment is conceptual in nature (Hunt and Benford 2008: 441).[5] This study seeks to address both research gaps. The in--depth study of a southern social movement and the inclusion of contemporary research by Latin American scholars seek to amplify Western social movement research and theorizing. Moreover, the study's analytical approach based on GTM is particularly suited to yield insight into non-Western conceptualizations

5 Hunt and Benford acknowledge the existence of individual case studies but call for more systematic empirical research (Hunt and Benford 2008: 441).

of identity. In order to avoid that theoretical concepts are "forced" upon empirical data without considering the specific context and connotations, the conceptual and analytical framework are tailored to the particular case study.

Of course, it is an obvious simplification to speak of Western and non-Western countries, especially as the terms do not simply denote geographic location but also allude to the economic, political, and cultural characteristics of the respective countries. There are differences with respect to these attributes not only between the so-called Western (that is, developed) countries and the so-called non-Western (that is, developing) countries but also among them. Nonetheless, the extant structures of domination in the political and economic realm imply that there are different "configurations of civil society" in developing and developed countries (Zinecker 2011: 2). From this point of view, the differentiation is reasonable and useful – at least on the analytical level – for a study that analyzes a social movement in a developing country. In this study, the term Western refers to North America and Europe, and to the concepts, theories, and methods of social movement research developed there. Non-Western refers to any other country (and Brazil, in particular) that becomes the object of research and the destination where Western theories and methods are applied. However, the terms Western and non-Western are used merely as shorthand for more complex ideas about the implications of the traveling of theories and concepts that are discussed throughout the study and specifically in Chapter 6.

In order to make said contribution to the theoretical debate, the study adopts an interdisciplinary perspective and draws from area studies, political science, and sociology with the objective of enhancing the explanatory value of the research. Area studies emphasize the cultural context of social phenomena, while political science and sociology provide comprehensive theories and solid methodological approaches for their systematic study.

1.2 Case Selection and Generalization

Knowledge about contentious politics and collective action in Brazil is increasingly relevant, as the challenges faced there are typical of developing economies that have to balance economic growth with social and environmental imperatives (Hochstetler 2011: 350). Of the vast number of potential case studies dealing with collective action against infrastructure projects in emerging economies, the social movement against the Belo Monte Dam is especially interesting and appropriate for analysis.

1. Why Brazil? Brazil is a dynamic emerging power that seeks to play a leading role in the international political and economic realm (Lima and Hirst

2006). While the country has historically been characterized by significant economic, social, and geographical disparities, it experienced remarkable economic and social development in the early 2000s (Coy 2012: 52–55; De la Fontaine and Stehnken 2012b: 13–14). However, Brazil's participation in the global economy has raised the demand for natural resources and, as a result, intensified conflicts over land and citizen rights (Carter 2009; Maihold and Müller 2012). These controversies have drawn attention to the organization of internal decision making processes and shed light on the social, cultural, and environmental implications of Brazil's rapid development.

2. Why energy politics? The Belo Monte Dam is a strategic infrastructure project in the realm of energy politics, which, in turn, is one of the most contentious policy fields in Brazil because of its strategic importance for the country's economic development. Projects in this policy field represent opportunities for establishing Brazil's international reputation and regional leadership with respect to energy technology and environmental sustainability (Hochstetler 2011: 350; Maihold and Müller 2012: 300; The Economist 2013).[6] However, economic progress and environmental protection are often portrayed as conflicting objectives, especially in developing countries (Zellhuber 2012), and "no other country is as profoundly implicated in both the problems and the solutions as is Brazil" (Franco 2010).
3. Why Belo Monte? With an estimated cost of 20.3 billion reais, the Belo Monte Dam is one of the biggest projects within the PAC.[7] It has a history of reevaluation and modification and of intense protest by national and international opponents. The collective action against Belo Monte has taken place under specific context conditions, including the strong heterogeneity of the activists, a sensitive ecosystem, and complex socioeconomic conditions. Knowledge about the mobilization of collective action

6 The increased share of votes for the Green Party (Partido Verde, PV) in the general elections in October 2010 (19.33%), the popularity of Brazil's most famous environmental politician, Marina Silva, in the general elections in October 2014 (21.32%) (this time, however, she ran for the Brazilian Socialist Party (Partido Socialista Brasileiro, PSB)), and Brazil's hosting of the fourth United Nations Conference on Sustainable Development, commonly known as Rio+20, in June 2012 are indicators of this trend in Brazil (election results retrieved from globo.com 2010, 2014).

7 This amount was estimated by the Brazilian Energy Research Company (Empresa de Pesquisa Energética, EPE) in 2011 (MME and EPE 2011). Recent media reports suggest that the actual cost amounts to 31 billion reais (Ordoñez and Fariello 2017).

under these conditions is highly relevant, as similar conflicts can be expected to arise in Brazil and other developing countries in the near future.

Previous research on large hydropower plants in Brazil has addressed social conflicts and dynamics in general terms (see, for example, Fearnside 1999; McCully 1996; Rothman 2001), social and environmental consequences in the Amazon region (see, for example, Fearnside 1999, 2006, 2008, 2012), and the strategies and alliances of the Anti-Dam Movement in Brazil (see, for example, Hochstetler 2011; McCormick 2006; Rothman and Oliver 1999). More specific studies have placed emphasis on science and technology (McCormick 2007a, 2007b, 2009, 2011) and the situation of dam affected people from a juridical point of view (Graeff 2012). All of these studies allude to the Belo Monte Dam as a case study; yet, they vary in depth. The most frequently cited assessment of the Belo Monte Dam is the volume *Tenotã-Mõ* that provides a comprehensive evaluation of the project taking into account its economic, social, and environmental consequences (Filho 2005). In a similar vein, the comprehensive and interdisciplinary report of the so-called Panel of Experts (Painel de Especialistas) evaluates the Environmental Impact Assessment (Estudo de Impacto Ambiental, EIA) of Belo Monte with respect to social, economic, cultural, technical, and environmental questions (Painel de Especialistas 2009).[8] Similar studies have been produced by nongovernmental organizations like the Conservation Strategy Fund (Sousa Júnior et al. 2006; also see Sousa Júnior and Reid 2010) and International Rivers and Amigos da Terra – Amazônia Brasileira (Hurwitz et al. 2011). Emphasis has also been placed on the social dynamics in the collective action against Belo Monte (Scholz et al. 2003) and the role of big enterprises involved in the financing, construction, and operation of the hydropower plant (Hall and Branford 2012). Other studies have addressed the relationship between society and nature in the Belo Monte context (Fleury and Almeida 2013) and the discourse of the Xingu Forever Alive Movement (Movimento Xingu Vivo Para Sempre, MXVPS) – an organization that is also the focus of this study (Silva 2011).[9] An interesting study on how political opportunities influence the advocacy strategies

8 The Panel of Experts consists of scholars from various disciplines and areas of expertise who are affiliated with diverse institutions of education and research. Their areas of expertise include biology, ecology, economics, electrical engineering and energy planning, family farming and sustainable development, history and civilization studies, geography, hydrology, political science, public health management, social anthropology, sociology, urban and regional planning, and zoology.

9 Throughout this study, I refer to the Xingu Forever Alive Movement as Xingu Vivo or the Xingu Vivo Movement.

and tactics of the social movement against Belo Monte was published by Bratman shortly before the completion of this study (Bratman 2014). Another relevant source of information are the works of anthropologists (see, for example, Forline and Assis 2004; Ramos n.d.; Turner and Fajans-Turner 2006). With the exception of Bratman (2014), the works cited above do not analyze the collective identities and collective action frames prevalent in the social movement against the Belo Monte Dam. This study fills the research gap by investigating the movement dynamics and the factors that enable the persistence of the collective action and the maintenance of movement cohesion.

But what exactly constitutes the case in this study? According to Ragin (1992) cases have to be defined and delineated in a process called "casing". This process involves the selection and narrowing of cases on the basis of theoretical interest and empirical focus (Ragin 1992: 218–222). In terms of the geographical scope, this study focuses on social movement organizations (SMO) in the municipality of Altamira and the state capital of Belém. However, frequent reference is made to incidents of collective action in the neighboring municipalities of Brasil Novo and Vitória do Xingu. These municipalities will be affected indirectly by the Belo Monte project. In order to explore the motives and objectives of the local people, the collective action at the community level, and the characteristics of a non-Western social movement, the study focuses on grassroots organizations based in these areas, and explicitly excludes other national and international organizations. The temporal scope of the study extends from 1989 to 2012, with a particular focus on the years from 2003 (the beginning of former President Luís Inácio 'Lula' da Silva's term[10]) to 2012 (the year of data collection[11]). The year 2003 has been chosen as the starting point for the investigation period because Lula supported the construction of Belo Monte and became a key antagonist to the social movement. Moreover, in hindsight, his administration had severe and lasting impacts on civil society activism in Altamira. In order to account for the dynamics throughout the years of his administration, his taking office in 2003 constitutes the starting point of this investigation. As the collection of data in retrospect involves the risk of memory lapses and the reinterpretation of past events, emphasis is placed on recent events and developments. Hence, the

10 The former president is internationally known by his nickname, Lula. Brazilians frequently refer to their politicians by their first names. In line with this habit, I refer to former President Luís Inácio Lula da Silva as Lula and to former President Dilma Vana Rousseff as Dilma throughout this study. Lula was president of Brazil from 1 January 2003 until 1 January 2011. Dilma succeeded him and served from 1 January 2011 until 31 August 2016.

11 The terms empirical material and (empirical) data are used interchangeably throughout the text.

study provides a snapshot of the social movement at a time when conflicts over the implementation of the Belo Monte Dam intensified.

While this study focuses on a single case, comparative elements are included because the empirical findings are systematically contextualized with existing knowledge. Hence, this study represents a "single-country study as comparison" according to Landman's classification. He argues that "a single-country study is considered comparative if it uses concepts that are applicable to other countries, develops concepts that are applicable to other countries, and/or seeks to make larger inferences that stretch beyond the original country used in the study" (Landman 2008: 28). This study does not just use concepts that are applicable to other countries; rather, it problematizes the fact that these concepts were developed in Europe and North America and are now being applied to a South American country. Moreover, Landman's classification raises the question of what constitutes comparison. In their assessment of comparative area studies, Basedau and Köllner distinguish between three types of comparison: intra-regional comparison considers entities within a region, inter-regional comparison analyzes processes affecting different regions, and cross-regional comparison examines entities from different regions (Basedau and Köllner 2007: 111–112). While the authors acknowledge that questioning the applicability of Western concepts in other contexts constitutes "some sort of comparison," they do not consider it "a comparison in the narrow sense" (Basedau and Köllner 2007: 111). In contrast, I claim that the comparison of theoretical concepts and empirical phenomena does constitute an essential form of comparison that is particularly relevant in the fields of area and comparative area studies.[12] Area specialists should question the applicability of Western concepts in non-Western contexts, precisely because of their sensitivity to the local language(s) and culture(s). Otherwise, they may be accused of imposing their Western ways of thinking and theorizing onto their research objects (cf. Szanton 2004: 23). This study emphasizes that comparison is always taking place, not only concerning theories but also with regard to methodologies and general conceptualizations of social science research. The inconsistencies uncovered by this form of comparison (a comparison in the broader sense) represent findings in and of themselves and inform the subsequent research. Moreover, identifying discrepancies between theoretical concepts and empirical phenomena contributes to refining theory and future research projects.

12 This view is shared by Cappai, who states that any investigation of foreign culture constitutes a comparison with the researcher's own culture (Cappai 2005: 48).

By their very nature, single case studies have a low level of generalizability. This forces the researcher to specify under which circumstances the findings are true. As area studies are generally limited in their geographical scope, they have been particularly criticized for taking a merely descriptive, ideographic approach that is unsuitable for generalization and theory building. However, area studies research is by no means less theory-driven than other social science research and can therefore contribute to "testing, critiquing, confirming, or marginally elaborating or refining, some larger (possibly theoretical) generalizations" (Szanton 2004: 21). Moreover, the explanatory power of studies can be improved by breaking down the unit of analysis and thus increasing the number of observations (Landman 2008: 91). Research on collective action has taken advantage of this strategy by investigating empirical phenomena at a lower level of aggregation – namely, the individual or a group of people (Landman 2008: 92). Landman's compilation shows that single-country studies on collective action have challenged popular wisdom and enhanced concepts and methods in the field of social movement research, thus supporting Szanton's claim (Landman 2008: 176–178).

Drawing on these insights, this study takes individual participants in the social movement against Belo Monte as the unit of analysis. It undertakes a micropolitical analysis of the social movement participants while at the same time considering the macro structures that influence them. This approach seems justified as the agent–structure debate in comparative politics indicates that the micro and macro levels of analysis are difficult to separate empirically (Landman 2008: 19–20).

1.3 Preliminary Study and Field Research

The study is based almost exclusively on original interview data that was collected during two field research trips to Brazil. During the first trip to São Paulo, Brasília, and Rio de Janeiro in the fall of 2011, 31 semistructured interviews with experts from different disciplines and three interviews with activists in São Paulo were conducted.[13] These interviews focused on civil society and collective

13 In the context of this study, an expert is a person who has experience in an occupation relevant to the Belo Monte conflict – be it through employment or volunteerism or both – and a reputation with other experts in the field. Experts can act in private enterprises, civil society organizations, foundations, think tanks, educational institutions, or in the public sector. The selection and recruitment of experts was based on a snowball system (Przyborski and Wohlrab-Sahr 2010: 72). A complete list of the interviews conducted with experts during the preliminary study is reproduced in Annex 1.

action, indigenous and civil rights, development, energy politics and hydroelectricity, environmentalism and sustainability, the Brazilian legal system, and Brazil's international relations. The interviews yielded a vast amount of data that was not analyzed systematically but informed the overall conduct of the research project.[14] Most notably, the findings and experiences from the first research trip resulted in substantial modifications to the theoretical perspective and methodological approach. The insights gained from field research and their implications for social movement research and theory building are discussed in Chapter 6.

During the second research trip to Altamira and Belém in the summer of 2012, data about the motives and objectives of local movement participants and the dynamics inside the social movement against Belo Monte was collected.[15] The interviews with local activists included a semistructured part about topics derived from social movement literature focusing on interpretive frameworks, the actors involved in the protest, identity and the perception of others, and the cooperation enabled by framing processes and identity work. Despite the thematic focus, the interviews allowed for extensive answers, thus enabling interviewees to explicate their understanding of the conflict and of the collective action, and to describe their personal involvement at length. In addition, the interviews included a standardized questionnaire asking about the relationships between people and organizations in the social movement against Belo Monte. With very few exceptions, the interviews were conducted in Portuguese.[16]

1.4 Theoretical and Methodological Positioning

Qualitative researchers are commonly concerned with the in-depth analysis of complex social structures. They "seek to identify and understand the attributes, characteristics, and traits of the object of inquiry" (Landman 2008: 20) rather than breaking it down into neatly separated variables (Mayring 2010: 19). In order to conduct thorough investigations of empirical phenomena, qualitative research often focuses on one case or a limited number of cases. The case study method is typically associated with the building rather than the testing of social

14 A systematic analysis of the interviews at a later point in time is entirely possible, due to the methodologically sound approach and the depth of knowledge of the interviewees.

15 The complete list of interviews with activists in Altamira and Belém is reproduced in Annex 2.

16 In Chapter 3, I discuss the benefits and challenges of doing interview research in a foreign language.

theory because it focuses on comprehending the processes that individuals use and create (Berg 2009: 319–320).

Qualitative research is typically exploratory and inductive, tends to follow a constructivist approach and to strive towards theory development or refinement. Qualitative researchers are likely to emphasize complexity, holism, and totality in their studies. Accordingly, the collection of qualitative data typically involves a low degree of standardization and quantification (Hollstein and Ullrich 2003: 33–34). In a critical review of the properties of qualitative research, Hollstein and Ullrich identify three properties they claim to be constitutive of and exclusive to qualitative research (Hollstein and Ullrich 2003: 34–37). These include, (1) in-depth understanding of meaning (*Sinnverstehen*), (2) openness to the empirical puzzle in the process of data collection, and (3) prevalence of interpretive approaches.

The in-depth understanding of meaning is the main objective of this study about the social movement against the Belo Monte Dam. Special attention is paid to the motives and objectives behind the collective action against the hydropower project, and to the meanings that activists attribute to the social conflict and their collective action. The focus on collective identities and collective action frames as central movement dynamics suggests that the study is based on a constructivist research paradigm (cf. Hollstein and Ullrich 2003: 37). According to Adler, constructivism is based on the belief that "the identities, interests and behavior of political agents are socially constructed by collective meanings, interpretations and assumptions about the world" (Adler 1997: 324).[17] As identities, motives, and objectives at the individual and the collective level are the main explanatory factors in this research project, constructivism provides an adequate analytical framework. As a social theory it only makes "minimalist social-theoretic claims" (Finnemore and Sikkink 2001: 394); therefore, it should be combined with more elaborate and specific theories in order to investigate and understand the processes that characterize a social phenomenon. Hjelmar (1996) seeks to provide conceptual clarifications on the constructivist view of social movements. He emphasizes that a constructivist perspective offers the opportunity to include human action into the analysis and thus add another dimension to the study of political and cultural opportunities and struc-

17 While Adler evaluates the contributions of constructivism in the field of international relations, his general discussion of its social-epistemological basis is informative for other fields of research, too. Adler emphasizes that constructivism is not a political but a social theory, making it applicable to various disciplines, not just international relations research (Adler 1997: 323).

tures. He further suggests that scholars should study the particular circumstances of collective action, as they might be perceived and exploited in different ways by different groups (Hjelmar 1996: 182). How social movements recognize and take advantage of opportunities depends on their interpretation of reality. Constructivism emphasizes that there is no "unifying political logic of society" (Hjelmar 1996: 182); hence, what is politically significant to one group may be irrelevant to another. Therefore, a constructivist approach to social movement research that reconstructs how a contentious issue gained political significance represents a bottom-up approach (Hjelmar 1996: 183). According to Finnemore and Sikkink, social movement researchers tend to be pragmatic in choosing and combining those methods that best suit their research problem (Finnemore and Sikkink 2001: 409). In a similar vein, this research project combines different concepts of social movement theory in order to arrive at an adequate theoretical framework.

The study adopts an exploratory design that requires the comprehensive analysis of the social movement against Belo Monte and the context conditions that influence it. Special attention is paid to the meaning that the conflict and the collective action have for local movement participants, to their individual and collective motives and objectives, and to the role of social movement organizations.[18] Still, this research is not merely descriptive. As Finnemore and Sikkink emphasize, "understanding how things are put together and how they occur" (Finnemore and Sikkink 2001: 394) is central to the constructivist research paradigm, since the structure and functionality of things determine political behavior and effects (Landman 2008: 5). In a similar vein, Corbin and Strauss emphasize that "description is the basis for more abstract interpretations of data and theory development" (Corbin and Strauss 2008: 54). In line with this understanding, the analysis in Chapter 5 focuses on the interviewees' perspective, while the evaluation in Chapter 6 takes the empirical findings to a higher level of abstraction.

In terms of the analytical method and procedures, this study is based on the grounded theory methodology. This is a well-developed approach that emerged in the 1960s in the field of sociology. GTM focuses on interpersonal relationships and the actions of individuals in groups and larger social settings

18 Throughout this study, the terms local activists, local movement participants, or interviewees are used to refer to participants in the social movement against the Belo Monte Dam who were interviewed during field research in Altamira and Belém. Unless explicitly stated otherwise, these terms do not refer to people who participate in other social movements in the region, nor to people who participate in the social movement against Belo Monte in other parts of Brazil or in other countries.

(Mey and Mruck 2009: 101–102). Due to its microsociological perspective, it has been applied in a variety of disciplines and in interdisciplinary research. However, its application in political science is a relatively recent phenomenon (Oertzen 2006: 146). The objective of GTM is to investigate individual and social practices by taking empirical findings to a higher level of abstraction and developing hypotheses and/or middle-range theories that are empirically grounded – hence the name grounded theory (Mey and Mruck 2009: 104; Oertzen 2006: 146; Strauss 1998: 50–51). As a comprehensive research program, GTM offers a variety of instruments and procedures that enable researchers to use it in the most diverse projects. However, this methodological freedom requires that the researcher explicate her approach and critically reflect upon the objectives, procedures, and results of her study. In line with these requirements, the method and procedures of this study are elaborated in Chapter 3.

1.5 Western Thinking in non-Western Cases: Conceptual Challenges

There is an extensive body of literature on civil society and social movements in Latin America in general, and in Brazil in particular. The works are authored both by area experts from Europe and North America and by scholars stemming from the region. Interestingly, social movement theories and concepts that were developed in the global North have entered the scholarly debate and are frequently applied to the local context. However, a number of Latin American scholars have demonstrated to be sensitive to the challenges arising from the European and North American influence upon academia in Brazil, and the applicability of Western theories and concepts in non-Western case studies (see, for example, Gohn 2008; Scherer-Warren and Lüchmann 2004; Scherer-Warren 2015).

Almost all of the contemporary literature on civil society and social movements assumes that civil society represents an autonomous sphere that is separate from the family, the state, and the economy (Kocka 2004: 68; Zinecker 2011: 3–5). Moreover, the term carries a strong positive connotation, as civil society is commonly associated with freedom, pluralism and social autonomy (Kocka 2004: 67–68). However, the implicit meanings and assumptions about the concept call its applicability in non-Western case studies into question (Zinecker 2011: 1; also see, Abers and von Bülow 2011; Alvarez et al. 1998). Empirical research shows that, due to different context conditions, civil society in non-Western countries often mingles with state institutions or commercial undertakings (Alvarez et al. 1998: 9; Zinecker 2011: 6). As a consequence, the study of contentious politics provides conceptual challenges because some Western presumptions (for example, about civil society's separation from the state) do not hold true (Abers and von Bülow 2011: 62–64). As Abers and von Bülow assert,

> *"[t]his assumption impedes the capture of some of the complex relationships that exist between people in the state apparatus and those that act on behalf of social movement organizations. If we think of the state as a homogeneous block that operates in a distinct organizational space we can hardly recognize networks that cross the boundaries between state and civil society as an important part of social movements"* (Abers and von Bülow 2011: 64, author's translation).

Hence, theories and concepts developed in the Western context cannot necessarily be applied to non-Western case studies without modification.[19] In many regions of the world the analysis of social movements requires an assessment of their relations with the state and political parties (Abers and von Bülow 2011: 64). The overlap of social movements and the state in many policy fields in Brazil can be traced back to the transition to democracy in the 1980s and the consolidation of democracy in the last two decades. In cases where social movements supported the creation of government agencies in the early years of democracy, activists were likely to be included in the staffing of key positions (Abers and von Bülow 2011: 67). Moreover, alliances between individuals inside and outside the state apparatus have led to the creation of new social movements (Abers and von Bülow 2011: 68). Hence, on the one hand, the transition to democracy and the Brazilian constitution of 1988 opened spaces for popular participation in governance processes in a number of key areas including health care, social assistance, the environment, and urban organization (Avritzer 2009: 2). On the other hand, there is disagreement among social movements about the implications of a close cooperation with the state. Some movements take advantage of their close ties with the state and seek to promote their demands, whereas other movements strictly reject these possibilities (Abers and von Bülow 2011: 66). In any way, a conceptualization of civil society that purports a strict separation of civil society, family, state, and economy is not suitable in contexts where social movements are likely to have close relationships with the state. As Avritzer claims,

19 It should be noted, however, that the division line with respect to the concept of civil society does not necessarily run between Western and non-Western countries. This means, civil society in Western countries is not always political, democratic and nonviolent as purported by the concept. At the same time, civil society in non-Western states is not always "uncivilized" as would be the converse argument.

> *"[p]olitical parties and political society remained undertheorized in most of the literature of participation, because of the elitist character of the literature or the antisystemic conceptions of social movements theory. Particularly in Brazil, where the Workers Party (called the PT) has led the way in introducing participatory arrangements, the connection between political parties and civil society in implementing forms of participation became a key variable – but one that is not explained in theory" (Avritzer 2009: 7).*

These findings demonstrate that scholars investigating civil society and social movements in Brazil should pay special attention to the definition of their key concepts. This study seeks to address the challenges in two ways. First, it problematizes the relationship between civil society and the Workers' Party. To that effect, I outline my assumptions about the relationship between the two in the sensitizing concepts (cf. Chapter 3) and address the issue throughout the analysis (cf. Chapter 5). Second, the analytical approach based on the grounded theory methodology, which focuses on building concepts from the data, ensures that empirical findings are not "forced" into existing theoretical categories. Rather, the categories that are developed throughout the analysis reflect the interviewees' understandings of the social phenomena that are addressed in the research.

1.6 Outline of the Study

The study is divided into six chapters. Chapter 2 presents the theoretical framework for this study. Based on a brief review of the relevant literature, I develop the theoretical concepts guiding the analysis. Although this study seeks to reconstruct the meaning of the Belo Monte conflict for local activists and the dynamics in the social movement, a purely inductive approach is unfeasible, as any research project has to determine its research interest, objective, and procedures. Hence, this chapter defines and operationalizes the theoretical concepts that are central in this study – namely, collective action, social movement, collective identity, framing, and collective action frames.

Chapter 3 discusses the methods and procedures applied in this study. The empirical analysis is based almost exclusively on original data obtained from semistructured interviews that were conducted in Altamira and Belém in 2012. In this chapter, I discuss my approach to data collection and data analysis in the context of the grounded theory methodology. Particular attention is paid to quality standards in qualitative empirical research and to the implications of conducting interview research in a foreign language. Moreover, I discuss my previous knowledge and assumptions, which I set forth in the sensitizing concepts.

Chapter 4 introduces the reader to the Amazon state of Pará and to the Belo Monte conflict. I give an overview of the settlement, national integration, and socioeconomic development of the region and discuss the legal basis for the implementation of large infrastructure projects in the Brazilian Amazon. Moreover, the chapter outlines the historic development of the Belo Monte conflict from the 1980s until 2012 and introduces the relevant actors. The objective of this chapter is to draw attention to the particular problems in the region and their implications for the development and maintenance of a social movement.

Chapter 5 is the centerpiece of this study. Here I present the detailed analysis of the empirical data along the lines of the existing theoretical concepts defined in Chapter 2 and the core categories that emerged from the empirical analysis. Section 5.1 outlines the historical development of civil society organizations in Altamira and introduces the relevant actors. In Section 5.2, I reconstruct the personal, social, and collective identities of local activists in Altamira and Belém from the original data. Identities form an integral part of the analysis, because they are assumed to contribute to the persistence of collective action and the maintenance of movement cohesion. Section 5.3 provides an in-depth analysis of the collective action frames and framing processes. It emphasizes the Belo Monte diagnostic frame, and the divergence of the collective action frame that eventually contributed to the fragmentation of the movement and to the definition of two different prognostic frames. In Section 5.4, I discuss the central dynamics within the social movement against Belo Monte and introduce the core categories of my study – that is, cohesion and fragmentation. The concept of fragmentation was not originally included in the theoretical framework and emerged from the original data as an in-vivo code. I briefly review the current state of research on factionalism in social movements in an excursus. Then I analyze the internal and external factors that promoted the fragmentation of the movement. The chapter closes with a preliminary conclusion on cohesion and fragmentation in the social movement against Belo Monte.

While Chapter 5 focuses on reconstructing meaning from the activists' point of view, Chapter 6 takes the empirical discussion to a higher level of abstraction. I present the insights I gained from the analysis of identity work, framing processes, cohesion, and fragmentation, and assess the study's contribution to the existing knowledge on social movements. Moreover, I evaluate my sensitizing concepts in terms of their relevance and adequacy, and discuss the extent to which social movement theory and concepts can be applied to non-Western case studies. Finally, I review the appropriateness of the method and procedures and discuss the study's implications for future research.

2 Theoretical Framework

What motivates people to dedicate time and effort to the collective action against Belo Monte – especially as the context conditions are adverse to the mobilization and maintenance of a social movement and chances for success are slim? What meanings do activists attribute to the conflict over hydropower projects at the Xingu River and to their collective action against them? These are the core questions in the analysis of the social movement against the Belo Monte Dam, and they can best be addressed with two theoretical approaches that focus on the movement participants: the collective identity approach and the framing approach. Collective identity refers to a feeling of belonging to other people, groups, organizations, or – in more abstract terms – institution(s). It is conceptualized in this study as an individual attribute based on a social psychological perspective. While the study analyzes whom the social movement participants identify with, it also considers how collective identity is integrated with an activist's personal and social identities. Framing, in turn, refers to the efforts that groups of people undertake for the purpose of developing common understandings of the world and the events surrounding them. Until the 1970s, framing processes and identity work were clearly subordinated to structures and processes in social movement research. However, they have come to prominence in recent years and seem particularly adequate for this research, as I will demonstrate in the following.

Given the exploratory character of this study and the research design based on grounded theory methodology, I argue that theoretical concepts cannot be "applied" directly to the empirical material. However, a purely inductive approach is not feasible either, because the researcher has to define her research interest, objective, and procedures. In this study, the collective identity approach and the framing approach are the theoretical perspectives that guide the analysis. Concepts stemming from the literature, such as collective action, social movement, collective identity, and collective action frame, are used to denote the phenomena I am interested in. They are operationalized so as to guide the sampling, the development of interview guides, and the data collection. However, they are disregarded in the initial phase of the data analysis (coding) in order to allow for an emergence of original concepts that reflect the interviewees' perceptions.[20] To this effect, the analysis focuses on the relevance systems of the research participants in order to understand how they make sense of the events, actions, and conditions around them.[21] In a later phase of the research, concepts stemming from the literature are systematically compared to the empirically grounded concepts derived from the analysis. The purpose of this comparison is to refine existing concepts and to evaluate the applicability of Western concepts in non-Western case studies. In Chapter 3, I discuss how a research design based on grounded theory methodology can be reconciled with the previous specification of a theoretical framework. Moreover, I reflect upon my previous knowledge and preliminary assumptions, which I set forth in the sensitizing concepts.

The present chapter focuses on the conceptualization of central theoretical concepts with a view to developing a conceptual framework that determines the research perspective and guides the analysis. Section 2.1 introduces the reader to the study of collective action, its research strands and conceptual backgrounds. Section 2.2 defines the concept of social movement and discusses its network character. The conceptualization of a social movement as a network entails a focus on collective identity. Therefore, the collective identity approach and the impact of collective identity on movement cohesion are discussed in Section 2.3. Section 2.4 elaborates on the framing approach and explains the characteristics and functions of the collective action frame. In Section 2.5, I discuss the differences between collective identity and framing because the concepts are closely related. The concept of cohesion is discussed and defined in Section 2.6. In the final section (2.7), I define the central theoretical concepts that guide the data collection and analysis.

---

20 It is impossible to completely neglect theoretical concepts in the course of the data analysis. However, in order to avoid the inconsiderate influence of my previous knowledge, assumptions, and beliefs on the interpretation of primary data, I reflect upon these concepts and disclose my previous ideas in the sensitizing concepts in Chapter 3 (also see Kelle 2011: 251; Kruse 2015: 479–484).

21 According to Alfred Schütz, all human actions are based on relevance structures. Relevance structures determine how people interpret situations and how they relate new experiences to existing knowledge (Schütz and Luckmann 2003: 253). All relevance structures taken together make up a person's relevance system. It is unique in that it comprises a person's attitudes, motives, past experiences, and extant knowledge (Schütz and Luckmann 2003: 305–312).

2.1 The Study of Collective Action

Social scientists are interested in diverse forms of collective action, including crowds, riots, interest groups, movements, gangs, revolutions, etc. The systematic study of these phenomena is based on analytical approaches stemming from social psychology, sociology, and political science. In the first half of the 20th century collective behavior was commonly associated with deprivation and social crisis (Klandermans et al. 1988: 2). However, with the emergence of so-called new social movements during the late 1960s and early 1970s scholars started to focus on the processes of mobilization and social movement activity (Della Porta and Diani 2006: 8).[22] Since the late 1980s, the collective identity approach and the framing approach have come to prominence in social movement theory and research (Benford and Snow 2000: 612; Snow and McAdam 2000: 41). These approaches are based on early works of symbolic interactionism, sociology, and social psychology; however, they break with the earlier perception of collective action as irrational and destructive behavior (Gamson 1992: 54; Polletta and Jasper 2001: 283; Snow and Oliver 1995: 573; Stryker et al. 2000a: 3–4). Instead, the collective identity approach and the framing approach adopt the focus on human interaction that is prevalent in these research traditions. Symbolic interactionism is based on the American philosophical tradition of pragmatism, and stresses that social meanings and social order are created and maintained though human interaction and negotiation (Sandstrom et al. 2010: 2).[23] People observe their environment; they interpret it and respond to it based on past experiences. In doing so, they give meaning to the people and objects around them. Erving Goffman, a scholar from the Second Chicago School, argued that people use frameworks to make sense of the events they see in daily life. Frameworks provide them with "schemata of interpretation" that give meaning to something that would otherwise be meaningless (Goffman 1974: 21; also see Münch 2004: 283–284). Frameworks have varying degrees of organization ranging from precise systems of rules to loose bundles of understandings (Goffman 1974: 21). In order to interpret a situation, people tend to use

22 New social movement theory is based on European traditions of political philosophy and social theory. It developed as a reaction to the failure of extant theories to explain the new forms of political participation that emerged in the 1960s. Major theorists of new social movement theory include Manuel Castells, Alain Touraine, Alberto Melucci, and Jürgen Habermas (Buechler 1995).

23 George H. Mead, a leading scholar of the Chicago School, is credited for having introduced the pragmatist philosophy to sociology (Sandstrom et al. 2010: 4–5). However, the term symbolic interactionism was introduced by his student Herbert G. Blumer (Sandstrom et al. 2010: 7).

several frameworks at the same time (Goffman 1974: 25). Hence, frameworks form a constitutive element of the belief system of a social group (Goffman 1974: 27). As a consequence, symbolic interactionists believe that research in the social sciences has to focus on human agency, interaction, and meaning in order to understand social life (Sandstrom et al. 2010: 2–3). This perspective had a significant impact on the study of social movements, in that scholars like Erving Goffman, Robert Benford, Francesca Polletta, and David Snow, among others, have integrated the key concepts into social movement theory and continue working on them (see below).

Among the different strands in social movement research, this study focuses on collective identities and collective action frames as the theoretical perspectives for analysis. These concepts seem most adequate to explain the persistence of the collective action and the maintenance of movement cohesion in the social movement against the Belo Monte Dam.

2.2 Social Movement Theory

Social movements are commonly perceived as a particular form of collective action. Defined in general terms, collective action is characterized by the joint action of at least two individuals who are pursuing a common goal (Snow et al. 2008: 6). As this is true for many forms of everyday behavior, scholars have introduced the differentiation between institutionalized and non-institutionalized behavior as a basic criterion for classification. While interest groups and political parties have access to or even form part of political institutions, social movements are considered challengers to established structures that pursue their objectives through noninstitutional means (Snow et al. 2008: 6–7; Staggenborg 2008: 5). Beyond this attribute, however, scholars have not been able to develop a common definition of the phenomenon they investigate (Gohn 2000: 11; Snow et al. 2008: 6; Staggenborg 2008: 5). While reviews of the relevant literature identify a number of common dimensions in the various conceptualizations of social movement (see, for example, Diani 1992; Opp 2009), they also find that definitions remain heterogeneous and "surprisingly unclear" (Opp 2009: 37). The Blackwell Companion to Social Movements identifies five conceptual axes that are present in most definitions (Snow et al. 2008: 6): (1) collective or joint action, (2) change-oriented goals or claims, (3) some extra- or noninstitutional collective action, (4) some degree of organization, and (5) some degree of temporal continuity. Based on these attributes, Snow and colleagues propose to define social movements as "collectivities acting with some degree of organization and continuity outside of institutional or organizational channels for the purpose of challenging or defending extant authority, whether it is institutionally or culturally based, in the group, organization, society, culture, or world order of which they are a part" (Snow et al. 2008: 11). Despite the conceptual rigor, these authors emphasize that social movements cannot always be clearly separated from crowds or interest groups. This is because social movements may support crowd behavior and/or cooperate with interest groups in order to promote their claims (Snow et al. 2008: 8). Diani proposes an alternative conceptualization of social movement that focuses on (1) conflictual collective action, (2) dense informal networks, and (3) collective identity as the central dimensions of social movements (Diani 2003: 301–306; also see Della Porta and Diani 2006: 20–21). He defines social movement as "a network of informal interactions between a plurality of individuals, groups and/or organizations, engaged in a political or cultural conflict, on the basis of a shared collective identity" (Diani 1992: 13).[24]

The two definitions presented above both emphasize that the existence of a social movement depends upon (1) a political or cultural conflict, and (2) a social or political opponent (Diani and Bison 2004: 283; Diani 1992: 13; Snow et al. 2008: 11). Moreover, Diani points out three aspects that seem particularly relevant for the study of the social movement against Belo Monte but are less prevalent in other conceptualizations. These are (1) the differentiation between social movement and social movement organization (SMO), (2) the network character of a social movement, and (3) the existence of a shared collective identity as the basis for interaction in a social movement.

The analysis of social movements with formal network approaches gained importance in the 1990s. However, the idea that people are embedded in larger structures (social networks) that influence individual and collective actions dates back to the 1950s.[25] Individuals, groups, and organizations maintain relations of various types with other people and organizations (Diani 2002: 189). These exchanges are by no means incidental – by contrast, they reveal dynamics of interaction between the different actors of a social movement that are of particular interest in social movement research.

But what exactly is a network? Everyday conceptualizations and a large number of scholarly works use the term to refer to a mode of organization that

24 Diani's work is also perceived in Brazil. A translation of his 2004 article with Ivano Bison (Diani and Bison 2004) was published in the Brazilian *Revista Brasileira de Ciência Política*, No. 3 in 2010.

25 Among the early proponents who are frequently quoted by social network researchers is sociologist George Simmel (Skvoretz and Faust 1999: 254; Diani 2009: 64–65; Scott 2000: 9; Wellman 1988: 23).

implies informal relationships or even the opposite of hierarchical structures (Christopoulos 2008: 475; Hafner-Burton et al. 2009: 561).[26] By contrast, formal Social Network Analysis works with a conceptualization that is based on mathematical graph theory and defines a social network as a "set of actors and the ties among them" (Wasserman and Faust 1994: 9). While appearing very basic, this definition rids the concept of any premature assumptions – for example, the absence of hierarchy between actors – and allows scholars to study the network structure and its impact on individuals and groups (Wasserman and Faust 1994: 9). The degrees of organization, formality, and hierarchy within a network can differ across actors, and they can be assessed at different levels of analysis – for example, at the level of the entire network, the subgroup, or the individual actor (cf. Snow et al. 2008: 10).

The network perspective ties in well with the differentiation between social movement and SMOs. While the social movement as a whole takes the form of a network, individuals, groups, and organizations represent the set of actors. The differentiation between social movements and social movement organizations was first proposed by McCarthy and Zald (McCarthy and Zald 1977) and has been followed by a number of scholars (Opp 2009: 36; Snow and Oliver 1995: 571). In this perspective, a social movement is conceptualized as "a set of opinions and beliefs in a population which represents preferences for changing some elements of their social structure and/or reward distribution of a society" (McCarthy and Zald 1977: 1217–1218). The social movement does not consist in people, but it is evoked by their shared opinions and beliefs. Individual activists enter into this comparatively abstract definition through their affiliation with a social movement organization – that is "a complex, or formal, organization which identifies its goals with the preferences of a social movement or a countermovement and attempts to implement those goals" (McCarthy and Zald 1977: 1218).[27] This definition of an SMO includes many of the aforementioned

26 This conceptualization also seems to be prevalent among the experts interviewed during the preliminary study in São Paulo, Brasília, and Rio de Janeiro in 2011.

27 The term organization is disputed and some authors prefer to offer examples of organizations instead of a definition of the term (Reinhold et al. 1997: 476). Basic agreement exists on the general characteristics of an organization. In a broad sense, an organization is "a type of collectivity established for the pursuit of specific aims or goals, characterized by a formal structure of rules, authority relations, a division of labour and limited membership or admission" (Jary and Jary 1991: 444). The existence of common goals is a particularly controversial aspect, as individuals and groups within an organization may hold diverse and competing goals. It is an empirical question how common goals are defined and who is involved in these processes. A general distinction is made between formal organizations that seek to establish common goals through rewards and punishment, and informal organizations that negotiate goals and

dimensions that are commonly referred to in definitions of a social movement (Opp 2009: 36; Snow et al. 2008). Diani emphatically promotes the differentiation between social movements and SMOs in his works (Diani 1992, 2003), claiming that social movements are less formal in terms of membership and less coordinated in terms of interaction and internal regulation than SMOs (Diani 2003: 302). From his point of view, the differentiation allows for a closer analysis of the relationship between social movements, parties, and interest groups, as it breaks with the treatment of social movements as a specific type of organization (Diani 2003: 304). The network perspective and the differentiation between social movements and SMOs shift the analytical focus from the attributes of individual organizations to the relationships between organizations, thus leading to a conceptualization that is inherently relational. According to Diani, SMOs are "all those groups who identify themselves, and are identified by others, as part of the same movement, and exchange on that basis" (Diani 2003: 305).

Diani's conceptualization, which emphasizes social movement organizations, the network character, and the existence of a shared collective identity, seems particularly adequate for the analysis of the social movement against the Belo Monte Dam. Secondary literature on Altamira shows that the city has an active civil society with some individuals taking decisive roles in its activities (Umbuzeiro and Umbuzeiro 2012). It is plausible to assume that participants in the social movement against the Belo Monte Dam know each other from earlier incidents of collective action and are thus connected through relationships of collaboration, friendship, opposition, etc. The conceptualization of the social movement as a network enables an in-depth analysis of local activists' personal backgrounds, their experiences with collective action, and their relationships. Moreover, this conceptualization contributes to solving a conceptual discrepancy in the analysis of the social movement against Belo Monte. While the collective identity approach is commonly associated with the study of new social movements, which promote postmaterialist values, the collective action against Belo Monte is characterized by materialist and postmaterialist values.[28] Consequently, one might question the usefulness of the collective identity approach

procedures within organizations (Jary and Jary 1991: 444–445). As I will discuss in Chapter 5, the organizations involved in the Belo Monte conflict include formal organizations like the Catholic Church, which relies heavily on hierarchy and lines of authority to define common goals and procedures, and informal organizations like the various grassroots organizations involved in the social movement against Belo Monte, some of which deliberately dispense with leadership.

28 In Chapter 6, I discuss how materialist and postmaterialist values are reconciled in the social movement against Belo Monte.

and the framing approach in this particular case study. On the contrary, I propose that the collective identity and framing perspectives are particularly adequate to address the heterogeneity and complexity that characterize this particular movement. As discussed in the introduction, the strong heterogeneity of movement participants, difficult socioeconomic conditions, and other obstacles to mobilization – for example, power asymmetries and repression, among others – hamper the mobilization and target-oriented interaction of movement participants. If we think of the social movement as a network of actors, we can imagine that people and organizations are connected to each other through various relationships. These relationships influence the interaction between local activists and their collective action against Belo Monte. According to Diani, the network perspective is inherently concerned with identity dynamics (Diani 2003: 305). It is therefore particularly adequate for assessing the impact of collective identities on the persistence of the collective action and the maintenance of movement cohesion in the social movement against the Belo Monte Dam.[29]

Beyond the differentiation between social movement and SMO, the study focuses on the individual social movement participant, defined as a person who is not necessarily affiliated with a group or organization but who participates in the collective action on a regular basis.[30] The study focuses explicitly on the "plurality of individuals, groups and/or organizations" (Diani 1992: 13) in the social movement against Belo Monte in order to study the dynamics of identity work on the personal and collective level. Moreover, the focus on individuals takes into account that, empirically speaking, SMOs seem to play a subordinate role in the collective action against the Belo Monte Dam.[31] The differentiation between the social movement, the social movement organization, and the individual social movement participant adds conceptual clarity and allows for a detailed analysis of the activists' motives and objectives.

29 However, it should be noted that Diani's conceptualization of identity is based on the work of Melucci who adopts a structural cultural perspective of identity. By contrast, this study builds on a social psychological perspective of collective identity, as I will explain further below. The different conceptualizations do not compromise the adequacy of a network perspective; however, they require a thorough discussion and conceptualization of identity.

30 Consequently, data is gathered and analyzed at the level of the individual (cf. Chapter 3).

31 I gained this insight during my field research trip to Altamira and Belém and discuss its implications in Chapter 6.

2.3 The Collective Identity Approach

Since the early 1990s, identity is considered a constitutive element of social movements (Daphi 2011: 13; Della Porta and Diani 2006: 21; Melucci 1988; Polletta and Jasper 2001; Snow and McAdam 2000). While the concept is frequently used in different disciplines and addressed from different angles, it remains an abstract and "slippery" concept that is left unclear and vague in many studies (Daphi and Rucht 2011: 2; Flesher Fominaya 2010a: 393; Stryker et al. 2000A: 5).

Sociologists and social psychologists generally differentiate between distinct types of identity, including personal identity and social or collective identity/-ies (Rucht 1995: 10). However, they disagree on the type and number of levels where identity formation takes places. For example, Simon identifies identity formations at the personal and collective level. He proposes to dispense with the term social identity as it implies that its counterpart, personal identity, was antisocial (Simon 2011: 40). Rucht, on the other hand, presents four types of identity: (1) physical identity, (2) role identity, (3) organizational identity, and (4) collective identity. He emphasizes that the latter three types are socially constructed and inherently unstable (Rucht 2011a: 26–27). Another conceptualization that is frequently used in social movement research and that I adopt for this study dates back to Snow. He differentiates between the personal, social, and collective identities of an individual (Snow 2001: 2213). According to Snow, personal identity is built up of self-designations and self-attributions, whereas social identity is attributed by others. The latter designates actors to a specific social space based on their social role (for example, their profession) or their belonging to a social group or category (for example, their ethnicity) (Snow 2001: 2212–2213). The concept of collective identity is particularly relevant for the study of social movements, as collective identities have been found to contribute to movement cohesion (Flesher Fominaya 2010b: 377). Snow defines collective identity as being "constituted by a shared and interactive sense of 'we-ness' and 'collective agency'" (Snow 2001: 2213). The sense of belonging to a collectivity (we) is based on shared attributes and experiences, and constructed in contrast to other actors (them). Scholars agree that the differentiation between in-group and out-group has a strong influence on the development of a collective identity. Moreover, the external environment pays an important role in the definition of movement boundaries. Social and political actors outside the movement may accept, deny, or oppose the in-group/out-group differentiation, thus recognizing the social movement as a relevant actor (Melucci 1996: 73). Inside the social movement, the shared sense of we-ness fosters collective agency (Rucht 1995: 10, 2002: 330; Snow 2001: 2213).

Besides the disagreement about the types and number of identity/-ies, social movement scholars base their identity concept on different perspectives – namely, the structural cultural perspective and the social psychological perspective. The structural cultural perspective treats collective identity as a collective attribute that becomes salient in rituals, styles, and narratives (Daphi 2011: 18–19; Hunt and Benford 2008: 434–435). For example, Alberto Melucci – who has made important contributions to social movement theory from a structural cultural perspective – defines collective identity as "an interactive and shared definition produced by several individuals and concerned with the orientations of action and the field of opportunities and constraints in which the action takes place" (Melucci 1988: 342). In contrast, scholars sharing the social psychological perspective refer to collective identity as an individual attribute and seeks to explain a person's identification with a collective (Daphi 2011: 18–19; Hunt and Benford 2008: 435–436). From their point of view, the structural cultural perspective tends to neglect individual actors' involvement in movement activities (Stryker 2000: 23). Hence, there is substantial disagreement on whether collective identity is a personal or a collective attribute (Daphi 2011: 18; also see Flesher Fominaya 2010a; Hunt and Benford 2008; Polletta and Jasper 2001; Snow and McAdam 2000).

This study adopts a social psychological perspective and builds on the conceptualization of personal, social, and collective identities proposed by Snow (2001). Accordingly, collective identity is treated as an individual attribute and analyzed at the level of the social movement participant. This approach seems to be most adequate for analyzing the actors' identities and the relationship between personal, social, and collective identities, as is the objective of this study. Snow's conceptualization of identity is appropriate for this research for two reasons. First, the differentiation between social identity, which is ascribed by others, and collective identity, which is based on a sense of belonging, is empirically relevant in the case of Brazil. The conceptual distinction between self-classification and ascription is missing in other conceptualizations – for example, in the work of Simon (2011). The practical value of this differentiation becomes apparent, for example, in the fundamental changes in Brazilian racial policy in recent years. In the early years of this century, the Brazilian government adopted measures of affirmative action in the public sector and in higher education. As a consequence, many Brazilian universities implemented quotas for the admission of disadvantaged students based on race and/or socioeconomic conditions. Most universities rely (at least partially) on self-classification for the evaluation of eligibility. However, as self-classification and ascription by others may produce different results, the procedures are contested (Htun 2004; Schwartzman 2008). As this example shows, the conceptual distinction between ascribed identity (that is, social identity) and a sense of we-ness developed by a group of actors (that is, collective identity) is empirically relevant in Brazil. Second, the conceptualization of identities on the basis of self-classification and ascription adds more analytical value than, for example, the distinction between role identity, organizational identity, and collective identity proposed by Rucht (2011a). These three types of identity refer to a persons' sense of belonging to a collective, be it a social group, an organization, a movement, or – in more abstract terms – an institution. Hence, they can be considered three different types of collective identity. But what is their analytical value? On the one hand, I agree with Rucht that a differentiation is useful when analyzing the processes of identity work in collectives, because it is plausible to assume that social movements have to engage in more identity work than formal organizations given the lack of clear boundaries and authorized representatives (Rucht 2011a: 27). On the other hand, I propose that it is even more important to ask: who identifies an actor with a collective? Does the actor identify him-/herself with a collective, or do others designate the actor to a specific social space? In this sense, self-classification and ascription should be understood as factors that influence the development of identities in a person. In contrast to Rucht, Snow offers a conceptual distinction between collective identity (based on self-classification) and social identity (based on ascription) that results in analytical clarity and parsimony. Hence, this study adopts the conceptualization of personal, social, and collective identity proposed by Snow (2001).

The social psychological perspective on identity and social movements has been further elaborated in recent years by Stryker, Owens, White, and others.[32] Polletta and Jasper conceptualize collective identity as "an individual's cognitive, moral, and emotional connection with a broader community, category, practice, or institution. It is a perception of a shared status or relation, which may be imagined rather than experienced directly, and it is distinct from personal identities, although it may form part of a personal identity" (Polletta and Jasper 2001: 285). This definition locates collective identity at the level of the individual and alludes to the relationship between personal, social, and collective identity. According to the social psychological perspective, people have multiple identities that are organized hierarchically and become salient in different situations. That is to say, identity is a cognitive schema pertaining to the expectations for behavior that we have of a person with a particular role and corresponding

32 See, for example, the volume edited by Stryker and colleagues (2000b) and the article by Polletta and Jasper (2001).

identity. Identity salience refers to the readiness of a person to act out a particular identity at a particular point in time when the person takes on the corresponding role (Stryker 2000: 33–34). While the relationship between the different identities of an individual remains unclear, scholars generally agree that the three different types of identities interact and overlap (Flesher Fominaya 2010a: 397; Polletta and Jasper 2001: 285; Snow 2001: 2213). Moreover, they propose that collective identity amounts to more than the aggregate of the personal identities of a group of people (Polletta and Jasper 2001: 298).

Much research has also been done on the emergence and construction of collective identity through a process of identity work (Rucht 2002: 331; Snow 2001: 2213). Identity work is defined as "the range of activities people engage in, both individually and collectively, to signify and express who they are and what they stand for in relation or contrast to some set of others" (Snow 2001: 2216). Rucht emphasizes that social movements depend on extensive identity work in order to avoid fragmentation (Rucht 2002: 331). Especially those social movements whose collective identities are not characterized by primoridial characteristics such as race or gender have to engage in discerning identity constructions (Rucht 1995: 19–20). As collective identity is constantly in the making it cannot constitute a precondition for social movements but rather represents "an (interstage) product of repeated interaction" (Rucht 1995: 14, author's translation). Nonetheless, empirical research suggests that collective identities also rely on the characteristics emphasized by primordialism and social structuralism. Moreover, they are influenced by similarity in personal characteristics, by common fate, and shared experiences of collective action (Klandermans 1997: 41; Snow 2001: 2215–2216). Interestingly, collective identity can arise from "the discovery of preexisting bonds, interests, and boundaries" (Polletta and Jasper 2001: 298). This implies a redefinition and renegotiation of existing relationships between actors and demonstrates the fluidity of collective identity.

As mentioned above, collective identity is constructed in social interactions with different kinds of audiences including bystanders, opponents, media, and authorities (Polletta and Jasper 2001: 298). It can even be constructed and ascribed to a collective by outsiders without the involvement of the individuals concerned (Polletta and Jasper 2001: 285). Collective identity becomes salient in cultural materials like symbols, rituals, styles, and narratives (Polletta and Jasper 2001: 285). These symbolic resources also mark the boundary between insiders and outsiders (Snow 2001: 2216). The delineation of boundaries, which is an integral part of collective identity, makes identity work a complex process. Social movements have to find a balance between internal cohesion and external differentiation, on the one hand, and openness and low entry barriers that allow for the recruitment of new movement participants, on the other hand (Rucht 2002: 331). Rucht suggests that diffuse external barriers and the admittance of heterogeneous groups to the movement implicate a risk of deadlock, loss of discriminating power and efficacy, and eventual fragmentation (Rucht 2002: 331–332). Moreover, he argues that the question of balancing internal cohesion against external openness is especially relevant for transnational social movements that have to reconcile cultures, styles, and practices when engaging in identity work (Rucht 2002: 332). Regarding the collective action against the Belo Monte Dam, I propose that the conciliation of cultures, styles, and practices is not only relevant in transnational social movement but also in smaller geographical unities (like regions or even communities) that are characterized by ethnic diversity and strong heterogeneity in social, economic, and cultural terms. According to Turner and Killian (1987), members within one social movement can have different identities based on their participation in local chapters or working groups. Being based on common activities, these identities are likely to be more concrete than the abstract collective identity of the entire social movement (Turner and Killian 1987: 136). Due to the coexistence of collective identities in a movement, Turner and Killan speak of social movements as "diffuse collectives" that allow for the inclusion of different identities that are consistent with the rather abstract collective identity of the broader movement (cf. Rucht 1995: 14).

Another factor that influences the development of a strong collective identity is the degree of opposition that a social movement encounters. Drawing on Touraine (1973), Rucht emphasizes that the existence of a conflict with another social group and the perception of common interests that meet external opposition are constitutive of a collective identity. They contribute to the contouring and structuring of the social movement as a distinctive and coherent social entity (Rucht 1995: 13, 2002: 331). This is also an important aspect for the analysis of the social movement against the Belo Monte Dam, as the movement is confronted with strong opposition from governments and companies.

2.4 The Framing Approach

Until the 1980s the beliefs and perceptions of social movement participants were dismissed as determinants for social movement emergence as they were considered ubiquitous. However, research has shown that social movements take on the important functions of carrying and transmitting existing beliefs and producing meanings through shaping and structuring the sociopolitical reality (Snow and Benford 1988: 198). Hence, framing processes have become a central explanatory factor in social movement theory alongside resource mobilization theory and political opportunity structures (Benford and Snow 2000: 612).

The framing approach is based on the works of interactionist Erving Goffman (Goffman 1974; see above) and was introduced to social movement theory mainly by Snow and Benford (Snow and Benford 1988, 1992; Snow et al. 1986; also see Haunss 2004: 36; Rucht 2002: 336). They refer to a frame as "an interpretative schemata that simplifies and condenses the 'world out there' by selectively punctuating and encoding objects, situations, events, experiences, and sequences of actions within one's present or past environment" (Snow and Benford 1992: 137). Hence, a frame corresponds to an extract or a certain perspective of reality that emphasizes some aspects while hiding others. It explains a movement's raison d'être and legitimizes the collective action (Snow 2008: 383). Regarding the Belo Monte conflict, one could think of a variety of possible interpretations of the historic and recent developments. For example, the collective action against Belo Monte can be framed as an indigenous struggle, a social and environmental conflict, or a general question of social and political order (see, for example, GfbV n.d.; Schulz 2013; Storm 2013; Survival International n.d.). The perception and subsequent presentation of the conflict as an indigenous, social, environmental, or ideological issue corresponds to the mindset and relevance system of the respective author. While frames are prevalent in everyday life, social movements employ them strategically in order to align their participants' perceptions of reality (Klandermans 1997: 121–122). Framing – as a process – refers to "the conscious strategic efforts by groups of people to fashion shared understandings of the world and of themselves that legitimate and motivate collective action" (McAdam et al. 1996: 6, emphasis omitted). This definition emphasizes that framing is a dynamic, interactive, and controversial process that may challenge existing interpretations of reality. If successful, it results in a shared understanding of a situation that has been identified as problematic. However, the framing activity is not limited to the interpretation of reality; it also aims to promote collective action. The term collective action frame refers to "action-oriented sets of beliefs and meanings that inspire and legitimate the activities and campaigns of a social movement organization" (Benford and Snow 2000: 614). These frames are typically addressed at constituents, antagonists, bystanders, and observers. They contribute to creating public attention, to disseminating information, and to mobilizing and legitimizing collective action (Benford and Snow 2000: 613; Hellmann 1998: 22). The framing approach adds a new dimension to the conceptualization of social movements in the present study. I argue that social movements are not only based on a shared collective identity, as proposed by Diani, but also on the continuous "production and maintenance of meaning" (Benford and Snow 2000: 613). Therefore, the study adopts the collective identity approach and the framing approach as the theoretical perspectives for analysis.

If frames are produced by ordinary people and are therefore prevalent in everyday life, what are the distinguishing features of collective action frames? How do they come to be shared by a group of people and promote collective action? According to McAdam and colleagues, framing is a deliberate process; its core tasks have been elaborated by Snow and Benford. The first task in the framing process is the identification of a problem in social life that needs alteration. The second task is for the social movement to propose a solution to the problem that has been identified. The third task is the development of a rationale for collective action and the formulation of an appeal to participate in the social movement (Benford and Snow 2000: 615–618; Snow and Benford 1988: 199). The process of identifying a social problem is called diagnostic framing and involves the development of a shared understanding of a problematic situation. Research has shown that many diagnostic frames are injustice frames, a concept introduced by Gamson and colleagues (1982). Injustice frames comprise the belief that the authorities' behavior violates the "shared moral principles" of a group of people (Gamson et al. 1982: 123). Apart from injustice frames, Benford and Snow emphasize that in general terms the identification of the sources and victims of a problematic situation is central to diagnostic framing. By assigning roles and responsibilities, social movements can identify the addressees of their claims (Benford and Snow 2000: 616). However, an injustice frame – or a diagnostic frame, in general – does not automatically lead to collective action. It has to be matched with other frames that propose and justify collective action as the only adequate solution to the problem (Gamson et al. 1982: 122–124; Sandstrom et al. 2010: 220). Hence, the second core framing task is concerned with the solution of the problematic situation and is therefore called prognostic framing. The prognostic frame that results from this process proposes solutions to the problem and outlines possible activities and strategies that contribute to achieving the proposed solution. However, the range of possible and reasonable solutions is constrained by several factors including the nature of the problem itself and the positions and strategies of the other actors involved in the debate. Social movements can be challenged by the counterframes of their opponents and by disagreement among SMOs within the social movement. Even if SMOs present concordant diagnostic frames that identify the same problem, they may propose different solutions and develop different prognostic frames (Benford and Snow 2000: 617). The third core framing task aims to motivate movement participants to take action, and is therefore called motivational framing. It emphasizes the agency of actors and provides them with a rationale and a vocabulary of motive for collective action (Benford and Snow 2000: 617).

Contemporary scholars have also evaluated the characteristics of collective action frames in terms of direction, flexibility and inclusivity, scope and influence, and resonance. Collective action frames address a wide variety of contentious issues. One hypothesis relating to problem identification developed by Gerhards and Rucht (1992) is particularly interesting for the analysis of the social movement against the Belo Monte Dam. These authors claim that "[t]he larger the range of the problems covered by a frame, the larger the range of societal groups who can be addressed with the frame and the greater the mobilization capacity of the frame" (Gerhards and Rucht 1992: 580). If this hypothesis is true, the converse argument would be that a frame with a strong mobilization capacity that is supported by a large range of societal groups is likely to address a large range of problems. More specifically, the successful mobilization of the heterogeneous social movement against Belo Monte should depend – at least in part – on a broad and inclusive collective action frame that addresses a variety of issues. Hence, the collective identity approach and the framing approach are adequate theoretical perspectives for analyzing the persistence of the collective action and the maintenance of movement cohesion in the social movement against the Belo Monte Dam.

Another important feature of collective action frames is their cultural resonance – that is, their effectiveness in connecting their contents to the experiences and beliefs of a target audience. As discussed above, frames are developed by groups of people in interactive and often controversial negotiation processes that eventually arrive at shared understandings of a problem. In order for a collective action frame to resonate with a target audience, these shared understandings must be credible and the frame must be salient. Credibility is evaluated in terms of frame consistency, empirical credibility, and the credibility of frame articulators (Benford and Snow 2000: 619–622). Salience, on the other hand, depends on the centrality of the beliefs, values, and ideas for the lives of the target audience as well as the frame's coherence with the people's everyday experiences (experiential commensurability) and cultural narratives (narrative fidelity) (Benford and Snow 2000: 619–622).[33]

The question that remains is: How do frames contribute to the mobilization of social movement participants? And how do different social movements come to connect their frames? Social movement organizations are interested in mobilizing society, recruiting new members, forging ties with other organiza-

33 See also Herkenrath (2011: 49) and Snow and Benford (1988).

tions, and acquiring resources. Benford and Snow have investigated the frame alignment process that social movement organizations employ when reaching out to potential adherents. They differentiate four basic alignment processes: frame bridging, frame amplification, frame extension, and frame transformation (Benford and Snow 2000: 624–625).

1. Frame bridging is suspected to be one of the most prevalent framing strategies. It occurs when "two or more ideologically congruent but structurally unconnected frames regarding a particular issue or problem" are linked (Benford and Snow 2000: 624). Frame bridging can take place on the individual level when social movement organizations reach out to unmobilized segments of society in an attempt to connect people's sentiments to the collective action frame. It can also occur across social movements (Benford and Snow 2000: 624).
2. Frame amplification seems to be particularly relevant to movements holding values that challenge those of the dominant culture. Social movements employing this process of frame alignment seek to mobilize new activists by appealing to their preexisting beliefs and values and by reassuring them about their sentiments. The amplification of beliefs and values typically "involves [their] idealization, embellishment, clarification, or invigoration" (Benford and Snow 2000: 624).
3. "Frame extension entails depicting an SMO's interests and frame(s) as extending beyond its primary interests to include issues and concerns that are presumed to be of importance to potential adherents" (Benford and Snow 2000: 625). While frame extension can lead to internal disputes about the ideological purity of a movement and may thus challenge movement cohesion (Benford and Snow 2000: 625), I propose that frame extension can also promote the mobilization of hitherto unmobilized segments of society and contribute to the development of (new) collective identities.
4. Frame transformation aims to overturn existing understandings and meanings prevalent in society by proposing a counterframe – that is, alternative understandings of a particular issue or problem (Benford and Snow 2000: 625).

The framing concept has been applied extensively to the study of social movements since the mid-1990s (Benford and Snow 2000: 612), and much research has been done on the core tasks of framing. According to Snow (2008), scholarly research on frames and framing processes typically focuses on "(1) enlargement and clarification of the conceptual architecture of collective action frames and framing processes [...]; (2) empirical research investigating the application and analytic utility of various framing concepts [...]; (3) exploration of the link between framing processes and other factors relevant to the dynamics of social movements [...]; (4) methodological issues and techniques relevant to conducting framing research [...]; and (5) critical assessment of the framing perspective" (Snow 2008: 386).[34] While this research falls into the second category, it also addresses the relationship between framing and collective identity (third category) as well as methodological questions of social movement research with a focus on non-Western case studies (fourth category). It reconstructs framing processes from original data, and then compares the empirical findings with Benford and Snow's theoretical concepts, with a view to advancing the theoretical debate.

2.5 The Difference between Collective Identity and Framing

The discussion of collective identity and framing shows that the concepts are closely related. Both are conceptualized as dynamic processes that demand actors to negotiate and construct meaning in order to create movement cohesion (Hellmann 1998: 19; also see Daphi 2011: 15). Therefore, research focusing on identity frequently considers framing processes in order to explain the mobilization and integration of activists in social movements (Daphi 2011: 15; also see Haunss 2004). What, then, is the difference between collective identity and framing? I propose that identities and frames are similar in that they are based on shared beliefs about the world. At the same time, they differ because they focus on distinct effects and implications of these beliefs. Collective identity is central to the self-assurance of a group and centers on the differentiation between in-group and out-group. Framing, on the other hand, serves to manifest this differentiation by creating group cohesion and a consistent behavior towards the outside world (Hellmann 1998: 16–17). Based on Gamson's insight that social movement participation contributes to the enlargement of personal identity (Gamson 1992: 56), Snow and McAdam discuss various forms of identity work and the role of framing in these processes (Snow and McAdam 2000). Drawing on Hunt and colleagues (Hunt et al. 1994), they emphasize that framing processes contribute substantially to the construction of identities (Snow and McAdam 2000: 53). As stated above, frames provide shared understandings of

34 Snow references a large number of theoretical and empirical studies falling into these focal categories (Snow 2008: 386). As this list is to serve illustrative purposes only, the references are not reproduced here.

events and the actors involved, thus "situating or placing relevant sets of actors in time and space and [...] attributing characteristics to them that suggest specifiable relationships and lines of action" (Hunt et al. 1994: 185). Likewise, Rucht emphasizes that the framing of the opposition, the contentious issues, and the role of the social movement are important for the development of a collective identity (Rucht 1995: 16). Framing processes are therefore consistent with processes of identity construction in that they organize the world in a way that actors can make sense of occurrences and actions, and define their identities accordingly (Snow and McAdam 2000: 54).

2.6 Cohesion in Social Movements

Social movement scholars assume that a sense of cohesion is fundamental for the development of collective action; however, they rarely define movement cohesion in their works (Flesher Fominaya 2010b; Hunt and Benford 2004; Polletta and Jasper 2001; Teune 2008).[35] Drawing from Pearlman (2011), I conceptualize movement cohesion as "the cooperation among individuals that enables unified action" (Pearlman 2011: 9). Cohesion does not imply that individuals have identical motives, objectives, ideas and beliefs (Pearlman 2011: 11); rather, it emerges "when the forces assisting cooperative behavior exceed the forces encouraging competitive or antagonistic behavior" (Pearlman 2011: 9). Pearlman attributes the development and maintenance of movement cohesion to internal command and control, which enable the unified action of autonomous individuals. In her analysis of the Palestine national movement she focuses on (1) leadership, (2) institutions, and (3) the population's sense of collective purpose as the three most important factors facilitating cooperation (Pearlman 2011: 9).

This study takes up the three factors identified by Pearlman; however, instead of measuring to what degree they are present in the social movement against Belo Monte, I reconstruct the local activists' understanding of each of the factors. To this end, I assess the movement participants' sense of collective purpose by analyzing their understanding of the conflict (framing) and the motives behind their participation in the collective action (identities). Moreover, I examine the role and possible leadership of social movement organizations and individual actors in uniting the activities of various civil society organizations. According to Gardner, "leadership is the process of persuasion or example by

35 Hunt and Benford (2004) and Polletta and Jasper (2001) use the term solidarity instead of cohesion. I agree with Flesher Fominaya (2010b) and Mizruchi (1992) that the terms are used interchangeably in social movement research. In this study I use the term cohesion exclusively.

which an individual (or leadership team) induces a group to pursue objectives held by the leader or shared by the leader and his or her followers" (Gardner 1993: 1). I use this as a working definition but focus on the interviewees' concept of leadership, which I reconstruct in Chapter 5 and evaluate in Chapter 6. Institutions – the third factor introduced by Pearlman – are generally understood as to provide rules for social interaction between individuals and groups (Pearlman 2011: 10). In this study, they play a subordinate role, due to the focus on individuals and the meaning they attribute to the Belo Monte project and the collective action. However, institutions enter into the analysis through the discussion of the strained relationship between civil society and the authorities on the local, state, and federal levels.

While collective identity has been identified as the basis for collective action and an important factor in the development and maintenance of movement cohesion (Flesher Fominaya 2010b: 377; Teune 2008: 533), the relationship between collective identity and cohesion remains vague. I argue that cohesion – defined as the cooperation between individuals and/or groups – is possible even between heterogeneous movement organizations, provided that they identify with a collective purpose and accept common institutions and leadership. I further propose that collective identity goes beyond collective action that is done in view of a collective purpose. This is because collective identity entails a sense of we-ness that is based on shared beliefs, interests, and experiences other than the collective purpose. While collective identity contributes to the development and maintenance of social movement cohesion, cooperation between actors does not automatically imply that they share a collective identity.

2.7 Definition of Central Theoretical Concepts

As the above discussion of the collective identity approach and the framing approach has demonstrated, there is a vast literature on social movements with a number of independent research strands. However, these concepts cannot be "applied" directly to the empirical data. In line with the grounded theory methodology, the collective identity approach and the framing approach are the theoretical perspectives that guide this research. For this purpose, the relevant theoretical concepts have to be defined and operationalized for data collection and analysis. In this section, I develop definitions of the central theoretical concepts based on the social movement literature discussed above. In Chapter 3, I operationalize these concepts for the purpose of data collection, and I explain how they inform the analysis.

(1) Collective action

In general terms, the protest activities against the Belo Monte Dam can be referred to as collective action. In line with Snow and colleagues (Snow et al. 2008: 6), the term collective action is deliberately used in a broad sense to refer to any kind of joint activity performed by at least two individuals who pursue a common objective in the realm of contentious politics.

(2) Social movement

More precisely, the collective action against the Belo Monte Dam is assumed to be a social movement. The conceptualization of social movement used in this study is based on the five axes developed by Snow and colleagues (2008) and the dimensions proposed by Diani (Diani 2003: 301–306; also see Della Porta and Diani 2006: 20–21; Diani 1992: 7). Based on Snow, I conceptualize social movements as "collectivities acting with some degree of organization and continuity outside of institutional or organizational channels for the purpose of challenging or defending extant authority, whether it is institutionally or culturally based, in the group, organization, society, culture, or world order of which they are a part" (Snow et al. 2008: 11). In order to specify the definition and to integrate the network perspective, I treat collectivities as "network[s] of informal interactions between a plurality of individuals, groups and/or organizations" (Diani 1992: 13). I further assume that collective identities play an important role in enabling collectives to work towards a common objective in an organized and lasting fashion. As Deaux and Reid propose, "[c]ollectivism implies an emphasis on group cohesion, common fate, distinction from out-groups, and shared norms and standards" (Deaux and Reid 2000: 186). Assuming that these dimensions are closely connected to collective identities and collective action frames, I adopt the collective identity approach and the framing approach as the theoretical perspectives for my analysis.

While this conceptualization of social movements seems adequate for the study of the collective action against the Belo Monte Dam, it should be stressed that before conducting the actual analysis it remains unclear whether the phenomenon constitutes a social movement according to the above conceptualization. Throughout this study, I treat the collective action against Belo as a social movement based on a preliminary assumption that is discussed in detail in the fist sensitizing concept (cf. Chapter 3).

(3) Collective Identity

The disagreement about collective identity being either an individual or a collective attribute has important implications for the research question and research design of a study (Daphi 2011: 19). If collective identity is conceptualized as a collective attribute, the level of analysis should likewise be the collective – for example, a social movement organization. Studies taking this perspective typically focus on rituals, symbols, and movement discourses (see, for example, Haunss 2004, 2011). On the other hand, if collective identity is conceptualized as an individual attribute, data collection and analysis take place at the level of the individual by means of qualitative interviews, surveys, observation, or experiments (see, for example, Simon 2011). As discussed earlier, this study takes a social psychological perspective and assumes that collective identity is an individual attribute that is embedded in the individual's identity hierarchy (Simon 2011: 40; Stryker 2000: 33–34). In line with this perspective, personal and social identities are included in the research in order to analyze how they interact with collective identity. Media reports and information material provided by SMOs tend to differentiate between different groups of people that are affected by the hydropower project. The groups most frequently referred to are riverine people, indigenous people, fishers, subsistence farmers, and townspeople. They can be expected to have different social identities based on distinct ethnic backgrounds and lifestyles. In order to gain further insight into their identities and the interaction between the different types of identities, I define collective identity broadly as the shared sense of belonging to a collectivity (we) in contrast to other actors (them). It is based on shared attributes and experiences, and leads to collective agency (cf. Rucht 1995, 2002; Snow 2001). This broad definition enables interviewees to explicate their relevance system. They can situate themselves in the context of various collectivities; and they can elaborate on their beliefs, experiences, objectives, and motives behind the collective action against Belo Monte. This kind of data es expected to provide further insight into framing processes and identity work, on the one hand, and the relationship between an actor's personal, social, and collective identities, on the other hand.

(4) Framing and Collective Action Frames

Based on McAdam and colleagues, framing is conceptualized in this study as "the conscious strategic efforts by groups of people to fashion shared understandings of the world and of themselves that legitimate and motivate collective action" (McAdam et al. 1996: 6, emphasis omitted). Collective action frames are defined as "action-oriented sets of beliefs and meanings that inspire and legitimate the activities and campaigns of a social movement organization" (Benford and Snow 2000: 614). The objective of this study is to identify the collective action frame that has been developed and promoted by the social movement against the Belo Monte Dam – that is, the story of Belo Monte. Moreover, the study seeks to trace how the local population adopts the frame and how different actors contribute to the framing process.

The central theoretical concepts defined in this section guide the sampling, the development of the interview guides, and the data collection. They also form the basis for the coding scheme, which was developed in a combined top-down and bottom-up procedure. In Chapter 3, I discuss the method and procedures of this research as well as my analytical positioning on the application of the grounded theory methodology.

3 Method and Procedures

This study seeks to explore the collective action against the Belo Monte Dam in order to find out if and how collective identities and collective action frames contributed to the persistence of the collective action and the maintenance of movement cohesion in the social movement. Following a qualitative research design, the objective is to develop empirically grounded concepts that advance existing theories and contribute to evaluating the applicability of social movement theory in non-Western countries.[36]

Qualitative research undertakes in-depth analyses of complex social structures.[37] By using interpretive approaches and reconstructing meaning from the subjective statements of individuals, the qualitative researcher seeks to analyze an empirical phenomenon in its own right, to acknowledge its specific structure and dynamics, and to develop an understanding of the same. Hence, qualitative research is particularly suited to exploratory research that aims to build theory and/or develop hypotheses. In line with this approach, this study presents five central findings that abstract from the specific case and offer more general explanations that contribute to theoretical debates and inform future empirical research.

This chapter presents the methods and procedures applied throughout the course of the study.[38] Section 3.1 provides a precise and comprehensive review of the constitutive characteristics, assumptions, and requirements of GTM

---

36 The term concept refers to "the building blocks of theories" (Shoemaker et al. 2004: 15). Concepts are derived from the empirical material, and represent abstractions of specific aspects of the empirical phenomenon that is being studied. In order to build theory, concepts have to be compared and related to each other (Corbin and Strauss 2008: 51–52; Shoemaker et al. 2004: 15). The term theory refers to "a set of well-developed categories (themes, concepts) that are systematically interrelated through statements of relationship to form a theoretical framework that explains some phenomenon" (Corbin and Strauss 2008: 55; also see Hage 1972: 34).

37 Qualitative research should be understood as an umbrella term for a vast number of methods and approaches applied in the social sciences (Flick 2005: par. 1). The special issue of *Forum: Qualitative Social Research* on "Qualitative Methods in Europe" discusses the methodological variety in detail, focusing on the European perspectives on qualitative research and their differences vis-à-vis the Anglo-Saxon literature (*Forum: Qualitative Social Research*, Vol. 6, No. 3, September 2005).

38 Parts of this chapter were previously published as a GIGA Working Paper (Peters 2014).

sensu Strauss and Corbin. Section 3.2 presents my approach to data collection, while Section 3.3 elaborates on the process of data analysis including interview transcription and coding. In Section 3.4, I explain my differentiated approach to the disclosure of methods and data and discuss quality standards in qualitative research. In the final section (3.5), I reflect upon the applicability of the theories that I use and my own assumptions and expectations.

3.1 Grounded Theory Methodology

Grounded theory methodology was developed in the 1960s by the U.S. sociologists Barney Glaser and Anselm Strauss with the objectives of disclosing their own research procedures and offering a formalized research program that emphasized openness and unbiasedness towards the empirical phenomenon. After a dispute and the parting of the two scholars, Glaser and Strauss (the latter together with Corbin) developed independent approaches to the analysis of qualitative data.[39] The data analysis sensu Strauss and Corbin is based on a coding paradigm and so-called sensitizing concepts that facilitate the deliberate use of previous theoretical knowledge in the data analysis. Researchers following this approach emphasize that references to existing literature throughout the research process contribute to the better understanding of one's own empirical work (Corbin and Strauss 2008: 75). At the end of the research project, the concepts and/or theories developed from the empirical data can be associated with and compared to existing theories (Mey and Mruck 2009: 108). Based on a literature review and experiences gathered in the process of the preliminary study, I developed six sensitizing concepts that explicate my expectations and assumptions and disclose my relevance system with respect to this research project (cf. Section 3.5).

Although GTM offers an entire research program, the methodology does not prescribe a precise procedure and can even be applied selectively throughout the research process (Mey and Mruck 2009: 148; Oertzen 2006: 146). Researchers are free to choose their instruments for data collection, the degree of abstraction of the theory they seek to develop, and their hermeneutic procedure (Oertzen 2006: 146). Yet, as Corbin emphasizes, they "should be very clear at the beginning of a study what it is they are setting out to do" (Corbin and Strauss 2008: x).

39 Kelle (2011) provides a detailed account of the controversy between Glaser and Strauss, also discussing the underlying theoretical traditions that have shaped their approaches.

Grounded theory methodology is based on two theoretical traditions: symbolic interactionism and pragmatism. As discussed in Chapter 2, symbolic interactionism stresses human agency in the creation of social meanings and social order (Sandstrom et al. 2010: 2). The philosophy of pragmatism in turn constitutes the basis for symbolic interactionism, as it assumes "that knowledge is created through action and interaction" (Corbin and Strauss 2008: 2).[40] Consequently, GTM emphasizes collective processes, human behavior, and interaction. It assumes that the world is complex, and that events result from multiple factors. Therefore, any methodology has to strive for a balance between capturing complexity and reducing complexity with the objective of developing concepts at different levels of abstraction (Corbin and Strauss 2008: 8). Mey and Mruck (2009) have structured the extensive literature on concepts and approaches in GTM and have select three elements they consider constitutive of the methodology:

1. Building of concepts instead of description: The principle task of GTM is the analytical step from data to concepts. It is assumed that any data segment – for example, an interview statement – points towards broader underlying ideas. Relevant data segments are therefore considered empirical indicators of theoretical concepts (Strauss 1998: 54). Concepts are developed through constant comparison, interpretation, and abstraction of data segments, and they eventually form the building blocks of an empirically grounded theory (Mey and Mruck 2009: 109).
2. Theoretical sampling and theoretical saturation: When GTM is used, data collection and analysis should be iterative, meaning that a first round of data collection should be followed by data analysis and a subsequent round of data collection based on the initial findings. This procedure contributes to the theoretical saturation of the concepts – that is, their gradual development based on the purposeful and selective collection of those data that contribute to the analysis. As the data collection for this study took place abroad, theoretical sampling could only be applied during the stage of data analysis (see below).
3. Writing of memos: GTM requires that the decisions regarding case selection, sampling, and analysis that are taken repeatedly throughout the research process be documented in memos. Therefore, I wrote extensive coding notes for each interview as well as analytical notes on the key

40 The philosophical orientation of grounded theory methodology is discussed in Corbin and Strauss (2008: 1–8).

concepts that emerged from the data analysis. The memos contributed significantly to the development of concepts and categories, the elaboration of the relationships between them, and the evaluation of the finding's generalizability.

The grounded theory methodology is the most suitable approach for the investigation of the social movement against the Belo Monte Dam for three reasons. First, the study aims to evaluate the applicability of Western theories and concepts in non-Western case studies and to contribute theoretically grounded concepts to the existing theoretical framework. GTM offers a systematic and rule-based approach to data analysis that emphasizes the constant comparison of original data – among itself and with previous knowledge. Therefore, it is an adequate tool for studies that seek comparison, both in the broad and in the narrow sense (cf. Chapter 1). Second, when applying Western theories to non-Western case studies, attention should be paid to possible differences in the meaning of concepts. This necessitates an open and unbiased approach that uncovers indexicality.[41] Third, GTM is particularly well suited to research conducted in foreign languages, as will be discussed in Section 3.4.

3.2 Collection of Original Primary Data

As argued in Chapter 1, this study focuses on the identities, motives, and objectives of the movement participants and their understanding of the social conflict and their collective action. Consequently, the study takes individual participants in the social movement as the unit of analysis. Qualitative data are particularly suited to the analysis of meanings that people attribute to structures, processes, and events. Moreover, they are especially useful in exploratory studies (Miles and Huberman 1994: 9–10). While social movement organizations and activists have produced written material about the Belo Monte conflict and the associated collective action, this material generally does not provide personal accounts of the individuals' identities, motives, and objectives. Therefore, original data had to be collected through semistructured interviews as part of this study.

The data collection was prepared thoroughly based on methodological considerations regarding the content, structure, and conduct of the interviews (cf. Helfferich 2009: 37–38). All interviewees were provided with information about the study and an informed-consent form stating the purpose of the inter-

41 Indexicality refers to the fact that language is vague, and that meaning depends on context (Garfinkel 1981: 204–205; Przyborski and Wohlrab-Sahr 2010: 29; also see below).

view and guaranteeing confidentiality to research participants.[42] During the preliminary field trip to São Paulo, Brasília, and Rio de Janeiro in the fall of 2011, 31 semistructured interviews with experts from different disciplines and three interviews with activists in São Paulo were conducted in order to gain background information about the case. These interviews were fairly structured with a focus on issues pertaining to the area of expertise of the interviewee. Emphasis was placed on the interviewee's status as an expert. Nonetheless, the role of the interviewer allowed for occasional references to previous knowledge during the interview. The collection of primary data about the motives and objectives of local movement participants and the dynamics inside the social movement against Belo Monte took place in May and June 2012 in Altamira and Belém. These interviews were fairly open and comprised narrative parts that allowed the interviewee to explicate his/her own relevance system and communicative patterns. Emphasis was placed on the interviewee's status as an expert of his/her own life (cf. Helfferich 2009: 163). According to her role, the interviewer neglected her previous knowledge and assumptions in order to remain open to the views and beliefs of the interviewee. Nonetheless, it is challenging for the researcher to fully comprehend the respondent's structuring of social reality (*Fremdverstehen* – understanding the other). The exact meaning of verbal and nonverbal expressions is always specified by context, making communication indexical (Przyborski and Wohlrab-Sahr 2010: 31). Indexicality refers to the fact that language is vague and that verbal expressions merely point towards meaning that is dependent on context (Garfinkel 1981: 204–205; Przyborski and Wohlrab-Sahr 2010: 29). Qualitative research seeks to uncover this indexicality by enabling research participants to explain their relevance system, and by systematically addressing potential differences in the interpretive frames of the researcher and the research participants (Przyborski and Wohlrab-Sahr 2010: 31). The interview guide for this study was developed in consideration of these issues. Moreover, special attention was paid to the so-called internal equivalence of the interview guide – that is, the consideration of cultural differences in the formulation of the interview stimuli in order to avoid bias in the data collection (Westle 2005: 151–152). Equivalence is a relevant issue for two reasons. First, as the study applies Western concepts to a non-Western case study, it is necessary to properly transfer the concepts of interest to the particular cultural setting of the case study (equivalence on the conceptual level) (cf. Westle 2005: 156–157). Second, as the interviews were conducted in Portuguese while the conceptual work took place in English linguistic inaccuracy arising from translation had to

42 For matters of research ethics and data protection see Helfferich (2009: 190 et seq.).

be avoided (equivalence on the linguistic level) (cf. Westle 2005: 159). The translation of the interview guide was supported by a research assistant who was properly informed about the research project and its objectives.[43] This enabled him to give substantial feedback on common formulations, connotations of words, cultural context, and potential misunderstandings in the interview guide.

The sampling strategy suggested by grounded theory methodology is called theoretical sampling and reflects the reiterative approach to data collection and analysis that is typical of GTM. In an ideal case, the researcher starts the analysis right after collecting the first piece of data, develops preliminary concepts and subsequent questions, and continues the data collection with a specific focus on the concepts she is interested in. Hence, the researcher is not sampling research participants but concepts (Corbin and Strauss 2008: 144). Theoretical sampling continues until data saturation is reached, meaning that all categories are sufficiently developed in terms of their properties and dimensions (Corbin and Strauss 2008: 148–149). However, as the data collection took place abroad, this study had to align the formal requirements with the practical constraints of the project. The sampling in Belém was largely based on a list of relevant organizations that was prepared beforehand. By contrast, the sampling in Altamira was predominantly conducted at the office of the Xingu Forever Alive Movement – an approach that is in line with Corbin and Strauss (cf. Corbin and Strauss 2008: 153). As the movement against Belo Monte is very heterogeneous, I deliberately selected interviewees from different places of residence and diverse socioeconomic backgrounds. Moreover, I applied theoretical sampling in the analysis of the interview data. To this effect, I used the principles of theoretical sampling to determine the order in which I analyzed my interviews (cf. Corbin and Strauss 2008: 150). Based on my knowledge of the interview contents and peculiarities, I always sought to select an interview for analysis that would contribute to the elaboration of the concept(s) that I was working on at that time. The selection was informed by the concepts of minimal and maximal contrasts, which suggest that the next piece of data should at first glance appear to be either similar to (minimal contrast) or completely different from (maximal contrast) the last collected piece (Keller 2005: par. 32; also see Corbin and Strauss 2008: 146–148). While minimal contrasts are helpful for the elaboration of concepts, maximal contrasts are helpful in determining the scope of validity of a concept. In the early phase of the data analysis, I hypothesized that activists affiliated with the Catholic Church were motivated by a desire to fulfill their vo-

43 The research assistant is a native Brazilian who was trained in linguistics and has extensive experience in the transcription of semistructured interviews.

cation and Christian mission. In order to substantiate the relevant concepts, I analyzed a number of interviews with movement participants working in the realm of the Catholic Church, and subsequently selected interviews with local activists working outside this realm.

During the interviews, participants were encouraged to give personal reports on relevant issues and to focus on any aspect they considered important. Questions were deliberately phrased as storytelling prompts with the objective of initiating descriptive narrations and giving interviewees the opportunity to express their holistic perception of the conflict. To that end, all but one of the interviews were conducted in Portuguese, the interviewees' native or working language. The interview guides comprised four sets of questions for social movement participants and seven sets of questions for key informants, with the additional questions demanding a higher degree of reflection about the social setting and the collective action. The questions for social movement participants focused on (1) interpretive frameworks; (2) actors involved in the protest; (3) identity, self-perception, and perception by others; and (4) cooperation enabled by frame alignment and collective identities. The additional questions for key informants addressed (1) the mechanisms of frame alignment; (2) adjustments in frameworks and identities as compared to the protests of the 1980s;[44] and (3) gender issues and the role of women in the social movement. In order to answer the latter three sets of questions, interviewees needed a basic understanding of recruitment processes, collective action, identities of activists, and interpretive frameworks, which could not be expected from the average interviewee.

In order to utilize the central theoretical concepts defined in Chapter 2 for the data collection, the concepts had to be operationalized. One challenge in the semistructured interviews was to prevent participants – and especially those with media experience – from giving standard or desirable answers. Rather, interviewees should be encouraged to explicate their personal understanding of the social conflict and the collective action. For this purpose, collective action frames were operationalized as the interviewees' perception of the "real meaning" of the Belo Monte Dam and the associated costs and benefits. In the opening question, interviewees were asked to describe what they perceived as the core issues of the conflict beyond the arguments prevalent in the public debate. Identity was operationalized as the personal motives behind the collective ac-

44 Differences between the collective action of the 1980s and the current wave of protest can be expected due to the redemocratization of the country, the withdrawal of the World Bank from the financing of the project, and significant modifications of the project, among others.

tion and the role of participants in the social movement. This operationalization was based on experiences from the preliminary study and the expectation that questions about motives would prompt people to make statements about themselves, their beliefs, and interests. Indeed, the question encouraged most activists to speak about their biography and to characterize themselves – for example, as a person of faith who fights Belo Monte to preserve the Creation, among others.

The data collection produced a comprehensive data set of good quality. Several factors indicate the authenticity of the research participants and their statements. For example, interviewees did not hesitate to talk about personal failure or to disagree with the interviewer, indicating that they sought to give honest rather than desirable answers. They spoke fast and used colloquial language, indicating that they perceived the interview setting as natural. Moreover, extraordinary reactions like interviewees struggling for composure or even crying were perceived as convincing indicators of authenticity (cf. Kruse et al. 2012a: 37–38). Despite the empirical richness of the interviews, one secondary source was included based on the recommendation of the interviewee himself.

3.3 Data Analysis

Since the development of GTM in the 1960s, a number of scholars have contributed to advancing the methodology, and various approaches have emerged.[45] Researchers are free to tailor their methods and procedures to their particular research project in order to develop an adequate analytical framework; however, they are requested to explicate their analytical approach and objectives. The process of data analysis includes interview transcription as well as coding and conceptualization.

The transcription of interviews is an important step in the research process that includes a number of decisions with respect to the transcription of verbal and nonverbal information (for example, utterances, gestures, and mimics), the representation of timing and sequence of speech (for example, overlaps, pauses, and silence), and the representation of dialects, among others. The purpose of the qualitative interviews was to focus on the subject matter and gather data about the issue(s) under investigation (cf. Behnke et al. 2006: 234). As the study does not pursue a linguistic analysis, simple transcription rules were applied in order to facilitate the transcription process and produce a legi-

45 For an overview of the method and its application in different disciplines, see Bryant and Charmaz (2007).

ble written document. It is important to note that it was not the transcripts but rather the research recordings – that is, the conversations held with research participants – that were considered to be data. Transcripts were used as a tool to help with the analysis of original data. However, whenever I had doubts about the completeness or reliability of a transcript, I turned to the original audio file in order not to lose contextual information. Of the 28 semistructured interviews conducted with activists in Altamira and Belém, 22 were selected based on the sound quality of the audio files and the relevance of the interview content. The transcription was outsourced to the same research assistant who had supported the translation of the interview guide. The transcription rules were based on Kuckartz (2010: 44); however, additional rules were developed in collaboration with the transcriber to accommodate the particularities of the study (cf. Lapadat 2000: 214–215). The focus of transcription was placed on the content of the conversation in order to allow for alignment with written language. Paralanguage (for example, gasps and sighs) and short pauses in the flow of words were considered irrelevant for the purposes of this study. However, longer pauses and exceptional reactions, such as crying and struggling to retain composure on the part of the interviewee, were considered relevant and therefore noted in the transcripts.

The central element of data analysis within GTM is the thorough coding of the empirical material. Coding refers to the development of concepts and categories and to the assignment of corresponding codes to the data (Kuckartz 2010: 74). The general aim of coding is to veer away from the empirical material (Kuckartz 2010: 96) by developing concepts on the basis of empirical indicators that capture the events and actions the researcher is interested in (Strauss 1998: 54). Once the analysis moves up the conceptual ladder, the concepts become broader and gain explanatory value, while at the same time losing some of their specificity. Consequently, higher-level concepts (= categories) have to rest solidly on lower-level concepts, which are in turn based in data (Corbin and Strauss 2008: 52). The term code refers to the word or short phrase that denotes an underlying concept or category (Mey and Mruck 2009: 114).[46] It can derive either from theoretical knowledge (conceptual code) or from the original data, in which case it uses the exact wording of the interviewee (in-vivo code) (Corbin and Strauss 2008: 65; Kuckartz 2010: 75; Mey and Mruck 2009: 114–155). Each type of code is analytic, in that it enables the researcher to abstract from the data and relate the concept to other concepts (Strauss 1998: 64). At the beginning of data analysis, concepts tend to be located at different levels of

46 Some scholars discard the term and speak directly of concepts and categories.

abstractions. Over the course of the analysis they are gradually refined, related to each other, and grouped into categories (Oertzen 2006: 149). This process involves the constant comparison of concepts and categories within and across documents – a procedure that is typical of GTM (Mey and Mruck 2009: 109).

The coding procedure introduced by Corbin and Strauss is characterized by three steps called open, axial, and selective coding (Corbin and Strauss 2008: 66, 159–160; Mey and Mruck 2009: 117; Oertzen 2006: 148). However, the differentiation between these steps is first and foremost an analytical one, as the three steps cannot be separated nor put into sequential order (Kuckartz 2010: 79). The first predominant task is for the researcher to immerse herself in the data by breaking up, investigating, comparing, conceptualizing, and categorizing the data (Kuckartz 2010: 75). The aim is to discover similarities and differences, develop and specify concepts, and identify their properties and dimensions (Corbin and Strauss 2008: 73–74; Strauss 1998: 100). This process can be facilitated by posing questions to the data, and making comparisons across data (Corbin and Strauss 2008: 67–68). Subsequently, the researcher can develop preliminary hypotheses, concepts, and categories that guide the theoretical sampling and the subsequent analysis (Strauss 1998: 42). The second predominant task of coding is the constant comparison of categories, concepts, and empirical incidents. This is mainly done using axial and selective coding. Axial coding aims to elaborate on the concepts and categories developed during open coding with the objective of establishing the relationships between them (Kelle 2011: 241; Mey and Mruck 2009: 117; Oertzen 2006: 150–151). As the transition from open to axial coding is fluent, the researcher can return to open coding and review codes and categories at any point in time (Mey and Mruck 2009: 129). The third step of coding refers to the theoretical integration of the interpretive work by identifying a core category and elaborating its relationships with all other categories (Corbin and Strauss 2008: xx; Kuckartz 2010: 77).[47] The aim is to develop a sequential and logic analytical story around a recurrent theme (Kuckartz 2010: 77–78). While the number of categories is reduced to a minimum in this process, special attention is paid to the properties and dimensions of the concepts; hence, the name selective coding. This step aims at developing a parsimonious but far-reaching theory (Strauss 1998: 66).

In this study, the in-depth analysis of 22 interviews led to the development of a comprehensive coding scheme that consists in 350 codes and was established in a combined top-down and bottom-up procedure. The coding

47 Most authors acknowledge that there may be more than one core category (Kuckartz 2010: 82; Oertzen 2006: 150; Strauss 1998: 65).

scheme is structured in four hierarchical levels of abstraction with higher-level categories being systematically built upon lower-level categories and concepts. Due to the hierarchical structure of the coding scheme, each level rests solidly on the respective lower levels of abstraction, and all categories and concepts are ultimately based on primary data. Considering the research question, theoretical perspectives, and sensitizing concepts, I started with a focus on collective identities and collective action frames, which form two out of three first-level categories.[48] The second-level categories reflect some of the central theoretical concepts (cf. Chapter 2). However, they were developed from the empirical data before they were compared to and labeled in accordance with existing concepts. For example, interviewees described processes that resembled the frame bridging process identified by Benford and Snow (2000), as the following quote illustrates.

> *"So, this understanding, which has a more individual origin, can, over time, advance towards a process of broader understanding, more collective; and this interaction, this relationship that the different peoples will have among themselves enables the understanding of the problem beyond the personal, individual, or specific problem." (P21)*

As this piece of data confirms previous research, I included the existing nomenclature into the coding scheme. The third-level categories emerged exclusively from the original data. For example, the following quote illustrates the "meaning of the river", which is a concept subordinated to the third-level category "regional context of Belo Monte".

> *"It is a major offense, it is very serious because you are directly affecting an entire history, an entire culture, an entire tradition, and entire array of signs and meanings that the river has. It is not the river, for the sake of the river. It is the river for the meaning that is carries for these peoples." (P1)*

While the concepts and third-level categories are unique to the Belo Monte case study, they abstract from the empirical incident and describe relationships and processes that could be relevant in other empirical cases too. In addition, each concept has different dimensions; for example, the concept "conflicts in Amazonia" has historical, geographical, and social dimensions, among others.

Oftentimes relevant statements in the interview transcripts can be interpreted and classified in different ways. I argue that the coding scheme serves to

48 The third fist-level category is called "movement and movement dynamics" and emerged from the data in a bottom-up procedure.

analytically separate and collect empirical indicators in order to analyze them in detail and elaborate the relationships between them. To this end, relevant statements were interpreted and coded according to the theoretical perspectives of the study and their relevance for the Belo Monte project and the collective action against it. As a general rule, I always assigned the most specific code possible to any interview statement. This enabled me to compare empirical incidents and elaborate on the relationships between concepts and categories at higher levels of abstraction. At the same time, any category can be illustrated with interview statements, as the hierarchical structure of the coding scheme guarantees that categories rest solidly on sub-categories and lower-level concepts, which are in turn based on data.

The inductive approach was particularly relevant in the structuring of the coding scheme and the relative emphasis of categories. For example, when cohesion and fragmentation emerged as central movement dynamics, I introduced another first-level category entitled "movement and movement dynamics" that comprises a large number of sub-categories and concepts specifying these dynamics.

Cohesion and fragmentation are the core categories in this study. Each of them builds upon a number of lower-level categories and concepts and is linked to the various concepts on identity and framing. The core categories capture the principal movement dynamics of the past years and contribute to explaining how the movement against Belo Monte entered into a process of fragmentation. Hence, the process of selective coding focused on the conceptualization of cohesion and fragmentation and on their relationships with the central theoretical concepts, identity and framing. The findings of the study abstract from the specific case with a view to informing social movement theory and future empirical research (cf. Chapter 6).

3.4 Standards in Qualitative Research

The case study and research design of this project require a differentiated approach to the disclosure of methods and data. On the one hand, there is a legitimate interest on the part of the research community and the public for the full disclosure of approaches and procedures regarding research design, data collection, analysis, and interpretation. On the other hand, there is a legitimate interest on the part of research participants for confidentiality and anonymity. Full disclosure of the research participants' beliefs and actions might expose these individuals and harm their integrity, given that activists in the research area suffer from criminalization, harassment, and insufficient law enforcement. Therefore, the study discloses as much information as possible and conceal as much information as necessary in order to ensure the interviewees' integrity and security. To this effect, the names of interviewees, organizations, and indigenous tribes have been removed. All interviewees, regardless of their status, are referred to as local activists, local movement participants, or interviewees. Pronouns that indicate the sex of the interviewee are avoided and "their" in the singular sense is used instead. In cases when interviewees refer to fellow activists in their responses, the names of the latter are spelled out in the analysis. This procedure seems reasonable, given that the general involvement of people in the collective action is a known fact within the region and does not require concealment.

The quality assessment of this study is tailored to the qualitative research design. Empirical studies are commonly assessed on the basis of their objectivity, reliability, and validity. However, many scholars consider these criteria inappropriate for the evaluation of qualitative research, because the analysis of meaning inevitably leads to subjectivity. While some scholars have sought to operationalize the above criteria for qualitative studies (Przyborski and Wohlrab-Sahr 2010: 35 et seq.), others claim that the classic quality criteria cannot be transferred to qualitative research given that the objectives and approaches of qualitative and quantitative research are different (Bergman and Coxon 2005: par. 8; Steinke 2005: 322). Grounded theory methodology sensu Strauss and Corbin makes a virtue of necessity in that it embraces subjectivity as natural and acknowledges the role of the researcher in the research process. Specific tools – for example, sensitizing concepts – are used to disclose the researcher's previous knowledge and assumptions and to evaluate the role of subjectivity in the analysis. In an attempt to elaborate quality criteria that are consistent with the epistemological underpinnings and methodological approaches of qualitative research, Steinke (2005) proposes a system of criteria that should be operationalized to meet the specificities of a particular research project (Steinke 2005: 322–324). Her system pertains to seven areas of quality assessment including (1) intersubject comprehensibility, (2) indication of the research process, (3) empirical foundation, (4) limitation, (5) coherence, (6) relevance, and (7) reflected subjectivity (Steinke 2005: 323–331). According to Steinke, several criteria should be met in order to ensure that quality standards in qualitative research are achieved. This study paid special attention to the following five criteria, which are also discussed in the literature on GTM:

1. **Intersubject comprehensibility** was sought through (1) the comprehensive documentation of the research process; (2) the introduction of sensitizing concepts; and (3) the thorough discussion of data requirements,

data quality, data collection methods, sampling methods, and transcription methods. Special attention was paid to the implications of doing interview research in a foreign language.

2. **Indication of the research process** refers to the appropriateness of research strategies, methods, and procedures, and depends on the proper documentation of the research process. The applicability of the GTM approach to the research interest and objective of this study was carefully evaluated based on the three constitutive elements of the methodology (cf. Section 3.1).
3. Qualitative research, whether theory testing or theory building, must have an **empirical foundation**. The thorough application of GTM, which aims to develop categories that rest solidly on lower-level concepts, which are in turn based on data, ensures the empirical foundation of the study's results.
4. Qualitative researchers should discuss the **limitation of their study's results**. A single case study cannot be representative of a universe of cases; yet, it can contribute substantially to the understanding of certain phenomena by identifying relevant concepts in understudied areas (Corbin and Strauss 2008: 319–320). The objective of this research is to provide an insight into the relevant issues and underlying theoretical concepts associated with the implementation of a hydropower plant in the Brazilian Amazon and to contribute to the debate about the applicability of Western theories and concepts in non-Western case studies (cf. Chapter 6).
5. As **subjectivity** is unavoidable in qualitative research, it should be reflected through self-observation and a critical assessment of one's own position vis-à-vis the research project and the possible research participants (Steinke 2005: 330–331). In this study, I critically reflect upon my own role as a researcher and on the impact of subjectivity on the analysis using the tools proposed by GTM – that is, sensitizing concepts and memo writing.

Corbin and Strauss suggest that researchers should not even try to create an objectivity that cannot be achieved. Instead, they should deliberately immerse themselves in the research and try to adopt the perspective of the research participants (Corbin and Strauss 2008: 32). In this study, I sought to achieve sensitivity by explicating and reflecting upon my own perspective using the sensitizing concepts and by seeking to interpret the results from the interviewees' perspective.

A key challenge of the Belo Monte study is the multilingual nature of the research: the interviews are conducted in Portuguese; the report is produced in

English; and the researcher's native language is German. As Kruse and Schmieder stress, reconstructive-hermeneutic procedures are especially appropriate for understanding meaning in foreign language situations (Kruse and Schmieder 2012: 251). GTM was therefore particularly well suited to this research project. Qualitative researchers agree that interviews should be conducted in the interviewees' native language, as research participants tend to feel more comfortable and express themselves more precisely in their native language (Kruse and Schmieder 2012: 248). To this end, I acquired adequate language skills for conducting the interviews in Portuguese and outsourced the translation of the interview guides and the transcription of the audio files to a native speaker. While this approach demanded additional effort in terms of quality control and the monitoring of the research assistant, it offered some interesting opportunities. Due to imperfect language skills, I reduced the pace of the conversation and made few interruptions, which enabled the interviewees to explicate their answers at length. Moreover, I used language difficulties deliberately as an excuse to request further explanations or examples, which resulted in more detailed narratives (cf. Kruse et al. 2012a). Another challenge of multilingual research is the presentation of the results in a written report. The translation of interview statements from Portuguese to English was limited to key passages intended to provide the reader with insight into the interviewees' thoughts and speech. I applied a set of rules developed by Nelofer Halai (2007) to the translation of interview statements. Halai seeks "inexact equivalence" in her translations. This approach focuses on conveying meaning and de-emphasizes the literal translation of statements (Halai 2007: 351–352; also see Kruse et al. 2012b: 14). A small number of Portuguese terms was not translated in order to prevent the reduction of meaning through inadequate translation and the forceful integration of data and concepts stemming from different cultural backgrounds (cf. Kruse et al. 2012b: 14). As the aim of qualitative research is to understand meaning, I decided to use translation rules that are open enough to enable an adequate and authentic expression of meaning given the linguistic and cultural context of the target language.

3.5 Sensitizing Concepts

Researchers applying GTM seek to base their arguments on empirical data – yet, they may also draw from existing theories and concepts. In doing so, they should reflect critically upon the underpinnings and implications of the theories they use and upon their own assumptions and expectations.

The ideas, interests, and previous knowledge of a researcher make up her relevance system and work like scanners on the empirical data (Kruse 2015: 482; also see Corbin and Strauss 2008: 32–33; Kelle 2011: 237). By highlighting certain elements in the data and omitting others, these scanners restrict the range of possible interpretations that the researcher is able to identify, thus threatening to constrict the analysis and to predetermine the research outcome. In order to remain as open and unbiased as possible, researchers should reflect upon their relevance system and disclose its elements in the sensitizing concepts (Kruse 2015: 481–484). According to Charmaz, sensitizing concepts "offer ways of seeing, organizing, and understanding experience" (Charmaz 2003: 259).[49] As the researcher is unable to dispense with her knowledge, she should apply it deliberately in order to be able to "respond to and receive the messages contained in data" (Corbin and Strauss 2008: 33).

Sensitizing concepts can only be used as a starting point for the analysis of data and the development of theory (Charmaz 2003: 259). In contrast to hypotheses, which can be tested using standardized methods, sensitizing concepts do not make predictions about the relationships between variables. They rather reflect the researcher's preliminary ideas about the research object and her research interest (Kelle 2011: 250; Kruse 2015: 480). The sensitizing concepts that I present and discuss below are derived from the social movement literature and from experiences gathered in the process of the preliminary study. They reflect my assumptions and expectations regarding the empirical incidents that I interpret; thus guiding the data analysis and the evaluation of the findings.

1. **The collective action against Belo Monte constitutes a social movement.** Based on Snow and colleagues (2008) and Diani (1992), this study conceptualizes social movements as collectivities that act outside of institutional channels in order to challenge extant authority (cf. Chapter 2). Participants and observers frequently refer to the collective action against Belo Monte as a social movement. However, if the analysis of the collective action reveals that it does not meet the criteria set forth in the definition it cannot be considered a social movement. Given that this study assesses the applicability of Western concepts in non-Western case studies, it would be necessary to determine what the collective action against Belo Monte is, should it not be a social movement according to the definition set forth in Chapter 2.

49 The idea is based on the work of Strauss' mentor Herbert Blumer. His work on sensitizing concepts is discussed in detail by Kelle (1997: 232–241).

2. **Collective identities and collective action frames are the object of analysis.** Based on the findings of the preliminary study, they are assumed to be central to the successful mobilization of actors and the maintenance of movement cohesion in the social movement against Belo Monte. As discussed in the introduction, the social movement is characterized by strong heterogeneity in terms of the participants' social and cultural backgrounds. Moreover, it aims to attract the attention of organizations and individuals working in various issue areas. It is reasonable to assume that the identities of prospective activists and the framing of the conflict play an important role in the mobilization of movement participants. The analysis of the social movement against Belo Monte gives insight into movement dynamics and the role of collective identities and collective action frames.
3. **Western theories and concepts need to be problematized.** Social movement theory is rooted in Western history and theorizing; hence, its application in non-Western case studies should be evaluated carefully in order to avoid conceptual stretching.[50] For example, the strict separation of civil society, family, state, and economy, which is central in the Western conceptualization of civil society, does not exist in many non-Western countries. In Brazil there are close ties between civil society and the Workers' Party, given that the latter emerged from grassroots activism (cf. Hochstetler 2008: 34–35). Moreover, my experiences from field research indicated that the interviewees might have a different understanding of the relationship between individuals and organizations, the concept of representation, and the role that organizations play in the coordination of collective action. Therefore, the data analysis seeks to uncover the indexicality of interview statements in order to reveal potentially different understandings of the underlying concepts.
4. **Amazonia constitutes a specific setting for social movements.** The Amazon region is very diverse in terms of settlement, living conditions, and sociocultural structures. The vast territory is difficult to populate, cultivate, and control – even with modern technology. Periods of intensive use took turns with practical abandonment and neglect on the part of the government (Coy and Klingler 2011; also see Chapter 4). I assume that underdevelopment, poor infrastructure, violence and vigilantism,

50 For a discussion of the applicability of Western concepts in non-Western case studies see, for example, Abers and von Bülow (2011), Mercer (2002), Zinecker (2011); for conceptual stretching see, for example, Sartori (1970).

among other factors, form adverse context conditions for civil society activism. Therefore, this study pays attention to the specific problems of the region and their implications for the development and maintenance of a social movement.

5. **The Catholic Church plays a central role in the lives of the local population.**[51] The Prelature of Xingu is administered by the Missionaries of the Precious Blood (Congregatio Pretiosissimi Sanguinis, C.PP.S.).[52] The congregation emphasizes the Christian mission, community, and spirituality; however, its work includes very practical aspects of building up communities and working with socially disadvantaged people. Scientific research and media coverage indicate that Erwin Kräutler,[53] who was Bishop of Xingu at the time of the study, and several organizations associated with the Catholic Church of Brazil play an influential role in the collective action against Belo Monte (see, for example, Silva and Miranda 2010; Stock 2013).[54] The sample of interviewees therefore includes clerics and employees of church organizations as well as Kräutler as a key informant and potential leader in the social movement.
6. **Women have taken on leadership positions in the collective action.** The list of organizations originally compiled for the sampling of activist interviews in Altamira and Belém indicated a strong involvement of women's movements in the collective action. Moreover, women have frequently been portrayed as coordinators and leaders of SMOs in the media (see,

51 While the Roman Catholic Church (as an institution) is often perceived as "one single worldwide entity" (Davies and Conway 2008: 38), it is a complex hierarchical organization. Throughout this study, I talk of "the church" when I refer to the collectivity of clerics and employees of church organizations in Altamira and Belém. However, when analyzing their participation in the social movement on the individual level, I refer to them simply as activists or movement participants.

52 The autonomous particular churches of the Catholic Church consist in dioceses or alternative organizational units such as territorial prelatures, as in the case of the Prelature of Xingu (Jones 2011: 59, 120). The Prelature of Xingu belongs to the Ecclesiastical Province of Belém and to the North II Regional Bishops' Council of the National Conference of Brazilian Bishops (Prelazia do Xingu 2010).

53 Erwin Kräutler, a native Austrian, has published several books about his life and work in the Brazilian Amazon, in which he alludes to the Belo Monte Dam, among other issues (see, for example, Kräutler and Bruckmoser 2014; Kräutler 2006, 2011, 2012).

54 Organizations associated with the Catholic Church of Brazil include, for example, the Pastoral Commission on Land (Comissão Pastoral da Terra, CPT), the Pastoral Commission on Fishing (Conselho Pastoral dos Pescadores, CPP), and the Justice and Peace Commission (Comissão de Justiça e Paz, CJP), among others. These organizations are officially affiliated with the National Conference of Brazilian Bishops.

for example, Irigaray 2014; Salazar-Lopez 2011). Although leadership and gender are minor aspect of this research, the key informant interviews address these issues. This sensitizing concept enables a close analysis of leadership in general, and the diverse roles of women in the social movement against the Belo Monte Dam in particular.

The sensitizing concepts support the process of data analysis, in that they structure the data and draw attention to those aspects that are relevant in view of the research question – that is, collective identities and collective action frames. Moreover, they facilitate the theoretical saturation of concepts and the evaluation of the study's findings in light of social movement theory and recent empirical research (cf. Kelle 2011: 253).

4 Collective Action in the Amazon State of Pará

> *"I also want to thank you, welcome you here in our country, especially here in Amazonia, our giant Amazonia, which is a continent, that we call "Planet Earth Amazonia" – Planet Earth, Planet Amazonia. It has its charms and disappointments. Amazonia is like this. It is beautiful, it has a friendly people. We appreciate your interest in our Brazil, in our Amazonia." (P16)*[55]

The warm words of welcome offered by one of my first interviewees gave me an impression of what I had to expect of my field research: a region full of charms and disappointments, and a friendly people willing to share their hopes and concerns. For me as a researcher wanting to uncover the deeper meanings of the Belo Monte conflict it was indispensable to meet my research object and my interviewees with an open mind. Likewise, I consider it indispensable for the reader of this study to familiarize himself/ herself with the context of the case study in order to truly understand the local movement and to appreciate its collective activities.

This chapter introduces the reader to the political, social, economic, cultural, and environmental context of the Belo Monte project. In Section 4.1, I given an overview of the settlement, national integration, and socioeconomic development of the Brazilian Amazon. Section 4.2 discuss the legal basis for the Environmental Impact Assessment, which is a precondition for the implementation of the Belo Monte Dam and a controversial issue in the conflict. In Section 4.3, I outline the historic development of the conflict over the exploitation of the Xingu River's hydroelectric potential from the 1980s until 2012 and offer facts and figures about the project. Then I present the key actors involved in its authorization and implementation, and I introduce the reader to the city of Altamira and its inhabitants who are at the center of this conflict.

---

55 Throughout the study, interviews with activists are referenced by a document ID that can be found in the list of activist interviews in Annex 2. The translation from Portuguese to English was done by the author of this study in accordance with the translation rules mentioned in Chapter 3. Words that were emphasized by the narrator are underlined. Distinct, lengthy pauses are marked by ellipses. Unfinished words and sentences are marked by a hyphen. Omissions in a quotation are marked by three periods in square brackets, while insertions are marked with the initials of the author of this study in square brackets.

4.1 Developmentalism and National Integration

The official Brazilian Amazon region consists of the seven states of the North region, namely Acre, Amapá, Amazonas, Pará, Rondônia, Roraima and Tocantins, plus parts of Mato Grosso and Maranhão.[56] This vast territory of approximately 5 million square kilometers is very diverse in terms of settlement and socioeconomic living conditions, the ethnic and cultural structure of its inhabitants, and other factors like environmental and climatic conditions (World Bank 2013).

The state of Pará, where the Belo Monte Dam is located, is considered a frontier state (Coy and Klingler 2011: 112; McAllister 2008: 30). Given its abundance in natural resources, Pará has been suffering substantially from deforestation and exploitation at least since the 1970s. The economic valorization of the region and its integration into the national territory have been at the core of Brazil's development model. The state has taken an ambivalent role in these developments. On the one hand, it has sought to stimulate the modernization of the region through large infrastructure projects such as railways, roads, and dams. On the other hand, it has failed to regulate the dynamic development. Today, intensive livestock farming, commercial logging, soybean farming, and mineral extraction place high pressure on the natural environment and the local population (Coy and Klingler 2011: 109–110). Conflicts over land have been at the center of these dynamics, as the state has failed to regulate and certify land acquisitions in Amazonia for decades (Coy and Klingler 2011: 123). As a consequence, development projects in the region raise a number of questions regarding property rights and rights of use, the reconciliation of diverging interests, and the balancing of social, economic, and environmental aspects of development (Coy and Klingler 2011: 113). Moreover, the dynamics of the pioneer front create unique context conditions for the development of an active civil society and the emergence and maintenance of social movements.[57]

The social and economic development of northern Brazil (including Brazil's Amazon states) has been a political project for decades. Civil and military governments have sought to populate the vast area and promote its social, cultural, and economic relations with other parts of the country (Reis 2012: 26). Between 1930 and 1964 major infrastructure projects were carried out with the objective of consolidating the Brazilian territory and turning the country into a major economic player (Cole and Liverman 2011: 151). The governments of

56 Throughout this study, I use the terms Amazon and Amazonia interchangeably.

57 The term pioneer front is used by geographers to refer to areas characterized by unconsolidated economic and social spaces that experience significant dynamics of change (Coy and Klingler 2011: 112).

Getúlio Vargas and Juscelino Kubischek developed programs for the economic valorization of the territory and established a development model that came to be known as developmentalism (*desenvolvimentismo*). This development model concentrates on (1) fostering vertical import-substitution industrialization (ISI) by focusing on basic industries, (2) promoting foreign direct investment, and (3) steering private investments into priority sectors (Sikkink 1991: 33; also see Reis 2012: 29). Emphasis was placed on the domination and the national integration of the vast territories in the Northeast and in the Brazilian Amazon. This included the concession of land to agricultural settlers at attractive economic conditions with the objective of creating a lasting immigration to the region (Reis 2012: 26). The extension of the Amazon pioneer front was continued and even strengthened under the military regime (1964-1985). Seeking to implement a prearranged social, economic, and cultural order, it attracted settlers (so-called *colonos*) to the region, and thus, contributed to its unique social and cultural diversity (Reis 2012: 29). During the Medici administration (1969-1974), the development model enabled average growth rates of 11.5% per year. However, it became detrimental when commodity prices deteriorated in the mid-1970s. Foreign debt and rising interest rates resulted in a recession and initiated a decade of stagnation, often called "the lost decade" in Latin America (Schmalz 2012: 266).

Nonetheless, the investment strategy of the 1930s to 1960s is reflected in current development programs like the Growth Acceleration Program, which was launched in 2007 under the second Lula administration. Dilma Rousseff, President of the Republic from 2011 till 2016 and Chief of Staff of the Presidency of the Republic from 2005 till 2010, was actively involved in the creation of the PAC. She has been emphasizing the importance of the PAC (2007-2010) and its successor PAC 2 (2011-2014) for the socioeconomic development of the country (Jungmann 2010; Macedo 2013; Marra 2007), and announced a third phase of the program in April 2014 (Lourenço 2014). The objective of the PAC is to foster Brazil's economic development by allocating resources to the following six investment blocs: (1) better city (*cidade melhor*), (2) citizen community (*comunidade cidadã*), (3) my home my life (*minha casa minha vida*), (4) water and electricity for all (*água e luz para todos*), (5) transport (*transportes*), and (6) energy (*energia*). In the energy sector, projects seek the diversification of Brazil's energy matrix with a view to ensuring the supply of electrical power throughout the country. Investments focus on increasing the share of renewable and clean sources in the generation of electrical power, promoting the exploitation of oil and gas in the pre-salt layer off the Brazilian coast, and fostering the production of petroleum based products (MP n.d.). Hydropower plants are promoted as a renewable and clean source of electricity and form a substantial part of the PAC. The program stipulates the development of 40 hydropower projects of different sizes in Amazonia. Moreover, four river basins in the region are being inventoried in order to assess their hydroelectric potential (MP n.d.).[58]

Scientists and movement participants claim that the infrastructure projects stipulated by the PAC for the Brazilian Amazon do not consider the needs and interests of the local population. Instead, they resemble the programs of past civil and military regimes that sought to "civilize" the Amazon and combat the "social backwardness" of its inhabitants – particularly, the indigenous peoples (Reis 2012: 26–27; Verdum 2011). Therefore, any assessment of the Belo Monte Dam should consider the region's historic social, political, and economic status and development vis-à-vis the central and southern regions of Brazil (Reis 2012: 30).

4.2 The Brazilian Environmental Legislation

Brazil's environmental laws are considered to be strong; yet, their enforcement is insufficient. An entire chapter of the Brazilian Constitution of 1988 is dedicated to environmental protection; and the environmental law stipulates the use of environmental impact studies and licenses, liability for environmental damages, and prosecution of environmental crimes. However, environmental agencies in Brazil tend to be unable to enforce this thorough and sophisticated legislation (McAllister 2008: 20).

The Brazilian environmental law includes federal and state law, the former of which tends to be more important for Amazonia. It addresses the protection of natural resources, among other things, which is a persistent issue in the region. Major advances in Brazil's environmental legislation were made in the 1980s. In particular, the National Environmental Policy Act (Lei da Política Nacional do Meio Ambiente) introduced environmental standards and instruments for environmental protection. It also provided the basis for the involvement of the Federal Public Ministry (Ministério Público Federal, MPF) in the prosecution of environmental crimes (McAllister 2008: 22–23). The MPF is an independent agency that monitors the compliance of public and private actors with those laws that are of collective interests. In the conflict over the Belo Monte Dam, the Federal Public Prosecutor of Belém is an important ally of the social movement. The MPF can start its own investigations and has the obligation to investi-

58 For a graphic overview of the distribution of hydropower projects, see the website Dams in Amazonia (International Rivers et al. n.d.).

gate cases brought to its attention by others – for example, by civil society organizations (Portal Brasil 2014a). The involvement of the Federal Public Ministry in the enforcement of the environmental legislation was specified in the Public Civil Action Law (Lei de Ação Civil Pública) of 1985 (McAllister 2008: 24). Moreover, the legislation on environmental licensing was strengthened throughout the 1980s and 1990s by resolutions of the National Environmental Council (Conselho Nacional do Meio Ambiente, CONAMA). For example, environmental permits for large dams became mandatory in 1985, and Environmental Impact Assessments and Environmental Impact Reports (Relatório de Impacto Ambiental, RIMA), which make the conclusions of the EIA accessible to decision makers and the public, became integral parts of the licensing process in 1986 (McAllister 2008: 23–24).

In recent years, Brazil has sought to implement an overall development strategy in its Amazon region. The Brazilian Ministry of Science and Technology (Ministério da Ciência e Tecnologia, MCT) emphasizes the substantial importance of Amazonia based on its biodiversity of plants and animals, its rich soils, and its relevance for climate change mitigation. The MCT itself seeks an important role in inducing a scientific and technological development that values biodiversity and combats the exploitative practices in the Brazilian Amazon (MCTI 2012). However, Brazil's behavior with respect to sustainable development and the use of natural resources in Amazonia seems inconsistent. Recent legislative procedures have reduced protection areas in order to promote large infrastructure projects such as roads and hydropower plants (Abranches 2013: 57). The number of prospective infrastructure projects in the region has increased accordingly (Fearnside 2009: 7). Moreover, extractivism – that is, the exploitation of natural resources for the purpose of generating rents from export – has gained importance as a development model throughout Latin America (Blanke 2013: 2). Extractivism on a grand scale produces severe conflicts over territorial and environmental questions, and affects primarily those segments of society that are marginalized already. In recent years, local conflicts exacerbated, as state institutions and mechanisms of representation and participation are insufficient to moderate them (Blanke 2013: 3).

4.3 The Belo Monte Conflict

Brazil's rapid socioeconomic development at the start of the new millennium has been paralleled by an increase in total primary energy consumption by more than one third within ten years (EIA 2014). Demand for electrical power is expected to grow further at an average 4.3% p.a. in the next ten years, amounting to a total consumption of 781.7 terawatt hours (TWh) in 2023 compared with a consumption of 514 TWh in 2013 (Oliveira 2014). The Brazilian Energy Research Company (Empresa de Pesquisa Energética, EPE) claims that 79.3% of domestically generated and imported electricity in Brazil stem from renewable sources. In 2013, the domestic hydraulic generation accounted for 64.1% of total electricity supply, although the sector experienced a decrease of 5.9% due to the persistent drought (EPE 2014: 15–16). While the authorities emphasize the need to diversify the energy matrix and reduce dependence on hydropower (Portal Brasil 2015), the development and implementation of large hydropower projects continues. In 2013, new hydropower plants accounted for 30% of the total increase in Brazil's electricity generation capacity (EPE 2014: 16). Most notably, the federal government considers the Belo Monte Hydroelectric Power Plant a strategic infrastructure project that is of national interest, as it will ensure the electrical power supply of the country (Jungmann 2010).

4.3.1 The History of Hydropower Projects at the Xingu River

The first plans to exploit the hydroelectric potential of the Xingu River emerged in the 1970s, when the newly created energy company Eletronorte started to map the river basin. The Xingu River originates in the Xingu Indigenous Park (Parque Indígena do Xingu) in the state of Mato Grosso and flows through the states of Mato Grosso and Pará for about 1 979 km before it empties into the Amazon River. It is home to approximately 25 000 indigenous people from 18 distinct ethnic groups (International Rivers n.d.). The original hydropower project, called Kararaô Dam, stipulated the construction of seven dams and the flooding of 18 000 km² of rainforest for the purpose of generating 19 000 megawatts (MW). It would have affected 7 000 indigenous people in twelve indigenous territories along the Xingu River, among other inhabitants of the region (Instituto Socioambiental n.d.a). From the outset, the hydropower project encountered resistance by CSOs, indigenous communities, national and international NGOs, and the local population. As a result, the original investors, including the World Bank, withdrew their support in 1989. The project was put on hold until 1994, when Eletronorte resubmitted a substantially modified proposal to the National Department of Water and Electrical Energy (Departamento Nacional de Águas e Energia Elétrica, DNAEE) and requested the concession for the hydropower project that was now called Belo Monte. The evaluation of the Belo Monte Dam as a strategic infrastructure project in the pluriannual plan 2000-2003 provided the basis for the heavy promotion and authorization of the project over the next years (Instituto Socioambiental n.d.a).

However, the authorization of the project has been severely criticized. The Brazilian constitution requires the national congress to approve of hydropower projects that affect indigenous peoples (Article 231, Paragraph 3). According to Fearnside, the approval of the Belo Monte Dam by Legislative Decree No. 788 was rushed through congress on 13 July 2005 without noteworthy debate (Fearnside 2006: 18–19). On 26 August 2005, the MPF instituted legal proceedings in the Supreme Court claiming that the authorization of the project and the conduct of environmental impact assessments were unconstitutional. The action was repelled by the Supreme Court in December of the same year. During the following years, legal battles continued and the authorization of the project was impeded by court injunctions time and again. On 20 April 2010, the consortium Norte Energia S.A. (henceforth: Norte Energia) won the auction for the construction of the Belo Monte Hydroelectric Power Plant. On 26 August 2010, Brazil's then President Lula signed a contract with Norte Energia on the construction and operation of the dam for a period of 35 years (Bitencourt 2010; Machado 2010). On this occasion, the then President of the Republic and the then President of Norte Energia, Carlos Nascimento, affirmed the dam's outstanding significance for the country's energy supply and its economic development. "I think this is a victory for Brazil's energy sector," Lula said on the occasion of the signing of the contract (Bitencourt 2010). On 1 June 2011, the license authorizing the installation of the Belo Monte Dam was issued (Deutsche Welle 2011); as a result, construction works started in July of the same year (Figueira 2011). The hydropower plant was scheduled to start its operation in January 2015 and to be completed in January 2019 (MME 2011). However, the constructions are delayed, which – according to Norte Energia – is the result of difficulties in the authorization of the project, legal actions, invasions of the construction sites, and blockades by environmental movements (Peduzzi 2015).

4.3.2 Consequences and Viability of the Belo Monte Project

After substantial modifications, the Belo Monte Dam is considered a scaled-down version of the original hydropower project at the Xingu River. The powerhouse will have an installed capacity of 11 200 MW, and the area that will be flooded has been reduced to 516 km². The project takes advantage of the natural downward slope of the river; in addition, two canals are built to divert the river water to the main powerhouse. According to the authorities, this innovative canal system reduces the land area required to generate power (MME and EPE 2011). However, experts warn that this will substantially reduce the water level in the so-called Volta Grande (big bend) – a 100 km stretch of the river.[59] This poses a threat to indigenous communities living along the river and its *igarapés* because fish stocks will be decimated, the navigation by boat will be hampered significantly, and stagnant pools of water will promote the proliferation of waterborne diseases like malaria (International Rivers 2010).[60] Figure 1 shows the course of the Xingu River, the canals and artificial reservoir, and the location of the main powerhouse.

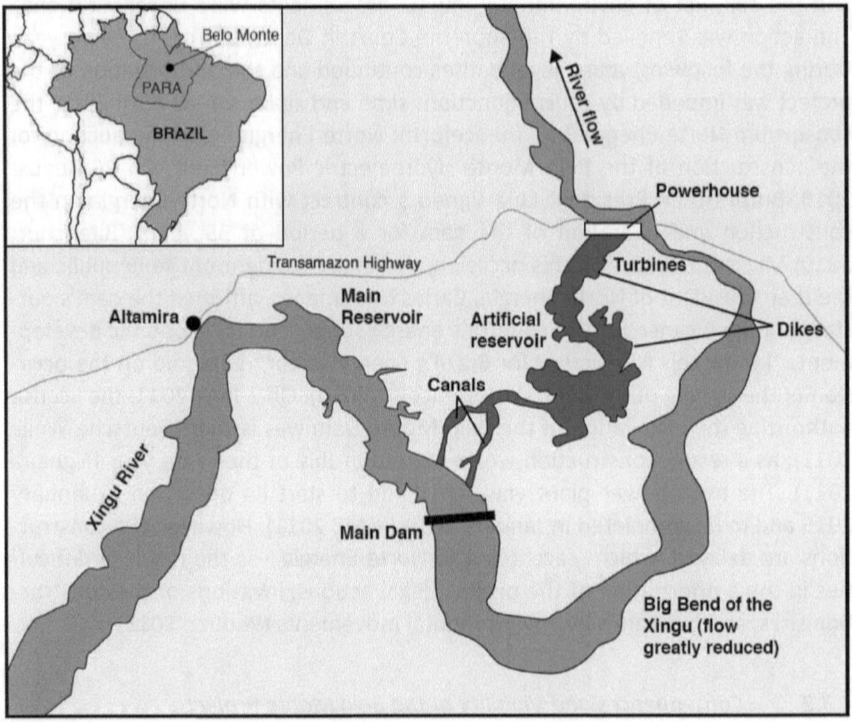

Source: International Rivers 2010
Figure 1: Project details of the Belo Monte Hydroelectric Power Plant

59 The term Volta Grande is used throughout this study to refer to the inhabited area along this 100 km stretch of the river. In this sense, it does not only denote the course of the river but also the Xingu's small distributary channels (called *igarapés*), its margins, and the land area between the river and the Trans-Amazon Highway that will be cut by the canals and the artificial reservoir.

60 *Igarapés* are small distributary channels of the rivers and streams in the Amazon basin. Due to their narrow width and dense vegetation, they can only be navigated with small boats. *Igarapés* are home to fishers and riverine people who often live in stilt houses on the river margin.

In line with the Brazilian legislation, an Environmental Impact Assessment was carried out by Eletrobras and the construction companies Andrade Gutierrez, Camargo Corrêa, and Odebrecht.[61] The findings were published in 2009 in the Environmental Impact Report (Leme 2009).[62] This contested report differentiates three areas of influence of the Belo Monte project: (1) areas of indirect influence, (2) areas of direct influence, and (3) areas that are directly affected.[63] While the first group comprises areas that are distant from the project and may suffer indirect modifications only, the second group comprises areas in the vicinity of the power plant and the reservoir. The third group includes areas that are occupied by engineering structures and the necessary infrastructure for the construction works, including construction sites, roads, and flooded areas (Leme 2009: 30). After the granting of the preliminary license (*licença prévia*), which included 40 conditions, the contracted Norte Energia consortium was obliged to develop a Basic Environmental Plan (Plano Básico Ambiental, PBA) based on the findings of the EIA in order to fulfill the requirements for the granting of the installation license (Norte Energia 2017a). Moreover, the Belo Monte project was included in the Xingu Regional Sustainable Development Plan (Plano de Desenvolvimento Regional Sustentável do Xingu, PDRS Xingu), a joint project of the federal government and the state government of Pará, which seeks to improve the living conditions of the population and to promote the sustainable development of the region (Secretaria Executiva do CGDEX n.d.). Norte Energia contributes close to 500 million reais (approx. 141 million euros) to the investment (Norte Energia 2017a). While the conditions stipulated in the preliminary license are supposed to prepare the region in advance for the Belo Monte project, the PBA and the PDRS Xingu are to be implemented simultaneous to the construction works.

---

61 Eletrobras (Centrais Elétricas Brasileiras S.A.) is the largest Brazilian company in the area of generation, transmission, and distribution of electrical energy, and one of the ten largest power utility companies in the world. The federal government holds 52% of the shares in Eletrobras; the rest is traded at different stock exchanges (Eletrobras n.d.).

62 The findings of the Environmental Impact Assessment are published in the Environmental Impact Report. Some interviewees combine the terms or use them interchangeably.

63 The quality of the EIA/RIMA is contested because it was financed and carried out by the companies that were later commissioned to construct and operate the Belo Monte Dam (Jagger 2012; also see Fearnside 2009: 6; Instituto Socioambiental n.d.a). Moreover, researchers involved in the study accuse Eletronorte of having controlled their research and edited their findings before they were submitted to the Executive Secretariat for Science, Technology, and the Environment (Secretaria Executiva de Ciência, Tecnologia, e Meio Ambiente, SECTAM; predecessor of the current State Secretariat of the Environment, Secretaria de Estado de Meio Ambiente, SEMA) (Forline and Assis 2004: 23).

A study from 2009 commissioned by civil society organizations and conducted by the Panel of Experts draws attention to flaws in the EIA regarding the evaluation of the project's social and environmental consequences, its impact on indigenous communities, and its technical feasibility and economic viability (Painel de Especialistas 2009). More specifically, the study questions the quality of the EIA, arguing that it is methodologically inconsistent, that it lacks adequate and consistent references, that the data collection was unsystematic and incomplete, and that data was misinterpreted. Moreover, the study criticizes that the RIMA uses a rhetoric that deliberately seeks to hide the negative consequences of the project. For example, the expression "stretch of reduced flow" (*trecho de vazão reduzida*), which refers to the Volta Grande, is considered an euphemism that conceals the project's direct impact on the indigenous territories Juruna do Paquiçamba and Arara da Volta Grande (Painel de Especialistas 2009: 11). From the panel's point of view, the RIMA underestimates the directly affected area, the affected population, the loss in biodiversity, and the compulsory displacement of the rural and urban population. Moreover, it denies the impacts downstream of the main dam and the powerhouse, it disregards threats to health and water security, and it overestimates the actual power generation of the plant, while underestimating the social, environmental, and economic costs of the undertaking (Painel de Especialistas 2009: 11).

The panel's criticism with respect to the project's technical and economic unfeasibility has been confirmed by other studies. Stickler and colleagues point out that the forests surrounding a hydropower plant have a significant impact on rainfall and river water flow, which in turn influence the energy generation potential of a facility. This is especially true in areas characterized by seasonal or erratic rainfall as is typical of the tropics (Stickler et al. 2013: 1). Past studies have already demonstrated a particularly strong effect of deforestation on hydrology in the Xingu River basin (Coe et al. 2009). The study by Stickler and colleagues substantiates the existing criticism of Belo Monte's inefficiency by confirming that the extreme seasonality of the river in conjunction with the small reservoir will reduce the energy generation potential to 33-38% of the installed capacity. Moreover, by simulating the indirect effects of deforestation within the Xingu and Amazon basins, the study demonstrates that the energy generation potential of Belo Monte could fall to as low as 25% of the installed capacity in the most extreme scenario (Stickler et al. 2013: 3).

While scientific research has shown that the Belo Monte Dam will have a substantial impact on the region, some of its consequences – especially the environmental and larger climatic consequences – remain unclear. Moreover, the authorities and Norte Energia are said to heavily promote the project and to deliberately conceal and neglect actual and potential drawbacks. As this study aims to uncover the deeper meanings that activists attribute to the conflict over Belo Monte, their perception of the impacts and consequences will be discussed in detail in Chapter 5.

4.3.3 Actors Involved in the Implementation of Belo Monte

Several organizations are involved in the assessment, authorization, construction and operation of the hydropower plant at the Xingu River. This section gives an overview of the actors and their involvement.

Norte Energia S.A. is a consortium comprising state-owned and private companies from the energy sector, pension and investment funds, and private sector participants. The largest shareholder is Eletronorte (Centrais Elétricas do Norte do Brasil S.A.) with approximately 20% of the shares (Norte Energia 2017b). Eletronorte is a subsidiary of Eletrobras, which holds 49.98% of the shares in the Norte Energia consortium (Norte Energia 2017b). On 20 April 2010, Norte Energia received the concession for the construction and operation of the Belo Monte Hydroelectric Power Plant for a duration of 35 years (Norte Energia 2017a).

The construction of the physical infrastructure was subcontracted to the Belo Monte Construction Consortium (Consórcio Construtor Belo Monte, CCBM), which consists of 10 enterprises with varying shares; among them the largest construction companies in Brazil: Andrade Gutierrez (18%), Odebrecht (16%), and Camargo Corrêa (16%) (CCBM 2014). Prefabricated parts are provided by domestic and transnational suppliers. For example, the consortium of Voith Hydro (Germany), Andritz AG (Austria), and Alstom (France) was awarded a contract with a total volume of 330 million euros to supply hydroelectric turbines, generators, and other equipment for the Belo Monte project. Other transnational companies are involved in the reinsurance of the undertaking (for example, Munich Re and Allianz) or provide equipment for the construction works (for example, Daimler). Their involvement has provoked protest at the headquarters and stockholders' meetings of the involved companies (Kleiber and Russau 2014: 27–35).

The authorization of the Belo Monte project rests with the Brazilian Institute of Environment and Renewable Natural Resources (Instituto Brasileiro do Meio Ambiente e dos Recursos Naturais Renováveis, IBAMA). IBAMA is a federal agency that was founded in 1989 to consolidate the federal agencies entrusted with environmental issues. It is responsible for the implementation of national politics pertaining to the environment and focuses on natural resource management, particularly in regions with abundant natural resources like Amazonia (McAllister 2008: 25). IBAMA's activities include environmental licensing, environmental quality control, authorization of the use of natural resources, and environmental monitoring and control. In this sense, IBAMA claims to act as an "environmental police" (IBAMA 2010).[64] On 1 February 2010, IBAMA issued the preliminary license for the Belo Monte project, which authorized the auction of the project (Gramacho 2010). The preliminary license stipulates the realization of public audiences and the fulfillment of 40 conditions related to water quality, wildlife, sanitation, social compensation, and the recovery of degraded areas, among others (Gramacho 2010; Norte Energia 2017a).

As several indigenous communities will be affected directly or indirectly by the Belo Monte project, the National Indian Foundation (Fundação Nacional do Índio, FUNAI) is involved in the authorization and monitoring of the Belo Monte project as well. FUNAI is a federal agency under the Ministry of Justice (Ministério da Justiça, MJ) that is responsible for establishing and implementing policies towards indigenous peoples in accordance with the Brazilian Constitution of 1988. Its responsibilities include the demarcation and protection of indigenous territories, the promotion of sustainable development in indigenous communities, and the inter-institutional communication. Its objectives are to guarantee indigenous people's civil rights and their access to education and health services, among others (FUNAI n.d.). In the process of the environmental licensing, FUNAI is responsible only for questions regarding the indigenous peoples affected by the Belo Monte project. It contributed 13 conditions pertaining to indigenous issues to the preliminary license (Programa de Comunicação Indígena – UHE Belo Monte 2011).

4.3.4 *The Municipality of Altamira and the Local Population*

The municipality of Altamira is located in the Xingu Valley (*Vale do Xingu*). With an extension of about 159 533.401 km² it is the second largest municipality in the world. Before the start of the Belo Monte project, Altamira had a population of approximately 100 000 inhabitants, 85% of which lived in the urban area (Umbuzeiro and Umbuzeiro 2012: 27). In 2014, the Brazilian Institute of Geography and Statistics (Instituto Brasileiro de Geografia e Estatística, IBGE) estimated that the population had grown to 106 768 inhabitants (IBGE 2014), while media

64 IBAMA's website provides comprehensive and detailed documents about the licensing of the Belo Monte project, such as technical reports, environmental impact assessments, reports of public consultations, terms of reference of the project, etc. (IBAMA n.d.).

reports suggest that the population had increased to at least 140 000 inhabitants in 2013 already (Folha de São Paulo 2013). This increase is commonly attributed to the arrival of migratory workers and new settlers who expect to benefit from the Belo Monte project (Folha de São Paulo 2013; Oliveira 2010). According to the newspaper Folha de São Paulo, 18 000 workers were expected to be employed at the construction sites during the peak time of the project; however, the number of workers increased to 25 000 already in the second semester of the construction (Folha de São Paulo 2013). Altamira has been referred to as the „eternal last frontier" (Umbuzeiro and Umbuzeiro 2012: 18). Throughout its history of approximately 130 years, the municipality has experienced different eras, "starting with the virgin front of the nineteenth century, the extraction of rubber for the Americans, passing through the conquest of the green ocean with the Trans-Amazon Highway, until arriving at the future big wall of Belo Monte" (Umbuzeiro and Umbuzeiro 2012: 18).

It is unknown since when Amazonia has been populated; however, the federal government acknowledges that the territory that became the Brazilian state was inhabited by indigenous tribes before the arrival of the Portuguese in 1500. The colonization initiated the immigration of people from various ethnic groups and the import of slaves from Africa. In the nineteenth and twentieth century, the number of immigrants seeking to escape economic problems, wars, or persecution increased. While African slaves where brought to the Northeastern region of the country, immigrants from Europe tended to settle in the South (Portal Brasil 2014b). These populational patterns are still visible today, despite the fact that the miscegenation of ethnic groups in Brazil was promoted by intellectuals and the state between the 1930s and the 1980s (Telles 2004: 33).[65] The development of the current populational pattern in Pará occurred in cycles. The colonization by the Portuguese colonial rulers caused the "depopulation" of the region, in that hundreds of indigenous tribes were eradicated and millions of indigenous people died of diseases (Portal Brasil 2014b). The arrival of African slaves and several rounds of both state led and private colonization attempts resulted in the mixture of various ethnics.[66] Today, the state is inhabited by people who combine indigenous, European, and African origin. In social terms they are

---

65 During most of the nineteenth century, miscegenation was believed to degenerate a people. However, towards the turn of the century, races mixture came to be understood as an instrument to whiten the Brazilian population and fight its backwardness (Telles 2004: 24). A very influential book by Gilberto Freyre called *Casa-Grande e Senzala* (English: The Masters and the Slaves) published in 1933 offered new perspectives on miscegenation as "a positive national characteristic and the most important symbol of Brazilian culture" (Telles 2004: 33).

66 The colonization of Amazonia with a focus on Pará is outlined by Foweraker (1981: Chapter 6).

often referred to as riverine people, indigenous people, rubber tappers (*seringueiros*), gold seekers (*garimpeiros*), fishers, and workers (Portal Amazônia 2017). Moreover, the region is inhabited by subsistence farmers who settled along the Trans-Amazon Highway in the 1970s and 1980s in the course of the Military Government's attempts to colonize the region. They base their livelihoods on small-scale farming, cash crops, and small-scale timber extraction (Toni 2007: 1).[67] Another relevant social group are so called *quilombolas*. These people are descendants of former slaves who have maintained their cultural and religious traditions, and their subsistence lifestyle over the centuries (Palmares 2017). Oftentimes, the inhabitants of the region are collectively referred to as forest people (*povos da floresta*). The Amazon Environmental Research Institute (Instituto de Pesquisa Ambiental da Amazônia, IPAM) defines forest people as "traditional inhabitants of the Amazon rainforest – indigenous peoples, rubber tappers, chestnut gatherers, etc. – who base their livelihood on the extraction of products such as rubber, chestnuts, *balata*, vegetable oils, and others.[68] Moreover, they engage in non-predatory hunting and fishing as well as subsistence farming. Forest peoples are social groups that require the forest and the rivers for survival, and know how to use natural resources without destroying them" (IPAM n.d., author's translation).

The analysis of the social movement against Belo Monte was informed by these social categories in that they structured the sampling of interviewees (cf. Chapter 3). However, in line with the research question and the hermeneutic research design, emphasis is placed on the reconstruction of people's personal, social, and collective identities from their own point of view (cf. Chapter 5).

67 According to the Merriam Webster Online Dictionary, a cash crop is "a crop (such as tobacco or cotton) that is grown to be sold rather than for use by the farmer" (Merriam Webster 2015).

68 *Balata* is an inelastic rubber-like material.

5 From Cohesion to Fragmentation: The Social Movement against Belo Monte

When I visited Altamira and Belém in May 2012, the social movement against Belo Monte stood at a crossroad. The construction of the Belo Monte Dam was starting to take shape, workers were occupying the construction site demanding the improvement of working conditions, and the social movement was facing criminalization and legal charges for alleged instigation of the workforce and interference in the construction. However, the obvious challenges that the social movement was facing at that time turned out to be only the tip of the iceberg. Inside the social movement a struggle over loyalties was posing a severe threat to movement cohesion.

The present analysis does not only provide explanations for the persistence of the collective action and the initial cohesion of the social movement, as was the intention of this study. It also reveals unexpected movement dynamics that are linked to recent developments in Brazil's civil society and that have interesting implications for the study of non-Western social movements.

The detailed analysis of the empirical material provides an insight into those movement dynamics that usually remain covert to outsiders. It reveals that Altamira's civil society benefited substantially from the grassroots work of the Catholic Church in the 1980s but suffered strong repercussions in the aftermath of the 2002 presidential elections and the coming into office of former President Lula on 1 January 2003.

This chapter analyzes the dynamics in the social movement against Belo Monte and advances the following central argument:

> **The election and coming into office of the Workers' Party, which is solidly based in grassroots organizations, altered the context conditions for civil society in Brazil. It had severe repercussions for the social movement against Belo Monte in that it induced a divergence of the collective action frame and an identity crisis among activists, which in turn resulted in the fragmentation of the social movement.**

The social movement literature discusses fragmentation as a regular phase in the life cycle of a social movement. According to Mauss, successful movements tend to experience what he calls a "normal fragmentation" after their claims have been officially included in the formal political process (Mauss 1975: 64).

However, the author acknowledges that conflict and pressure may cause a social movement's fragmentation at any point in time (Mauss 1975: 64 referencing Smelser 1962: 304–305; also see Oberschall 1973: 143). Without denying the success of the social movement against Belo Monte in raising awareness and challenging the authorities, its recent divergence cannot be considered a "normal fragmentation" sensu Mauss. It rather resulted from a combination of internal and external factors that challenged the cohesion and promoted the fragmentation of the movement. Internal factors referes to factors arising from internal movement dynamics that can be instrumentalized by activists, whereas external refers to factors arising outside the social movement. The differentiation emerged from the original data by means of constant comparison.[69] While the dynamics of cohesion and fragmentation are at the center of this study, they can only be understood through an in-depth analysis of the collective action frames and the personal, social, and collective identities prevalent in the movement.

In line with the interpretive approach, the central argument advanced in this chapter derives from the interviewees' perceptions and narrations of the conflict. The study does not aim to find an absolute truth. Rather, it seeks to reconstruct the meanings that activists attribute to the social conflict and their collective action. Their personal accounts of the occurrences are complex, in that they include extensive information, which the interviewees structure and present in accordance with their particular relevance system. The aim of this chapter is to reduce the complexity of the empirical phenomenon by breaking it down into smaller units that can be analyzed in detail. The separation of individual aspects is an artificial, yet analytically useful, method to raise empirical findings to the level of theoretical concepts. However, in order to acknowledge the complexity of the phenomenon, the individual aspects will be related to each other throughout this chapter, and they will be evaluated in light of social movement theory in Chapter 6.

This chapter is structured as follows: Section 5.1 starts with a discussion of the historical development of civil society organizations in Altamira. I introduce the Movement for the Development at the Trans-Amazon Highway and Xingu (Movimento pelo Desenvolvimento da Transamazônica e Xingu, MDTX), which united a large number of grassroots organizations in their collective ac-

69 Only in a second step did I compare my understanding of the fragmentation process in the Belo Monte conflict to existing research on factionalism. A review of the literature confirmed that other studies, too, have differentiated between internal and external factors driving fragmentation in social movements.

tion against hydropower projects at the Xingu River before it entered into a crisis in the early years of this century and eventually split in early 2008. Then I introduce the principle SMOs that emerged from the fragmentation of the MDTX, and other organizations that participate in the struggle against Belo Monte. The section also includes an introduction of the relevant state and business actors, and a brief discussion of the local population's opinion and mobilization for collective action. While the study has a clear focus on the municipality of Altamira, I make occasional references to the adjacent municipalities of Vitória do Xingu and Brasil Novo. The preliminary conclusion at the end of this section contributes to building up the central argument presented above.

Section 5.2 provides an in-depth analysis of the personal, social, and collective identities of local activists in Altamira and Belém. Identities are assumed to contribute to the persistence of the collective action and the maintenance of movement cohesion, as the social movement against Belo Monte is very heterogeneous and actors are expected to have different believes and interests. In discussing the personal identities of local activists, I focus on their typical characteristics and their motivation for collective action. I also elaborate on the motivation and contribution of female activists in the social movement. The discussion of social identities starts with an analysis of the interviewees' use of the term peoples. Then I elaborate on the social identities and self-identifications of the fishers, riverine peoples, and indigenous peoples that inhabit the Xingu River basin.[70] Finally, I propose that the definition of a collective identity is a central dynamic that promotes movement cohesion. Therefore, I introduce the collective identity of local movement participants in this section, and resume the discussion in Section 5.4.

In Section 5.3, I present an in-depth analysis of the collective action frames and framing processes prevalent in the social movement. The section starts with a detailed discussion of the Belo Monte diagnostic frame, which is shared in large parts by the two factions of the social movement. In discussing the framing process, I explicate how a divergence of the diagnostic frame contributed to the fragmentation of the movement and to the definition of different prognostic frames, which are discussed subsequently. At the end of this section, I draw a preliminary conclusion about the role of framing in the social movement. I propose that framing processes play a particularly important role

70 Riverine people are one of the so-called traditional peoples and communities (Povos e Comunidades Tradicionais, PCTs) of Brazil. These groups occupy traditional territories, either permanently or temporarily, and use natural resources for their economic, social, cultural, and religious reproduction (MDS 2016).

in movement cohesion and fragmentation. This discussion is resumed in Section 5.4.

Section 5.4 focuses on movement dynamics, and draws on the previous discussion of identities and collective action frames. I introduce the core categories of my study – that is, cohesion and fragmentation. I argue that between 1989 and the early years of this century, a collective identity and a collective action frame contributed substantially to the persistence of the collective action and the maintenance of movement cohesion in the social movement against the Belo Monte Dam. However, the movement suffered strong repercussions in the aftermath of the 2002 presidential elections. In order to contextualize the developments in Altamira, I briefly review the current state of research on fragmentation in social movements. Then I move on to an in-depth analysis of the internal and external factors that promoted fragmentation in the social movement against Belo Monte. The section further elaborates on the dynamics of the fragmentation and its results – that is, the factions and movement boundaries that emerged from the process. The section closes with a preliminary conclusion on cohesion and fragmentation in the social movement against Belo Monte, which substantiates the central argument presented above.

Sections 5.1 through 5.3 focus on reconstructing the meaning that activists have attributed to the social conflict and their collective action. While I structure and categorize the arguments of the interviewees by means of constant comparison and classification, I do not evaluate the statements in terms of their truthfulness, adequateness, and significance, nor do I introduce my own opinion and assessment of the issue. In Section 5.4, I draw on sections 5.1 through 5.3 for the purpose of analyzing the dynamics of movement cohesion and fragmentation. This section presents a synthesis of the previous arguments and demonstrates (1) how collective identities and collective action frames work together to create movement cohesion, and (2) how a divergence of the collective action frame and infringements of the collective identity result in the fragmentation of the social movement against Belo Monte. My own interpretation and assessment of the issue only become relevant in Chapter 6. There I take the empirical findings to a higher level of abstraction and present insights about identity, framing, cohesion, and fragmentation that can inform future research. Moreover, I relate my findings to the social movement literature and evaluate my sensitizing concepts in terms of their relevance and adequateness.

5.1 Conflict Parties: Background and Relationships

The spectrum of actors in the Belo Monte conflict is large and diverse. Given the research interest and design, this study was restricted to the investigation of identity and framing processes within the social movement against the Belo Monte Dam in Altamira and Belém. However, the definition of identities and the negotiation of shared beliefs and understandings always take place with reference to other actors. The establishment of boundaries between one's in-group and various out-groups is a defining aspect of identity work that contributes to movement cohesion (Teune 2008: 533). Therefore, reference is made to the supporters of the Belo Monte Dam – such as the government, the construction and operating consortia, and the business people of Altamira – with a view to their attitudes and their behavior towards the social movement against Belo Monte.

5.1.1 Origin and Development of the Social Movement in Altamira

In order to understand the emergence of the collective action against hydropower plants at the Xingu River, it is important to know that Altamira's civil society looks back on a history of social struggles (P19). The development of an active civil society was induced by the Christian Base Communities (Comunidades Eclesiais de Base, CEB) that emerged throughout Latin America after the Second Vatican Council and were established in Altamira in the 1980s.[71] Scholars agree that the Catholic Church, and more specifically the CEBs, exercised substantial pressure on the military regime and thus contributed to the redemocratization of the country (Della Cava 1989; Encarnación 2003: 112–115).[72] According to the interviewees and confirmed by church documents, the CEBs in Altamira educated people about their rights and the link between secular problems

71 The Second Vatican Council was opened under Pope John XXIII on 11 October 1962 and closed under Pope Paul VI on 8 December 1965 (Davies and Conway 2008: 44). It has been characterized as "one of the most important ecclesial events of the twentieth century" (Davies and Conway 2008: 54 emphasis omitted), because it significantly altered the Roman Catholic Church's understanding of its nature, structures, procedures, and relationships, thus creating opportunities for reform and lasting change (Davies and Conway 2008: 53–54).

72 Mainwaring defines the base community as "a small (15-25 people) group that usually meets once a week, generally to discuss the Bible and its relevance to contemporary issues" (Mainwaring 1986: 108). The objective of CEBs was to "enrich human relationships, facilitate more effective evangelization, develop better religious education, and promote more active lay participation" (Mainwaring 1986: 108). Yet, over time CEBs gained a political relevance that was initially unintended and unexpected (Mainwaring 1986: 109).

and religion, and they supported them in organizing the first interest groups (Provinzialat der Missionare vom Kostbaren Blut 1992; P9, P35).[73] Over time, a variety of grassroots organizations including associations, unions, and cooperatives emerged with the objective of promoting the interests of farmers, rural workers, women, and students. Oftentimes the members of these organizations were affiliated with the Workers' Party (P9). The strong interconnectedness between civil society and the PT in Altamira later fueled the conflict of SMOs in the social movement against Belo Monte.

The interests and claims of the early civil society organizations were diverse; yet, all of them were influenced by and reacted against the political, social, and economic effects of the government's colonization strategy (P16). Interviewees recount that in the 1960s and 1970s the military regime developed and implemented a plan for the national integration of the country (Plano de Integração Nacional, PIN). It focused on the resettlement of people from all over Brazil, but especially from the Northeast of the country, to Amazonia, and particularly along the Trans-Amazon Highway (P55). However, the region was poorly prepared for the arrival of the new settlers. Infrastructure was insufficient and land rights were not addressed properly. To make things worse, the authorities practically left the region along the Trans-Amazon Highway and the Xingu River to its own devices in the following years. The 1980s are therefore frequently referred to as the "period of abandonment" (P41). The authorities' neglect of the region created grievances in society that became politicized in the 1980s and let to the emergence of civil society organizations (P55). Rural workers' unions, associations, and cooperatives concentrated on economic development, modes of farming, and wage labor, while neighborhood organizations and movements in Altamira fought for the provision of basic state services such as public safety and civil rights (P31, P39, P41).[74]

> *"It was always this fight for the government to care for us, to care for the people, to find a way to avoid leaving the people vulnerable to mismanagement – for example, to violence, [...] to the suffering, to which it was exposed." (P31)*

---

73 The religious aspects of collective action will be discussed in more detail in Section 5.2.

74 It should be noted, that local activists often use the term movement to denominate a collectivity that is actually a social movement organization, according to the definitions given in Chapter 2. Thus, the differentiation between social movement and social movement organization proposed in this study is not mirrored in the narratives of local activists. However, as an analytical perspective it contributes to the reconstruction of collective action in Altamira and the assessment of recent movement dynamics.

According to interviewees the pervasive violence against women and children in Altamira, which culminated in the disappearance and emasculation of young boys between 1989 and 1992, was one of the most pressing grievances leading to the mobilization of civil society and the creation of the first civil society organizations in the realm of the CEBs (P9, P31). Looking back on their historical struggles, interviewees proudly say that they were able to establish an active civil society in Altamira and to enforce many of their claims – for example, the creation of a local office of the Federal Public Ministry (P19).

Early on, the civil society organizations emerging in and around the city of Altamira forged ties among each other and combined their forces in a regional movement (P55). Originally named Movement for Survival on the Trans-Amazon Highway (Movimento para Sobrevivência na Transamazônica, MPST), this movement called for public services and development programs claiming that "the Trans-Amazon Highway cannot wait any longer" (P41). However, the movement was perceived as limited to the interests of the people living in the catchment area of the highway. In order to open up to a larger constituency and address the interests of people living in remote rural areas and adjacent municipalities, the movement underwent profound changes throughout the 1990s and early 2000s that were reflected in name changes (P35, P37) and developed as follows:

> *"At that time, we were called the Movement for Survival on the Trans-Amazon Highway [...]. Then in the 1990s until 2000 we were called MDTX, Movement for the Development at the Trans-Amazon Highway and Xingu, and now, more recently – these names still involve a lot of fantasy – we adopted this matter of the Live, Produce, Preserve Foundation.*[75] *Hence, we experienced different times: the period of survival, the period in which we began to propose and establish development initiatives, and now the current period in which we are consolidating most of these development initiatives and building a new scenario for the future through the plans that we call medium- and long-term plans." (P41)*

Thus, unlike other municipalities in the region, Altamira generated a vivid civil society that was already well organized when plans about the exploitation of the hydroelectric potential of the Xingu River became public in the 1980s (P21, P31).

> *"So, when Belo Monte emerged, this big undertaking, not only this region but the Amazon as a whole started to raise a number of questions: Why a*

75 Throughout this study, I refer to the Live, Produce, Preserve Foundation (Fundação Viver Produzir e Preservar, FVPP) as the Foundation.

project like this at the Xingu River? Why a project like this in the Amazon basin if we have so many resources here, natural resources, which could well be exploited in a sustainable fashion, and that might yield a higher income both for the families that live here and for the development of the state, of the country? Then, throughout the '80s, '90s they criticized and continued their questioning. Only that from the 2000s the proposal for the construction of the plant started to take on contour." (P39)

The intense struggle over hydropower plants at the Xingu River that has occupied Altamira's civil society since the late 1980s strained the movement and eventually caused the separation of the MDTX into the Xingu Forever Alive Movement (MXVPS, which I refer to as Xingu Vivo) and the Live, Produce, Preserve Foundation (FVPP, which I refer to as the Foundation). Figure 2 illustrates the development of the social movement organizations from the 1980s until the end of the investigation period (June 2012).

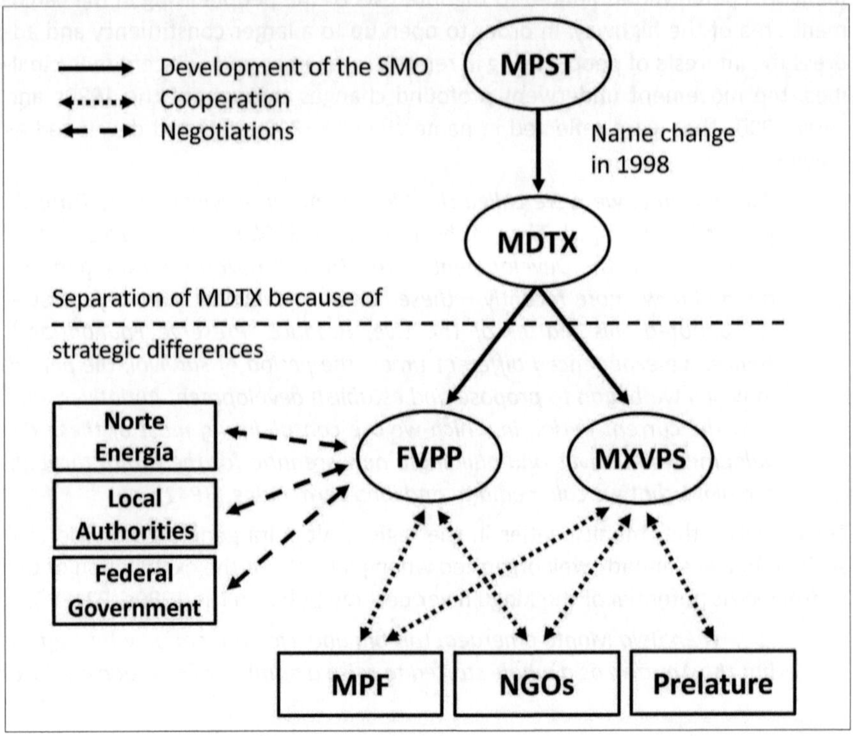

Figure 2: Development of principle SMOs in Altamira

Today, Xingu Vivo and the Foundation both claim to oppose the Belo Monte Dam despite their substantial differences in strategy and the tense relationships between some of their members. The strategic differences, which are illustrated in Figure 2 and will be discussed in detail in Section 5.3, resulted in the fragmentation of the social movement against Belo Monte and the emergence of two factions. The first faction consists of Xingu Vivo and its partner organizations; its objective is the prevention of the Belo Monte Dam (Plan A). These organizations refuse any negotiation with the authorities and enterprises involved in the Belo Monte project, claiming that it would constitute a compliance with the project. Due to their focus on the protest against the Belo Monte Dam, I refer to these organizations as the protest SMOs. The second faction is formed by the Foundation and its partner organizations. These SMOs negotiate with the Norte Energia consortium, the local authorities, and the federal government about mitigation measures, compensation schemes, and development projects to counteract the negative consequences of the project (Plan B).[76] I refer to this faction of the social movement as the monitoring SMOs, because these organizations focus on monitoring the events and negotiating the conditions of Belo Monte with the government and Norte Energia. However, both factions have historic ties with the Federal Public Ministry in Belém, which provides support in juridical questions and files lawsuits against government agencies, the Belo Monte Construction Consortium, and Norte Energia in the case of misdemeanor. Both factions have their respective support networks and cooperate with various national and international nongovernmental organizations. The Prelature of Xingu is the principal supporter of Xingu Vivo. While its members do not refuse dialog with other actors (P31), they emphasize that the strategies of Xingu Vivo and the Foundation are mutually exclusive; thus legitimating an exclusive cooperation with Xingu Vivo (P43).

Figure 3 illustrates the differences between the two factions in the social movement against Belo Monte; it lists the organizations of each faction as well as their purpose and activities. The organizations' general perception of the contentious issue – that is, (1) the characteristics and general meaning of Belo Monte, (2) its regional context, (3) its consequences, and (4) the controversial implementation procedure – is largely congruent. Therefore, the description of the diagnostic frame in Section 5.3 does not differentiate between the two factions of the movement.

76 Plan A of the protest SMOs and Plan B of the monitoring SMOs are discussed in detail in Section 5.3.

	Protest SMOs	Monitoring SMOs
Organizations	• Xingu Forever Alive Movement • Metropolitan Committee Xingu Forever Alive • Catholic Church, incl. church organizations in Belém, and the Prelature of Xingu in Altamira	• Live, Produce, Preserve Foundation • Movement of Dam Affected People • Socio-Environmental Institute
Purpose	• Stop Belo Monte (Plan A)	• Mitigate the consequences of Belo Monte (Plan B)
Activities	• Legal action • Protest letters, street protest (marches, sit-ins), talks and presentations, etc. • Celebrity diplomacy[77] and international support • Information and support for affected citizens	• Monitoring of the fulfillment of the conditions stipulated in the preliminary license • Participation in the steering committees of various development projects • Information and support for affected citizens
Self-perception	**What do protest SMOs think of themselves?** • We are the real (one interviewee said, the "serious") movement because we remain true to our principles.	**What do monitoring SMOs think of themselves?** • We are the responsible organizations because we admit the reality of Belo Monte and adapt our strategy. • We are still fighting for the shared aim: the improvement of living conditions along the Trans-Amazon Highway and the Xingu.

77 The term was introduced by Andrew F. Cooper in his book of the same title (Cooper 2008).

	Protest SMOs	Monitoring SMOs
Ascription	**What do other actors think of protest SMOs?** • Opinions are divided. • Some actors say that the protest is legitimate and helpful. • Other actors say that the protest SMOs are acting irresponsibly as they are not preparing the population for what is coming.	**What do other actors think of the monitoring SMOs?** • The monitoring SMOs have betrayed the movement. • Their members are merely interested in personal benefits. • They are not fighting for the shared aim anymore: stopping Belo Monte.

Figure 3: Overview of protest SMOs and monitoring SMOs

The disagreement between the SMOs refers primarily to (1) the current status of Belo Monte,[78] (2) the social movement's role and influence in the conflict, and (3) the advantages and disadvantages of the mitigation measures. The controversies in the collective action frame resulted in the development of different strategies, tactics, attitudes, and forms of conduct vis-à-vis third parties. Accordingly, the self-perception and ascription of the two factions in the social movement differ. While the protest SMOs believe that they are the real movement against Belo Monte, the monitoring SMOs claim to be the more responsible actors in civil society. Both factions are skeptical of the mindset and behavior of the respective other. Nonetheless, all actors appreciate the shared history of social struggles. Moreover, the long-term solutions to the regional challenges that the protest SMOs and monitoring SMOs offer in their respective prognostic frames are very similar. Therefore, I conclude that the protest SMOs and the monitoring SMOs should be seen as two factions within one movement, rather than two separate movements.[79] Nonetheless, questions arise as to what the separation of the MDTX into two factions means for Altamira's civil society in general, and for the collective action against Belo Monte in particular.

The following sections introduce the parties involved in the Belo Monte conflict and describe their respective positions on the issue.

78 Throughout the analysis, current refers to the time of the data collection (May to June 2012).

79 The argument is elaborated in Chapter 6.

5.1.2 *Xingu Forever Alive Movement*

Since its official inception in 2008, the Xingu Forever Alive Movement has become the most prominent and internationally visible actor in the relentless struggle against the construction of the Belo Monte Dam. The SMO was founded in the course of the Second Encounter of the Peoples of the Xingu (Segundo Encontro dos Povos do Xingu), taking place in Altamira on 20 May 2008. Its name goes back to the outcry of an indigenous leader at a meeting that took place in 2007 at Betânia, the educational center of the Prelature of Xingu: Nós queremos o nosso Xingu vivo para sempre! – We want our Xingu forever alive! (P13; also see P9). However, the creation of the SMO does by no means constitute the beginning of the collective action against the Belo Monte Dam. Much to the contrary, the social movement was able to stage the event Xingu +23 in order to celebrate 23 years of resistance in June 2012.[80]

According to its website, the Xingu Vivo Movement "is a collective of social and environmental organizations and movements in the region of Altamira and in the areas of influence of the Belo Monte project in Pará that have historically opposed its installation at the Xingu River" (MXVPS n.d., author's translation). Interestingly, interviewees refer to the Xingu Vivo at times as a movement or campaign and at other times as an organization or entity (P9, P16), which draws attention to the indiscriminate use of the terms.

From an analytical point of view, Xingu Vivo should be considered a social movement organization, as it identifies its goals with a set of opinions and believes, and attempts to implement the goals of the movement through collective action. Moreover, Xingu Vivo fulfills the general characteristics of an organization in that its members follow a certain code of conduct, divide tasks, and work towards a common goal. In particular, the organization has office space in Altamira, permanent – yet unpaid – staff, a coordinator who represents the Xingu Vivo externally, and a liaison office in São Paulo (P13). The organization is headed by Antônia Melo, who has been an active and recognized member of Altamira's civil society for the past 30 years. However, local activists often refer to Xingu Vivo as a network, because it provides structures and resources for the interaction of organizations, groups, and individuals (P9, P29, P51). This denomination contributes to the perception of Xingu Vivo as a proper social movement. The linguistic inaccuracy shows that the conceptualization of social movements as networks contributes substantially to the analysis of the collec-

80 The name alludes to the United Nations Conference on Sustainable Development, also known as Rio+20, that took place simultaneously in Rio de Janeiro from 13 to 22 June 2012.

tive action against Belo Monte. Not only the social movement but also the social movement organizations are perceived as networks that enable interactions between a plurality of individuals, groups, and organizations (cf. Chapter 2).

Many activists claim that the creation of Xingu Vivo as a distinct entity initiated profound changes in the collective action against Belo Monte in terms of its organization, cooperation between SMOs, and external visibility:

> *"And today, the Xingu Forever Alive Movement, even though it is coordinated by Antônia Melo, today it has a much greater visibility as a total movement, as a whole. So it left the focus of Antônia Melo and became a specific movement of the struggle; because when they talked about the struggle against Belo Monte, the people used to associate it only with Antônia Melo. Today this is no different, but now there is also a movement that accounts for this struggle, that also represents many entities – several other entities – in this struggle [...] So, these were separate struggles. Common but isolated. And the Xingu Forever Alive Movement came to make this a common and joint fight [...] So that is- the big change in this struggle is that." (P19)*

By creating a forum for interpersonal and interorganizational exchange and cooperation, Xingu Vivo contributed to the unification of hitherto unconnected struggles against hydropower projects at the Xingu River (P9, P19, P21) and facilitated the involvement of a variety of organizations and individuals (P9, P21, P27). It was created at a decisive point in time, at a "moment of all or nothing", for the purpose of reviving the collective action and creating a new spirit among activists (P31). Due to its openness and low hierarchies, the social movement against Belo Monte allows for the participation of entire organizations and of individuals. Local activists emphasize that organizations working in distinct thematic areas use the forum provided by Xingu Vivo to identify common interests and objectives and to coordinate their activities (P21). From their point of view, the specific structure of Xingu Vivo enables the cooperation of the most diverse organizations ranging from workers' unions, political parties, student organizations, international NGOs, church organizations and laity groups, to the indigenous movement, and other social movements like the movement of vegetarians, and the punk movement (P1, P3, P19, P31, P51, P53, P55).

While Xingu Vivo is the most prominent actor in the collective action against Belo Monte, local activists disagree about its size and actual influence. Interviewees in Belém perceive the Xingu Vivo Movement in Altamira as a large and influential entity, connected to an extensive and complex network of local organizations (P51, P55). However, some movement participants in Altamira take a modest position and acknowledge that the organization struggles to mobilize the masses. They describe Xingu Vivo as an elite organization that – even though its members are intelligent, competent, strong, aligned, and ready for the struggle – remains small in numbers (P47).

5.1.3 Metropolitan Committee Xingu Forever Alive

In 2009, the Metropolitan Committee Xingu Forever Alive (Comitê Metropolitano Xingu Vivo Para Sempre, henceforth: Metropolitan Committee) was created in the state capital of Belém as a representative of the Xingu Vivo Movement. Its purpose is to strengthen the movement in Altamira and to revive the struggle against Belo Monte by facilitating its cooperation and interaction with partner organizations in the state capital (P3, P21). The committee focuses on improving the visibility of the conflict and involving the population of Belém in the collective action (P3). This is done by means of seminars, debates, street activities, and legal action in cooperation with the Federal Public Ministry (P3). Like Xingu Vivo in Altamira, the Metropolitan Committee in Belém brings together a vast array of civil society organizations, such as the women's movement, youth organizations, unions, and nongovernmental organizations (P1, P3). It is therefore perceived as a network; however, from an analytical point of view the Metropolitan Committee is a social movement organization that identifies with the objectives of the larger movement. According to interviewees, the organization's greatest success is the creation of a public space where people with completely different ideologies – who even confront each other outside the committee – can meet and coexist (P3). This space is open to organizations and individuals alike, and it allows them to accept responsibility in the collective action, to advance their opinions, and exhibit leadership (P3).

> *"We always say that the task of the committee is first of all to enable the meeting of the largest possible number of organizations; make sure that they have a forum, a place, a time for the various organizations that have a critical view, that do not accept the construction of Belo Monte, to meet, to dialogue based on their diverse and different views, and to define common paths and common alliance." (P21)*

Today, both Xingu Vivo and the Metropolitan Committee are important points of reference for organizations and individuals in the collective action against Belo Monte (P19, P25, P37).

5.1.4 *Live, Produce, Preserve Foundation*

The Live, Produce, Preserve Foundation is the second organization (besides Xingu Vivo) that emerged from the Movement for the Development of the Trans-Amazon Highway and the Xingu. Despite the change of name, many locals still refer to the Foundation by its old name, and its members confirm that the Live, Produce, Preserve Foundation is primarily the legal entity representing the MDTX (P35).[81] According to its website, the Foundation brings together 113 organizations that are based in the municipalities along the Trans-Amazon Highway and the Xingu River. It comprises the farmers' movement, the women's movement, associations, unions, cooperatives, and student organizations (P9, P13). The common goal of these organizations is to promote the development of the region by demanding public policies in the areas of youth and education, technical assistance, agriculture and forest economy, and fishery (FVPP 2008). In contrast to Xingu Vivo, the Foundation does not only cooperate with nonstate actors but also with state actors in order to achieve these goals. Accordingly, the Foundation considers the structural changes that the MPST/MDTX underwent throughout the 1990s, and which eventually led to the separation of the organization, a significant shift in strategy from a "movement of claims and denunciations" towards a "movement of transformation and development" (MMA 2006: 6).

Regarding the Belo Monte conflict, interviewees from the ranks of the monitoring SMOs acknowledge the increased interest of the federal government in the region; yet, they caution that this interest and presence have to result in tangible actions (P41). Interviewees claim that civil society should be granted ownership of the process, in order to benefit from the development of the Belo Monte Dam and to enjoy a minimum of continuity after its zenith (P41). In line with this argument, the Foundation and its member organizations work towards ensuring that the region does not only carry the burden but can also reap the fruits of the hydropower project. Several interviewees characterize the Foundation as a strong actor (P13) that engages in a struggle for the rights of the local population (P37), the fulfillment of the conditions set forth in the preliminary license, and the implementation of public policies (P41). To that effect, the Foundation participates in the steering committees of the various development

81 When interviewees speak of "the movement in Altamira", they may be referring to different groups, depending on the time period they speak about. When speaking of the time before 2008 (founding of Xingu Vivo as a separate entity) interviewees are likely to be referring to the MDTX. When talking about the recent activism, context is usually required in order to determine which faction of the movement they are referring to.

projects, claiming that its presence demonstrates the enduring mobilization of civil society in Altamira (P41).

> *"And we are well respected within these spaces. There are natural weaknesses, of course, because we neither- We are not a mega-structure, but with our criticism, with our suggestions, with the accumulated 20 years of experience that we have in the region, we are trying to examine the things and to criticize in due time, to denounce in due time, to make claims." (P41)*

The monitoring SMOs anticipate that the various development projects and mitigation measures will reduce the negative impacts of the Belo Monte project and offer development perspectives for the region. They seek to contribute to the proper implementation of the development projects in the region by offering their expertise and experience (P41). Their main concern is to ensure that the strategic planning of the federal government reaches the local level and effects positive changes for the population (P39).

> *"The government thinks globally, it thinks nationally, and we, in turn, think of our dynamic here, of how to ensure that the processes of development do not pass over the heads of society." (P41)*

Interviewees report that the monitoring of the current developments is difficult because civil society organizations are excluded from the negotiations between Norte Energia and the municipal administration (P35).

Summing up, the Live, Produce, Preserve Foundation and the Xingu Forever Alive Movement share a number of characteristics:

1. Xingu Vivo and the Foundation both emerged from the Movement for the Development of the Trans-Amazon Highway and the Xingu. Therefore, they share a history of common struggles and successes.
2. Both organizations bring together a large number of organizations and provide structures and resources for their interaction. Therefore, Xingu Vivo and the Foundation are both perceived as networks.
3. Both organizations perceive of themselves as movements, while in effect they are social movement organizations that identify with a specific set of opinions and believes, and organize collective activities in an attempt to implement the common goals of the social movement.

In the course of fighting Belo Monte, the organizations have arrived at distinct interpretations of the conflict and have elaborated different strategies and tactics for confronting it. This study shows that collective identities and collective action frames are central for understanding the dynamics that led to the fragmentation of the social movement. While the identities of local activists and large parts of the collective action frames of both SMOs are very similar, disagreement on a limited number of issues eventually separated the members of the MDTX. The process of fragmentation – that is, the changes in people's mindsets, and the movement dynamics it effected – form a central part of the analysis. They contribute to our general understanding of movements dynamics and provide an insight into recent developments in Brazil's civil society.

5.1.5 The Catholic Church as a Political Actor

The Prelature of Xingu was founded in 1934 and has since been administered by the Missionaries of the Precious Blood. The congregation has contributed substantially to the social and economic development of Altamira and the surrounding area – an achievement that is also acknowledged by the local population. The Prelature of Xingu belongs to the Ecclesiastical Province of Belém and maintains close ties to various church organizations in Belém and in other municipalities. These include the Pastoral Land Commission and the Caritas, among others. Besides the bishop's see, several organizations affiliated with the National Conference of Brazilian Bishops have offices in Altamira, among them the Pastoral Land Commission and the Justice and Peace Commission.

Erwin Kräutler, Bishop of Xingu from 1981 till 2015, is an active and accessible member of Altamira's society and an outspoken opponent of the Belo Monte project. President of the Indigenous Missionary Council (Conselho Indigenista Missionário, CIMI) from 1983 till 1991 and again from 2006 till 2015, Kräutler is dedicated to the defense of indigenous rights and the protection of the natural environment. Throughout the 1980s he was particularly active in the struggle for human and civil rights and the establishment of indigenous rights in the Brazilian Constitution of 1988 – despite repression, death threats, and a presumed attempt on his life.[82] In 2010 he received the Right Livelihood Award for his enduring commitment (Prelazia do Xingu 2010). However, the involvement of the Catholic Church in social struggles in Altamira is by no means limited to the personal interest and dedication of its former bishop. Indeed, the National Conference of Brazilian Bishops (Conferência Nacional dos Bispos do Brasil, CNBB), several church organizations, and "important parts of the Catholic

82 On 16 October 1987, Kräutler was involved in an alleged car accident that left him severely wounded and killed his colleague Padre Salvatore Deiana. The circumstances of the accident have never been clarified, and Kräutler himself has repeatedly indicated that he considers the accident an attempt on his life (Kräutler 2011: 172–173).

Church" (P21) in the region have taken a stance against Belo Monte (P16, P51, P53). Moreover, a number of clerics participate in the social movement and in other acts of collective action (P13, P16, P47). The involvement of the Catholic Church in social and political struggles in Altamira is based on a particular self-conception that one interviewee describes as follows:

> *"First you have to understand what the church is. The church is not an entity that is outside the world. Sometimes people speak about the religious dimension as if it was something separate, completely separate from the world, from the men and the women. The same people who participate in the procession today, who are in the church, tomorrow will be challenged by this kind of thing. So the church has to speak up. The church has an obligation; even based on the very gospel 'I came that they may have life, and have it abundantly.' So we cannot separate things." (P43)*

While this statement confirms that clerics in Altamira consider the Catholic Church as a political actor, it also raises questions as to the relationship between the Church and the authorities. The self-perception of the Catholic Church as a political actor is based on Liberation Theology, a movement within the Catholic Church that emerged in Latin America in the 1950s and 1960s as a reaction to unjust political, social, and economic conditions, which drove many people into poverty. Taking the perspective of the poor, many clerics and lay religious workers called for the state to assume responsibility for its citizens, especially in poor rural areas of the country (Hoffman French 2006: 1–2). In Altamira, Liberation Theology had a significant influence on the development of an active civil society, which became a precondition for the mobilization against hydropower projects at the Xingu River in the late 1980s. According to interviewees, the Christian Base Communities, which sought to put the theology into practice, encouraged locals to assess their living conditions, to learn about their rights, and to make demands on the government (P9, P13, P35, P49). Several local activists state that they were mobilized into civil society through the CEBs, before they started to found particular interest groups and movements (P9, P35, P49). This interference from the Catholic Church was anathema to the Military Regime, which sought to control the clergy and the message they conveyed to the people (P13). The repression and abuse of power by the Military Regime led to a particular relationship between the authorities, the Church, and the population, which interviewees describe as follows:

> *"Since that time the people learned to shut up and accept, because it was the mayor who spoke. For them the words of a mayor are much stronger*

> *than the words of the Bible. For them- They cannot disobey, because it was the authority who spoke. So, a policy that is several centuries old and that has failed to change until today. The blind obedience to a political or economic authority, because the merchant also has a lot- is very respected. And, if a priest was to say something, they will still say the following: 'He should talk about the Bible, but not about these things'." (P13; also see P27)*

Interviewees from the ranks of the clergy in Altamira and Belém believe that the Church – and not only the Catholic Church (P16)[83] – has the obligation to consider the economic, social, political, and personal aspects of people's lives (P13) and support them in making claims on the authorities (P16). The clerics' commitment is generally based on the belief that convents should not be shut off from the world, that clergy should have an interest in people's lives (P13), and that "it is not sufficient to go on mission" (P49). As a result of its steadfastness and frankness vis-à-vis the authorities, and its trustworthiness among the people, the Prelature of Xingu is considered a predominant actor in the struggle against Belo Monte (P16, P35, P53):

> *"Among these actors, the one that was able to give the most legitimacy to the action may have been the Church, represented by its Bishop of Altamira, Dom Erwin. [...] Because over the years, the Church has been able to build a form of legitimacy in the region. It talks like someone from within the region, someone who knows the community, someone who has lived with indigenous people, someone who experiences the region. So this has given the church a legitimacy of discourse." (P53)*

It should be noted that the Catholic Church – despite its complex hierarchical organization – cannot be considered a single entity, and the above mindset is not shared by all clerics in Altamira and Belém (P31). However, as the latter do not undermine the collective action against Belo Monte, this study focuses on those clerics that participate in the social movement against Belo Monte. Their motivation is often based on believes and attitudes that also influenced their choice of profession (cf. Section 5.2).

83 In contrast to this interviewee, some activists believe that most other churches have withdrawn from the struggle (P31, P47). However, a discussion of the relationship between the churches is beyond the scope of this study.

5.1.6 Other Social Movement Organizations in Altamira

The Socio-Environmental Institute (Instituto Socioambiental, ISA) is a civil society organization founded in 1994 with the objective of "propos[ing] solutions to socio-environmental questions with a focus on the defense of social, collective, and diffuse goods and rights in the realm of the environment, the cultural heritage, human rights, and the rights of the peoples" (Instituto Socioambiental 2014a, author's translation). It emerged from the Ecumenical Center of Documentation and Information (Centro Ecumênico de Documentação e Informação, CEDI) and the Nucleus of Indigenous Rights (Núcleo de Direitos Indígenas, NDI), which where among the principle organizations concerned with indigenous issues in the 1970s (Instituto Socioambiental n.d.b). Today, ISA has offices in São Paulo, Brasília, and several cities in Amazonia, including an office in Altamira. The organization follows five lines of actions, each of which includes a number of projects (Instituto Socioambiental 2014a). The Belo Monte Dam is an issue in the realm of ISA's Xingu Program, which seeks to contribute to the regional planning in the Xingu River basin by offering expertise on socio-environmental questions and promoting intersectoral dialog. In doing so, the program aims to preserve the natural environment and the living conditions of indigenous and riverine communities through a variety of projects that support family agriculture (Instituto Socioambiental 2014b). Local activists explain that the history of ISA in Altamira is closely linked to the collective action against Belo Monte. In the late 1980s various people, who later became members of the local division of ISA, came to the region for the purpose of organizing the First Encounter of the Indigenous Nations of the Xingu (Primeiro Encontro das Nações Indígenas do Xingu) taking place in Altamira from 20 till 25 February 1989. These people shaped and were themselves shaped by the struggle against the Belo Monte Dam and the incremental development of an active civil society (P37). Local activists describe the mission of ISA as

> *"a struggle for having different cultures, different peoples, different ways of seeing the world, forms of technologies, ways of dealing with health, with money, and relationships, and so on." (P37)*

This appreciation of diversity is shared by many activists in Altamira and Belém. Based on its longtime involvement in the struggle against Belo Monte, ISA has been able to establish itself as an important regional actor.

A rather recent actor in Altamira is the Movement of Dam Affected People (MAB), which established a local division in 2009 in order to support affected people in claiming their rights related to the construction of the Belo Monte Dam (P23). MAB was founded in 1991 based on grassroots activism that had emerged since the 1970s in reaction to infringements of individual and land rights in the course of dam projects in several places throughout Brazil. The organization focuses on promoting the interests of landowners, leaseholders, rural landless workers, and other people that are directly or indirectly affected by dam projects. However, MAB also fights for the conservation of nature and the creation and implementation of a just, participatory, and democratic energy policy in Brazil that considers the needs and wants of the affected people and guarantees their involvement in dam projects (MAB 2011a). Its strategy is based on bringing together the affected people ("join the oppressed"), explaining the issues ("clarify concepts"), and increasing awareness for their cause ("alert the people") (MAB 2011b, author's translation). MAB's activism in Altamira is based on the experiences with Tucuruí Dam (P16).[84] Interviewees acknowledge that the organization's strategy includes radical activities, such as the blocking of roads and the occupation of construction sites (P23). They are proud to report that MAB has been able to mobilize and empower affected families in similar struggles throughout the country with a view to achieving their resettlement and the provision of basic services (P23). Yet, with respect to the Belo Monte conflict, local activists seek to dampen high expectations, claiming that MAB is only starting to grow in the region, and its growth and influence will depend on its ability to organize the population (P49). In contrast to some activists' positive perception of MAB, some interviewees show skepticism about the organization's involvement in the Belo Monte conflict. From the critics' point of view, MAB has ceased to be a protest SMO because "with the passing of time and the advancement of the construction, MAB adopted the focus of action that it has today" (P19) – that is, a focus on the mitigation of negative effects, rather than the prevention of hydropower plants. Critics claim that this strategy constitutes an implicit acceptance of the construction of large dams (P19), thus placing MAB outside the protest SMOs.

Summing up, members of the protest SMOs have become increasingly skeptical of ISA and MAB's activities; and their relations have deteriorated despite the latter organizations' struggle for the local population's rights. As the protest SMOs focus on the prevention of hydropower plants, they consider ISA and MAB's focus on mitigation and compensation a tacit consent to the construction of large dams. From their point of view, the strategy of ISA and MAB does not reflect their interests.

84 Tucuruí Dam is a hydropower plant at the Tocatins River, and it is located about 300 kilometers east of the Belo Monte Dam. Tucuruí started operating in 1984 (International Rivers et al. n.d.).

"[ISA] has a line of action of monitoring the conditions, and this is not our role – to be negotiating, mitigating. So, for us, we do not have these interests. They entered the struggle of the movement at the very beginning with the Xingu Vivo Movement, as a struggle against that undertaking; and today they are entities in which we do no longer perceive that fight, that focus, that the Xingu Vivo Movement has." (P19)

The activists' understanding of the Belo Monte project and their perception of the attitudes and behavior of the various actors play a central role in the development of movement dynamics, as I will argue in Section 5.4.

5.1.7 State and Business Actors

The state actors involved in the Belo Monte project are the federal government, the government of the state of Pará, the administrations of the affected municipalities, and a number of state agencies. In general, the relationship between the local population and the authorities on various levels is strained. Interviewees report that ever since the colonization of Amazonia by the Portuguese – and especially during the time of the military dictatorship – politics have been characterized by authoritarianism and civil obedience (P13, P47). On the other hand, the various administrations of the federal government have shown little interest in the region – except for the economic exploitation of its natural resources and questions of national security and integrity (P35). Interviewees lament that the social policies have always been insufficient, and suspect that the situation of the poor will deteriorate with the construction of the Belo Monte Dam (P13, P27).

The population's opinion of the authorities has further deteriorated since the authorization of the Belo Monte project. Local activists are particularly disappointed with their local administration and denounce its mismanagement and irresponsibility. From their point of view, the municipality should defend the interests of the local population and even argue against the federal government, if necessary, in order to assure that local demands are met (P31). Instead, the local administration of Altamira is criticized for having handed over the city and its administration to the Norte Energia consortium (P19).

"The administration is acting with great irresponsibility, a poor administration, which does not know what its role is. It got carried away by the propaganda of Norte Energia, of the federal government; so, it is handing over all these responsibilities to Norte Energia, it stops doing all its administrative responsibilities, its attendance to the population, and

> *the public policies. There is no responsible planning of the occurences, of the public policies, including the management of the municipal resources that are allocated to the city to meet our demand." (P9)*

Interviewees denounce that the municipality stopped fulfilling its role and ordered Norte Energia to provide public goods and services – whose supply is commonly in the responsibility of the government – as part of the conditions of the preliminary license (P9, P19). However, Norte Energia has been failing to comply with the requirements and has frustrated the expectations of the authorities and population in Altamira (cf. Section 5.3). As a consequence, the municipality has initiated legal action against Norte Energia (P19), and has sought alliance with the social movement (P31). Local activists believe that the federal and state governments have entered into a "promiscuous relationship, and this word is to say, a gamble of interests" (P35) with the Norte Energia consortium. Roles and responsibilities have been confused to the point where the population is no more able to tell whether it is the municipality, the state government, the federal government, or even the Norte Energia consortium that is responsible of public policies in the areas of, for example, health and education (P35). Interviewees denounce the transfer of government responsibilities to a private enterprise as an irresponsible act to the detriment of society and particularly of indigenous peoples.

> *"So, it is Eletronorte, which is an enterprise specialized in building dams, that is assuming, in practice, the indigenous policy of the state. This has very strong social consequences that may result in the weakening and even loss of the culture of these people, who are- often they are already quite fragile, because these peoples have been suffering substantial pressure for quite a long time already. So, you have a lot of pressure and lack of policies; this results in cultural loss, and this gains momentum in a frightening way, because they [Norte Energia, I.P.] are allocating things to the indigneous in an arbitrary way." (P37)*

Local activists allege that the government has never been dedicated to the indigenous cause (P19, P29) and that Belo Monte is a systematic attempt to destroy the native ethnic cultures (P43). From their point of view, the authorities have always neglected the indigenous and abandoned them to their fate (P43). Interviewees critizice that the political representation of the native ethnic groups in Brazil is insufficient, as there are no secretariat for indigenous issues at the state level and no representatives of indigenous origin in the Senate and the Chamber of Deputies (P29).

Moreover, local activists denounce the status and performance of government agencies involved in the authorization and implementation of the Belo Monte project. FUNAI, whose task is to ensure the rights of native ethnic groups, is considered a "deteriorated institution" that has tolerated the approval of the Belo Monte project and the bribery of the communities instead of defending the rights and interests of the native population (P29, P35). As a consequence, indigenous communities have lost their trust in the institution and question its purpose and effectiveness in general (P29).

> *"FUNAI has a very complicated, very delicate role because FUNAI is the government and the government wants Belo Monte, and the government claims that Belo Monte is an example, and it has to sustain this discourse that Belo Monte is an example." (P37)*

In a similar vein, interviewees denounce the role of IBAMA in the Belo Monte conflict. They criticize the agency's double moral standard because, on the one hand, it penalizes the local population for illegal logging and fishing during the period of the fishing closure; on the other hand, it authorizes the construction of the Belo Monte Dam, which will cause significant damage of the flora and fauna (P13, P23, P31). Local activists believe that IBAMA and FUNAI – despite their legal status as autonomous public entities – are not sufficiently independent from the federal government to effectively represent the interests of the population in the face of a project like Belo Monte (P37). They claim that the domestic construction industry, which contributes substantially to the financing of political campaigns, is influencing the government to exert pressure on the agencies involved in the licensing of the project (P31).

5.1.8 *Opinion and Mobilization of the Local Population*

The opinion of the local population about the Belo Monte conflict constitutes an important context condition for the social movement. It shows whether the collective action frame resonates with the believes of the people and influences their evaluation of and reaction to the collective action. According to local activists, people react to the project and the associated social struggle in different ways.

> *"Some accept this as something – in quotations marks – 'natural'. Others, like me, believe that this is not natural, [...] that this is not how it should and how it could be." (P21)*

Traditional peoples evaluate the Belo Monte project against the background of their respective understanding of the world, their living conditions, shortages, and difficulties, and either choose to accept the project and its impacts or to react upon it (P21). Interviewees claim that many of the affected people in the rural areas accept Belo Monte because they lack the political power to oppose the project (P47). They know from experience that they have little influence on the development cycles that pass the region.[85] The exposure to foreign domination and authoritarian rule coupled with the experience of powerlessness in political decisions-making have created a fatalistic mindset in many people, who now seek to silently endure what they perceive as yet another development cycle (P25, P47).

The urban population of Altamira was initially divided into two groups: the first group supported the project in anticipation of economic progress, while the other group remained inactive and waited for the government to fulfill its promises (P43). Businesspeople were particularly interested in Belo Monte as they expected the project to create economic progress and additional opportunities for their businesses. Yet, these expectations did not materialize, and storeowners suffer from higher rents instead of increasing their sales (P55). Likewise, the population's approval for the Belo Monte project dropped when it became clear that the city as a whole would not be "overflowed by money" and that Norte Energia is neglecting the conditions of the preliminary license (P43).

While the local population's opinion about the Belo Monte project changed over time, their mobilization has remained difficult. Local activists admit that they have not been able so far to mobilize "the public power, the power of the street" (P3; also see P47). Their reports of failed attempts at mobilizing the masses indicate that mobilization is hampered by a number of factors, some of which are specific of the region. I propose that these factors can be classified into the following categories:

1. a lack of information and/or a lack of understanding of the issue (P25, P51),
2. the education of the population towards obeying the authorities (P13, P27),
3. feelings of powerlessness and self-identification as the weakest player in the conflict (P25, P47),
4. economic dependence and vulnerability to the consequences of collective action (P13, P25, P35), and
5. susceptibility to compensation and bribes (P27, P47).

85 The notion of development cycles in the Amazon is discussed as part of the Belo Monte diagnostic frame in Section 5.3.

Interviewees are clearly disappointed about the population's apathy in the face of Belo Monte (P29, P35). Yet, they sympathize with the people, claiming that their reluctance to participate in the collective action and their focus on material benefits are results of the abandonment and structural deprivation of the region (P13, P21, P55). One activist explains the dilemma of the population and the restraints of mobilization as follows:

> *"I always make a comparison: A poor family on the riverbank, in a suburb, the father is unemployed, the mother does the laundry for other families, five children, no means to provide for the necessary, then they are hit by a disease, they are in despair, et cetera, et cetera; and suddenly I arrive there and put down one thousand reais. And then I say, 'Look, there is a car outside. It is yours. And now you will refuel it in the gas station – I will pay. You will have to go shopping for your daughters because they are growing and the girls want nice clothes – so, you can go to that store, and it is being paid. What do you need? The house is in this and that condition. Do you have a stove- We will buy another stove. And you do not have a refrigerator. Of course, we will get you a refrigerator. I will pay for light and energy.' Who? Tell me. Which family will say, 'I am <u>against</u> it!'?" (P43)*

While local activists are sympathetic to the population's needs and wants, they criticize the authorities' way of dealing with the structural problems of the region (P13). Beyond that, interviewees report that the mobilization of the public is hampered by remoteness and lack of personal contact. It is complicated for SMOs to organize large protest events because of poor infrastructure and high costs of travel (P55). As a consequence, meetings of the social movement tend to be small and intermittent. Daily work is facilitated by communication technology, which helps activists overcome the geographical distance at least in part (P55).

In contrast to the active civil society in Altamira, there is no history of collective action in the neighboring municipality of Vitória do Xingu (P47). The social movement against Belo Monte has been trying to mobilize the local population there – but to no avail (P47). Interviewees claim that the political context of the municipality – that is, authoritarian politics and economic dependence – and the vulnerability of the population hamper the development of an active civil society in Vitória do Xingu (P47). Nonetheless, a small group of fishers meets regularly to discuss the implications of the Belo Monte project on their fishers' colony (P49). This initiative has been able to mobilize the population on specific occasions but has not succeeded in sustaining a mass movement (P49).

On the other hand, the municipality of Brasil Novo has an active civil society that emerged from the CEBs. Like Altamira, Brasil Novo engaged in the struggle for development when the Trans-Amazon Highway was built in the 1970s (P49). Nonetheless, there is no significant collective action against Belo Monte in Brasil Novo. Interviewees explain that the city of Brasil Novo will only be affected indirectly through increased migratory pressure on the region. However, the rural areas of Brasil Novo will be directly affected by the reservoir of the Belo Monte Dam (P49). It is reasonable to assume that mobilization in the city of Brazil Novo is hampered by the difficulty to predict and to communicate the expected social consequences to the urban population.

5.1.9 Preliminary Conclusion

As the discussion has shown, the Belo Monte project evokes a range of different expectations, opinions, and reactions. Local activists who had already been active in Altamira's civil society for many years were the first to question and oppose hydropower projects at the Xingu River, and they remained alert even after the prevention of the Kararaô Dam. They critically followed the modification of the project throughout the 1990s, and resumed their fight against the newly named Belo Monte Dam at an early stage of planning. While local activists were not convinced of the modification of the hydropower project, the local authorities, business people, and many citizens developed high hopes of progress and prosperity when the revised plans were made public. Yet, with the advancement of the project, their expectations were repeatedly frustrated. Activists claim that today one can hardly find citizens who support Belo Monte – they are either apathetic about the issue or have come to oppose the project (P3). In a similar vein, local authorities and business people have changed their mind and their behavior vis-à-vis the developers of the Belo Monte Dam once they realized that it was not generating the benefits they expected. Nonetheless, the mobilization of the local population for collective action against Belo Monte remains difficult. Interviewees attribute this to the geographical context and the colonial and authoritarian heritage of the region. The key actors in the social movement in Altamira today are the Xingu Forever Alive Movement; the Live, Produce, Preserve Foundation; and the Prelature of Xingu, among smaller organizations affiliated with the aforementioned entities. The key actor in the social movement in Belém is the Metropolitan Committee Xingu Forever Alive that represents the Xingu Vivo Movement in the state capital. All of the organizations in Altamira share a history of common struggles, and the majority of their members were initially mobilized through the Christian Base Communities. Yet, over time these activists developed different opinions about the meaning and consequences of the Belo Monte project, which eventually led to the fragmentation of the social movement into two factions.

In order to reconstruct step by step the movement dynamics of the recent past, the following section will analyze the identities of local activists. Collective identity is assumed to play an important role in the persistence of the collective action and the maintenance of movement cohesion in the social movement against the Belo Monte Dam; thus serving as one of the main explanatory factors of the social movement's fragmentation, which is discussed in Section 5.4.

5.2 Identities of Local Activists

As discussed in Chapter 2, this study differentiates between personal, social, and collective identities by drawing on the conceptualization proposed by Snow (2001: 2213). While personal identity is built up of self-designations and self-attributions, social identity is ascribed to a person by others based on primordial attributes and/or social roles (Snow 2001: 2212–2213). Collective identity is conceptualized in this study as an individual attribute based on a social-psychological perspective of identity (Simon 2011: 40; Stryker 2000: 33–34). Therefore, the study also takes into account the relationship between personal and collective identities.

Based on the in-depth analysis of interview data, I propose that the natural environment constitutes an important reference point of the activists' identities. By shaping people's characters and motivation to participate in collective action, and by defining the lifestyles[86] and economic activities of social groups, the natural environment has a significant impact on the personal, social, and

86 In his analysis of the pedagogical practices of the Brazilian Landless Workers Movement, Hammond questions the applicability of collective identity theory to movements in rural Brazil. Claiming that "[t]he terminology of collective identity theory reflects its origin in advanced industrial societies" (Hammond 2014: 379), he cautions against the uncritical use of terms and concepts. For example, from his point of view the term lifestyle implies that people can choose between different options – a connotation that does not hold true for poor rural workers in Brazil (Hammond 2014: 379). As outlined in the introduction, this study seeks to critically assess the applicability of Western theories and concepts in non-Western case studies. Nonetheless, I use the term lifestyle throughout this study when discussing the characteristics of a person's way of living. It certainly depends on a person's ethnic background, social status, and other socioeconomic factors, which often are not subject to the person's choice. In this context, my use of the term is not meant to imply that a person has possibilities and means to deliberately choose a certain lifestyle.

collective identities of the local population. In the preparation of this study, I assumed that the social and cultural heterogeneity of the local population was likely to result in different identities, cultures, interests, knowledge, and behavior, which would hamper collective action against Belo Monte. The data analysis shows that interviewees do differentiate between social groups, and that these are also relevant in socio-legal terms. Yet, interviewees de-emphasize the differences and instead allude to similarities in lifestyle, a common fate, and shared experiences as a basis for collective action. The concept of an Amazonian Identity – that is, a collective identity, which I reconstructed from the interview data – captures the characteristics that from the interviewees' perspective define the local population and distinguish it from the Brazilian majority population.

In the first part of this section, I discuss the personal identities of local movement participants. I propose that beyond some commonly shared attributes there are a number of characteristics that further define their personal identities and allow for a classification of actors into four categories. As female activists are said to possess some unique characteristics, I dedicate a section to female activism. In the second part, I present the notion of the peoples of the Amazon (*povos da Amazônia*) before I elaborate on the social identities and self-identifications of fishers, riverine, and indigenous peoples. The third part introduces the Amazonian Identity as a collective identity that is deliberately created by the local activists to facilitate the identification of the population with the social movement. The Amazonian Identity serves as an internal factor promoting cohesion, and will therefore be discussed in more detail in Section 5.4. After having discussed the personal, social, and collective identities of local activists, I analyze the motives behind their collective action against Belo Monte, and I elaborate on the repercussions of the conflict on local movement participants. The section closes with a preliminary conclusion that summarizes the study's findings on the identities of local activists and on the motives behind their participation in the social movement against Belo Monte.

All categories of the analysis emanate from the interviewees' perspectives and were elaborated by means of constant comparison and classification of interview statement. While focusing on the individual, the study acknowledges that professional affiliations and the identification with a certain social group are important for understanding activists' participation in the social movement, given that it "takes place in a wider context" (Klandermans 1997: 9). By analyzing movement participation on the level of the individual, the study seeks to shed light on the relationship between personal, social, and collective identities and their respective contribution to movement cohesion.

5.2.1 *Personal Identity*

One section of the interview guide focused explicitly on the identities of local activists with the objective of exploring how actors see themselves in relation to the Belo Monte conflict. In order to induce interviewees to explicate the motives behind their participation in collective action in general, and in the social movement against Belo Monte in particular, they were asked, "What are the personal motives for your work in these movements and organizations? And how is your work linked to the protest against Belo Monte?".

The analysis shows that activists in Altamira and Belém share a number of typical characteristics. The most prominent attributes are a great sense of volunteerism and an extensive dedication to the social struggle. A large number of activists participate in meetings and activities during their free time, each of them committing as much time as they can (P3, P13, P21, P25). One interviewee describes the character of the activists as follows:

> *"Individually, looking at each and every one, we are people who dedicate ourselves to this process, because here we do not receive a salary. We live on a small allowance, and if you follow our work for one week, you will be- you will ask: 'But these people are half crazy because they do not stop, they travel-'" (P41)*

Activists are said to be unpretentious in that they dedicate themselves to the cause instead of trying to build their own patrimony (P41, P43). Only few interviewees, who are employed at organizations that participate in the social movement against Belo Monte, say that they are allowed to use some of their working hours and ressources – for example, computers – to support the work of the social movement (P1). The majority, however, works without a salary or comparable benefits.

Beyond volunteerism and dedication, which are strong in all interviewees, there are a number of characteristics that further define the personal identities of activists. Most interviewees place their activism against Belo Monte in a larger context. They describe their personal background and their mobilization into civil society in general, and they identify the Belo Monte conflict as one struggle among others. This reasoning is consistent with the perception of Belo Monte as representative of something larger or a symbol of a certain kind of thinking (cf. Section 5.3). Based on interviewees' statements about themselves and their work, I have grouped them into one of four categories accroding to the most salient atttribute of their personal identity.

1. Regional identification: This group of activists demonstrate a strong emotional connection to their natural environment and base their personal identity on their Amazonian heritage (P1, P23, P25).
2. Religious Faith and Lifestyle: These activists base their commitment on their religious faith, and more specifically on the principles of liberation theology (P13, P16, P49, P51).
3. Organic Intellectualism: This group of actors have a strong desire to understand social situations and processes, to assess them in terms of their moral appropriateness, fairness, and sustainability, and to intervene in reality in order to counteract what they have identified as detrimental developments (P21, P35).
4. Political resistance: These activists disapprove of Brazil's economic, social, and environmental politics and show a general attitude of noncompliance. They frame their activism as a continuous struggle with the government and act immediately on misguided social developments (P41, P55).

Given the separation of the social movement into protest SMOs and monitoring SMOs, one could expect that activists affiliated with the protest SMOs base their activism on a more general indignation about the positions and actions of the authorities, while members of the monitoring SMOs are motivated by the desire to implement concrete development projects. Yet, the analysis shows that many activists who fight for the fulfillment of the conditions and the implementation of the development plans today started their activist careers with the objective of effecting societal change. Only one interviewee appears to be driven primarly by professional and technical considerations in their[87] work for the monitoring SMOs (P39).

The initial reactions of interviewees to questions concerning their motives provide insights into the persons' self-conceptions and identity salience. Some interviewees take the question for their personal motives literally in that they talk about their personal development, behavior, and way of thinking; thus alluding to their personal identity. Other interviewees focus on the detrimental effects of the Belo Monte project, and essentially imply that their motives are to counteract these effects. Yet another group of interviewees refer to the interests of a particular social group or the purpose of the social movement as a whole, and explicitly identify with these believes. While these

87 For reasons of confidentiality, I avoid using pronouns that indicate the sex of the interviewee and use "their" in the singular sense instead.

interviewees allude to collective identities, they seek to convey personal information in an indirect way. Throughout the analysis, the form of response was neglected and direct and indirect statements about one's motives were considered in equal measure.

In the following sections, I discuss the four categories describing the most salient attributes of a local activist's personal identity. These attributes are present in the identities of both male and female activists. Interestingly, female activists are said to possess a number of additional characteristics that are particularly helpful in the collective action against Belo Monte (see below).

5.2.1.1 *Regional Identification*

Amazonia constitutes a unique living space for humans, flora, and fauna. Especially those interviewees who live in rural areas and lead traditional lifestyles comment extensively on the living conditions in rural Pará, their relationship to the natural environment, and the effects of the Belo Monte project on their lives. The relationship to the river – and in this sense, any river in the Amazon basin – is a defining element of the people's personal identities.

> *"I was born in Santarém, on the banks of the Tapajós River, I was raised in the river, I went to the river every day, and my family comes from the river, my mother comes from the river, we have a very strong connection to the river." (P1)*

Likewise, other interviewees state that they are a "native of the river" (P23) or that they were born and lived on an isle as children of fishers (P25). In order to understand the strong connection of indigenous peoples, fishers, and riverine communities with the natural environment in general, and with the river in particular, one needs to understand the centrality of nature in the population's everyday life and its influence on their identities. As the following statement nicely illustrates, the traditional populations use nature

> *„to feed not only the physical body, but especially to feed our soul, because we – given that we are traditional populations – have to catch our fish in order to feed ourselves, we generate our income from agro-extractivism; but it is also in the midst of nature that we constitute ourselves as persons. It was with nature, with the interaction that we had – that I had, that my brothers had – with nature, that made us the people that we are today, that made us fight for what we believe in, that gave us strength to not be silent in view of the circumstances, in view of*

> *what is happening. So, nature has favored us a lot in what it taught us." (P25)*

The motivation to defend their environment and their living space derives from these people's sense of self, which in turn is constituted in close interaction with nature. According to the interviewee quoted above, the destruction of the environment does not only deprive people of their livelihood; it also means the loss of identity for the individual and the entire community, as everything they inherited and built up by themselves will be destroyed. As a consequence, future generations will not have the possibility to build the kind of relationship to nature described above (P25). Interviewees with a strong emotional connection to their natural environment feel that their living space and lifestyle are threatened by the authorities' attitude and politics towards Amazonia, and have therefore committed themselves to the collective action.

5.2.1.2 Religious Faith and Lifestyle

The defense of nature is also a central motive for religious activists and those affiliated with the Catholic Church. As discussed in Section 5.1, many activists in Altamira were initially mobilized through the Christian Base Communities of the Catholic Church. While not all of them name religious motives behind their activism, references to the Creation and the preservation of life and nature are quite common. Especially those interviewees who are strongly religious and/or affiliated with the Catholic Church in a professional way state that faith gives their lives a sense of meaning (P13), and that their faith in God motivates them to take action on behalf of others (P16). Religious activists also frame their criticism of neoliberal politics and the current development model as an offense against God's will.

> *"God said, that in the beginning he gave us everything and asked us to take care of it, and today man is destroying out of greed, out of ambition. Everything for money. Nowadays, it is no more for the well-being of life, it is for the money, it is the issue of wanting to own more and more." (P23)*

As discussed above, the Catholic Church in Pará has been particularly active in raising the local population's awareness of injustice, in educating people about their rights, and in fighting for marginalized people. This work towards *conscientização* – which can broadly be translated as "the act of acquiring knowledge about"[88] – has its ideological roots in liberation theology and grew in importance in the 1970s and 1980s (P13). Religious interviewees tend to have a holistic view of the individual and respect people's yearnings, anxieties, wills, and desires as part of their personalities (P43). As a consequence, they refuse to limit religious education to religious topics, claiming that the faith in God, and the Catholic Church as an institution matter in the economic, social, political, personal, and in all other other areas of life (P13; also see P43).

> *"And there I learned that the gospel, that the faith cannot be separated from our lives, from our reality, from the problems, and all that. And this issue stimulates and leads the person- and it led me to become who I am today. I cannot be a Christian, be here as a Christian, and the problems and situations surrounding me, and I let them be, because they are not mine. It is not like that. The struggle is part of faith and part of life." (P9)*

As this quote and other statements indicate, religious participants in the social movement against Belo Monte believe that faith is inherently linked to the defense of life and of the Creation. They consider it their vocation and religious mission to not only preach the gospel but to put it into action (P13, P31, P43). These activists participate in social struggles in general, and in the collective action against Belo Monte in particular, for the purpose of fighting for marginalized and disadvantaged people (P19, P27, P31) and in order to defend life and nature (P13, P16, P53).

5.2.1.3 Organic Intellectualism

Interviewees affiliated with either faction of the social movement frequently claim that they are dedicated to civil society because they want to intervene in reality. While some of them take an intellectual approach, others take a more hands-on or even militant approach to achieving social change. The interviewee who describes the attitude and work of the former group claims that

> *"I coordinate, nowadays I coordinate, and I am- I feel affilated with each base. I feel affiliated. Why? Because it is what we call [...] the organic intellectual. He can be here, but he- Physically he is here, but his spirit, his mind is there at the base, in the struggle. So, this is what we call the organic intellectual." (P16)*

---

88 Translation derived from the online dictionary *Michaelis Moderno Dicionário Inglês & Português* (UOL 2009a).

The objectives of the organic intellectuals are twofold: on the one hand, they seek to use their knowledge to the benefit of the people, and to contribute to a more equitable society. On the other hand, they seek personal growth in their intellectual work and dedication to civil society (P21). The term organic intellectual emerged from the data as an in-vivo code before I compared it to the theoretical concept introduced by Antonio Gramsci in his *Prison Notebooks* (Gramsci 1971).[89] Although the term appears only once in the data, other interviewees share the self-conception of the organic intellectual, as the following quote illustrates.

> *"As an organization for research and for the support of other community organizations, labor unions, it is our task, first of all, to understand the process, to analyze the process, to analyze and to understand; but not only that. It is also to evaluate how we can, in practice, contribute to a change in the reality that we consider unfair or unsustainable, incorrect." (P21)*

This interviewee endorses the organization's efforts to provide scientific and practical support to the collective action against Belo Monte (P21). Moreover, the concept of the organic intellectual seems to have influenced the educational work in the CEBs. Interviewees describe that clerics in the base communities were convinced that it did not suffice to analyze the situation and talk about it without taking action (P35). They rather encouraged people to "see, judge, and act" (P35) towards the various unjustices in the communities.

89 In his *Prison Notebooks*, written between 1929 and 1935, Antonio Gramsci elaborates on what he calls the organic intellectuals, their characteristics, and their role in society. Based on a Marxist viewpoint, he claims that every social group creates its own intellectuals, which give the group "homogeneity and an awareness of its own function not only in the economic but also in the social and political fields" (Gramsci 1971: 5). Gramsci argues that the working class needs to create, from within, organic intellectuals and acquire political consciousness in order to achieve a leadership role in society (Simon 1991: 97). The concept of the organic intellectual prevalent among activists in Altamira and Belém is consistent with Gramsci's theoretical considerations. Interestingly, clerics identify themselves as organic intellectuals – despite the fact that Gramsci considered them traditional intellectuals because they emerged from the feudal aristocracy and controlled a number of "important services" for a long time (Gramsci 1971: 7). A comprehensive analysis of the interviewees' practical use of Gramsci's concept would not only have to consider this aspect; it also ought to evaluate the applicability of the concept in the Belo Monte case study, as Gramsci developed the concept in a very different context. As a theoretical debate about the concept itself is beyond the scope of this study, I treat the concept as an in-vivo code and focus on reconstructing the meaning that local activists in Altamira and Belém attribute to the term.

The creation of political awareness in the CEBs and the spirit of liberation theology among clerics may have contributed to the interest in learning and development that characterizes not only the organic intellectuals but also the rank and file of the social movement against Belo Monte.

> *"I think that to help does not mean to pick you up and give you a job, to satisfy your hunger at that moment, but it means to enlighten you, to open your eyes to other worlds, to open your eyes to another time, because we no longer live in times when everyone was innocent, when everyone trusted everyone else." (P25)*

The openness for other lifestyles and ways of thinking is particularly important in a heterogenous movement like the one against the Belo Monte Dam. Interviewees explain that their work has enabled them to get to know the indigenous world, and to broaden their minds towards the living conditions and realities of marginalized people (P19). Moreover, they attach great importance to education, claiming that it enables them to acquire knowledge and make new experiences, which in turn will help them to support their communities and fight for their rights (P29). This attitude coincides with a skepticism towards the government and government agencies, and with preparedness for civil disobedience (P29).

5.2.1.4 Political Resistance

While the organic intellectuals focus on understanding social processes in order to be able to intervene in reality, the political resisters act more immediately on misguided social developments. They fight for human, economic, social, cultural, and environmental rights, and oppose the Belo Monte Dam because of its detrimental effects in all of these areas (P3, P9, P29, P37, P41, P47, P55). Yet, they consider the conflict over Belo Monte as only one struggle among others (cf. Section 5.3). Political resisters explain that they grew into activism during their adolescence when they were confronted with various injustices (P31, P55) and/or discovered alternative models of thought through education. The following statement illustrates how the growing awareness of social problems may lead a person to become an active member of civil society.

> *"Personally, since university, since high school, I always revolted against various injustices. I was outraged over the corruption in the country, I was outraged over the unequal distribution of wealth in our country, over the privileges for a minority at the expense of the majority, over this political practice of prioritizing the financial market to the detriment of*

> *social issues, and this outrage grew. It grew, and to the extend that I matured and grew personally, intellectually, and professionally, I could see that we would only solve the problems of our society by overcoming this capitalist mode of production. So, personally, I revolt against the capitalist mode of production. I am an anti-capitalist, an anti-imperialist, I am a militant of the socialist left wing." (P3)*

While only few interviewees identify themselves as anti-capitalists, anti-imperialist, or even militants, many of them subscribe to a left-wing ideology and seek fundamental changes in the Brazilian socioeconomic system. They believe that social movements have the capacity to contribute to social change (P49). Some of these actors also show tendencies towards militancy in that they approve of illegal actions in order to prevent the Belo Monte Dam (P13). On a personal level their mobilization and participation in social movements seem to follow a predetermined developmet – and indeed one interviewee claims that he could not do any other work but fight for human rights (P55). Moreover, the vocubulary used by interviewees is meaningful in terms of their self-conception and positioning in the social movement against Belo Monte. Political resisters claim to be "na luta" – that is, "in the struggle" (P16, P55). While the term alludes to the general mindset and activism of this group of people, the struggle against Belo Monte has become particularly important.

> *"It is a movement that never tires. It is a movement that is ready for the fight. And I think it is the movement that puts into action the part of the National Anthem that goes 'that a son of yours may not escape from the fight'. So, I think the Xingu Vivo Movement will never escape from the fight against the injustices, against this whole issue." (P19)*

Political resisters claim to share a common ideology, to engage in regular debates about their view of reality, and to develop their collective action strategies from there (P41). They work tirelessly towards their objectives, they resist social and political pressure, and find strength in the "spirit of revolt" (P28; also see P3 and P25). Passion and the will to change things are the main drivers of their action (P55; also see P16).

5.2.1.5 Female Activism

Gender relations among local activists are ambiguous and complex. As discussed in the sixth sensitizing concept, I expected female activist to play a prominent role in the social movement against Belo Monte, as I observed many women in leadership positions (cf. Chapter 3). Interviewees in Altamira and Belém confirm that "the struggle for justice and against this dam has the face of the local women" (P9). Female activists – just like their male counterparts – show a great sense of volunteerism and dedication to civil society. Moreover, they can be classified into the four categories discussed above according to their most salient characteristics. However, interviewees emphasize that, in contrast to male activists, women possess a number of unique attributes and capabilities that they bring into the struggle against Belo Monte.

Women are considered the stronger sex in the Belo Monte conflict and an integral part of the social movement (P3, P9, P31).

> *"So, the women who are in this fight, I would say they are much more militant than the men, because often they receive much more pressure from this conservative society, and not even this intimidates them, quite the contrary, they continue standing strong and accept distinguished positions in the leadership of the movement." (P3).*

The local women – and particularly those in Altamira – are considered to be strong and warlike (P1, P3, P35). Yet, it should be noted that women also suffer from repression (P1) and inequality (P29), which indicates that gender relations in Amazon societies are complex (P29) and merit a separate discussion that goes beyond the scope of this study.

Many interviewees attribute the strong involvement of women in the social movement against Belo Monte to the project's particular impact on women and children (P9, P35).

> *"We believe that women feel the impacts more intensely on their skin. It is the children who are vulnerable [...] to prostitution. It is the women who have the smallest jobs [...] the majority do not have the profession to take on these jobs, so they serve as cheap laborers and slave laborers. It is the women who are more frequently in line for health services and education, seeking vacancies, seeking attendance for their children and so on. It is the women who lose their children in these dam constructions, in these projects. And they are the ones who benefit the least from it. And there are more problems. There are much more illnesses that affect women. Illnesses like breast cancer, like uterine cancer. There is stress in the classrooms, they earn little. So it is the women- It is proven by studies that it is the women who are most affected in their lives by the construction of these dam projects." (P9)*

Interviewees point out that dam projects in general do not only affect the local population but also families in other parts of Brazil. Women have to bear the absence of their husbands who work at construction sites throughout the country

(P35). Interviewees conclude that the project's particular impact on women is an important factor in the mobilization of female activists, creating strong incentives for women to fight against the perceived threat (P9).

In the indigenous and traditional cultures of the region, women are seen as to possess the power to create life – by giving birth to their offspring, by producing foodstuff, and by raising animals – whereas men merely reap the fruits. As women take responsibility of the daily chores and the heavy work, they form the base of every community and develop a much better understanding of what is needed to sustain life (P27, P29). Moreover, they maintain a close connection to the water and take responsibility for the water management of the family (P27). On the other hand, men are described to be somewhat disconnected from these issues, and to take longer to develop consciousness of the fundamental value that water – and thus, the Xingu River – has for life (P27). Moreover, interviewees claim that women are less susceptible to manipulation (P29; also see P25). They are perceived to focus more on long-term developments and maintain a strong connection to future generations, while men are described as naive in their efforts to gain short-term benefits (P45). However, interviewees emphasize that these characteristics do not apply to every man and woman, as there are men who are very committed to the fight for life (P27) as well as women who do not live up to these expectations (P29). One interviewee describes the special characteristics of the local women at length:

> *"But the woman is connected to the next generation – through her being, through her heart, and through her phsyche. A woman puts people in the world, she gives birth, and she is almost instinctively concerned with the future of the offspring. This assumption is supported by anthropology and psychology. Over the years, I have noticed that women always have a clearer vision of the future because it is their son, daughter, grandson, granddaughter, whose lives are at stake. And the man thinks about the money, about the immediate. I am not saying all men, but a large part." (P45)*

Interviewees claim that female activists are able to resist the pressures and the emotional stress associated with the Belo Monte conflict because they know what is at stake. As one interviewee describes, "the one who creates, knows the value of life. [...] There is no way for you to put something in the world, and not fight for it" (P29).

5.2.2 Social Identity

The concept of social identity was introduced in this study in order to understand the diverse backgrounds of local movement participants in the heterogeneous social movement against Belo Monte. According to Snow, the social identity of a person is attributed by others based on the person's social role or belonging to a social category or group (Snow 2001: 2212–2213). At the same time, people identify with social groups, which means that personal identities (self-attributions) and social identities (attributions by others) can be overlapping. In this study, the social identities of various groups in the Volta Grande were derived from interview statements by means of constant comparison and classification. The comparison of statements about (1) the interviewee's in-group, (2) other interviewees' perceptions of this group (which is their out-group), (3) and group members' assumptions about how members of the out-group perceive of them, was particularly interesting in that it contributed to the interpretation of the social identities of indigenous nations and traditional peoples.

Throughout the interviews, local activists frequently refer to the local population as the "forest peoples". In this section, I explain what characterizes forest peoples from the interviewees' point of view. Then I introduce the social identities and self-identification of fishers, riverine people, and indigenous peoples.

5.2.2.1 Os Povos da Amazônia: The Peoples of the Amazon

Recurrent themes in the interviews are the regional context of Belo Monte, the special characteristics of the local people, their traditional ways of life, and the ways in which they are affected by the hydropower project.[90] Interviewees generally use the term peoples (*povos*) in the plural when they talk about the local population, and they connect it with different adjectives. They speak of forest peoples (*povos da floresta*) (P3, P16, P37), indigenous peoples (*povos indígenas*) (P1, P3, P9, among others), and make reference to a temporal and spatial context – for example, the peoples of the Xingu (*povos do Xingu*) (P1, P45), the peoples of the region (*povos da região*) (P21), or the peoples of Amazonia (*povos da Amazônia*) (P1, P3, P21, P31).[91] The use of the term emphasizes the strong

90 The regional context of Belo Monte plays a major role in the diagnostic framing and will be discussed in detail further below.

91 Sometimes the term peoples (*povos*) is substituted by populations (*populações*), which is used in the same sense and also in the plural form.

geographical component in social identities, which I also found in personal identities. Moreover, it includes a time component, as interviewees frequently refer to the centuries-old history of indigenous and traditional peoples in the area (P1, P13). The following statement shows the diversity of the social groups that interviewees identify to be native of the region, and it emphasizes the temporal and spatial components of social identities.

> *"It does not recognize that there are already- that at this moment and historically there have always been the native peoples, the indigenous peoples, but also the traditional populations; farmers have always been here, gatherers, rubber tappers, and several others, fishers, and many more." (P21)*

The geographical component of identities is particularly relevant in defining the boundaries between in-group and out-group. While the Brazilian society is characterized by an interethnic composition, interviewees emphasize that there are different peoples in the Brazilian Amazon (P43). They acknowledge that the people of one town differ from the people of another town, given the long distances between settlements (P16). However, at the same time, interviewees speak of themselves and the people in the region as one people (*o povo daqui*) (P16). The differences between the people from different towns within Amazonia seem to diminish when they are placed in a larger context with people from the south of Brazil or from other countries (P16). This implies that the differentiation between in-groups and out-groups depends on the point of reference, thus allowing the different peoples of the Brazilian Amazon to feel as one people – at least in certain situations.

In a similar vein, interviewees describe the identities and lifestyles of indigenous peoples, fishers, and riverine peoples to be strikingly similar. They all rely on a combination of fishing and farming in order to make a living (P25). Moreover, these groups share a strong dependence on nature and close ties to their natural environment as part of their personal identities. The differentiation between these groups essentially is attributed by others, and thus constitutes a social identity in the strict sense. One interviewee explains that the social categories were introduced to the region by outside agents, and that they are largely irrelevant in daily live.

> *"Agents – that is how we call them – the agents come from outside and engage in that dialogue with these peoples and that is how it starts. And we no longer see it only with our own eyes. We see it with the eyes of the researcher, with the eyes of the politician, etc." (P25)*

The social movement against Belo Monte seeks to unite the struggle by de-emphasizing the differences between the social groups. On the one hand, interviewees claim that differences exist between riverine peoples, fishers, and native ethnic groups – especially in terms of their official recognition and legal rights.[92] On the other hand, they stress that these groups have common interests and objectives because of their similar lifestyles and their mutual dependence on the river for survival (P25).

In the following sections, I characterize fishers, riverine people, and indigenous peoples as social groups, and discuss the consequences of the Belo Monte Dam for the survival of their cultures.

5.2.2.2 *Social Identity and Self-Identification of Fishers and Riverine People*

According to interviewees, the legal differentiation, which grants special rights to indigenous and traditional peoples, creates some dissent between the social groups but no open conflict (P25). In view of the attendance and support that indigenous communities have been receiving from Norte Energia and the government since the start of the Belo Monte project, interviewees from the ranks of the fishers complain about the neglect of their own social group and the unequal treatment of said social groups (P25). Interviewees claim that fishers are a highly neglected social group that lacks access to education and health care services. In contrast to indigenous people, they are not eligible to measures of affirmative action. Moreover, they are frequently confronted with prejudices, scrutiny of their identities, and demoralization (P25).

> *"And for society, the fisher has to be toothless, not have any teeth. He has to walk with dirty fingernails, with torn clothes and flip-flops, and smelling of fish. If he does not have these characteristics, the society does not consider him a fisher." (P25)*

As social identity is created by means of ascription, members of the out-group identify a person as a fisher if he or she meets the criteria that they believe are characteristic of fishers. This leads to a reinforcement of existing prejudices and

92 While indigenous people and *quilombolas* were officially recognized in the Brazilian Constitution of 1988, other traditional populations of Brazil were only recognized by presidential decree no. 6.040 of February 2007 (MDS 2016). A detailed discussion of possible differences in the official recognition and legal rights of riverine people, fishers, and indigenous peoples is beyond the scope of this study. However, it is important to note, that interviewees experience a differentiated treatment, which they consider unfair because of the similarities in the social groups' lifestyles.

limits the possibilities of fishers to express their identities through their outward appearance.

> *"Because even when you apply for the fishing closure allowance, the agent of the ministry looks you up and down.*[93] *With his gaze he already wants to tell you that you are not a fisherman, that you are not a fisherwoman. [...] So on the day of the fishing closure you practically have to go in rags and tatters to make sure that you are not discriminated against." (P25)*

While interviewees claim that fishers face discrimination in daily life, they also lament that this social group is doomed to disappear because of the detrimental consequences of the Belo Monte Dam (P25).

In a similar vein, interviewees from the ranks of the riverine people claim that they are going to lose their history and their identity as a social group because of the Belo Monte Dam (P23). Riverine people living in the area that is directly affected by the dam project feel uprooted in a physical and emotional sense. They do not only have to leave their houses and territories but have to give up some habits and customs.[94] Interviewees emphasize that the lifestyle of the traditional peoples is very pleasant because of the close contact to nature, the tranquility, the coolness of the forest, and the rich soil that allows them to plant foodstuff (P23). They note that the conflict about different paths for development is based on a different perception of traditional lifestyles, among other things.

> *"There is nothing positive about this issue [Belo Monte, I.P.]. There is nothing positive. And they keep lying. Telling us lies that we will have a normal life, calling us impoverished, that we have a miserable life. On the contrary, we have a very healthy life, very good, strong, and I say this: I have nothing to complain about my life there." (P23)*

Interviewees explain that outsiders associate the traditional lifestyle with sadness and loneliness (P23), while the traditional peoples themselves believe that they enjoy a high quality of life (P23). They are afraid of losing their lifestyles, which are an important part of their identity as a distinct social group.

---

93 During the period of fishing closure, fishers registered in fishers' colonies are eligible for an allowance (the so-called *seguro defeso*) that substitutes the incurred loss in income (Controladoria-Geral da União n.d.).

94 The socioeconomic consequences of the Belo Monte project on individuals are discussed in detail in Section 5.3.

5.2.2.3 *Social Identity and Self-Identification of Indigenous Peoples*

Indigenous people are probably the most visible social group in the collective action against Belo Monte, due to their presence in the national and international media. In 1989, various native ethnic groups from Pará and Mato Grosso met for the First Encounter of the Indigenous Nations of the Xingu and contributed substantially to the prevention of hydropower plants at the Xingu River (P9, P37). The indigenous female warrior Tuíra raising her machete against the former director of Eletronorte, José Antônio Muniz Lopes, not only convinced the World Bank to withdraw its financial support for the dam project (P19), but also contributed to the social identity that people in Altamira and Belém attribute to the indigenous. With reference to the resistance to hydropower plants at the Xingu River, interviewees describe the indigenous culture and behavior as brave (P9), more radical, and more aggressive than the non-indigenous (P23, P31). The attributed militancy is one aspect of their social identity that indigenous activists confirm. Yet, they criticize that the non-indigenous population tends to leave the struggle against Belo Monte to the indigenous precisely because of their attributed fighting spirit.

> *"When I say, 'It looks like they dump it on us.' Because the people believe that the indigenous have all the power, because we indigenous really fight, we are not afraid of fighting. This is something that not every society has. I do not know- This is something that comes from ourselves. It comes from us. We are not afraid of really fighting for what is ours. And the other populations are different. They are afraid. They are more afraid. They are very different. That is what it amounts to, what makes the difference." (P29)*

Indigenous activists claim that all native ethnic groups in Brazil are militant, but emphasize that they differ substantialy in terms of their capacities. While some indigenous communities receive support from outside agents and/or from other native ethnic groups, others are severely neglected and therefore more fragile and susceptible to manipulation (P29). Since the beginning of the construction works, the government and Norte Energia have offered financial and material support to some indigenous communities of the Xingu River. Interviewees from the ranks of the protest SMOs consider this bribery and a deliberate strategy of the government to weaken the resistance to the Belo Monte Dam.[95] They claim that these policies promote the dependence of indigenous communities on

95 As the financial and material support of indigenous communities contributed to the fragmentation of the social movement, this discussion is resumed in Section 5.4.

public assistance, instead of empowering them to use their knowledge and resources with a view to maintaining their independence (P29).

As regards the general reputation and role of the indigenous in society, interviewees lament that the authorities and parts of the Brazilian majority society disrespect the native culture and lifestyle (P29). According to interviewees, Lula once called the indigenous an "impediment" to progress (P1, P43). Local activists claim that the population in the South and Southeast of Brazil believes

> *"that you have to clear the forest, that you have to kill the indigenous, that you have to dam the rivers in order to generate development there." (P1)*

Interviewees insist that native ethnic groups and traditional peoples have a specific knowledge of the forest and capabilities that could be employed to make the use of natural resources more sustainable (P1, P13, P29). From their point of view, the indigenous knowledge could be a valuable asset for the country's development, as the following statement illustrates.

> *"We are capable. Owing to the knowledge that we have of the forest, of the plants, of everything. Up to this very water. We are able to contribute to the development of this country, only that we are not listened to. Our knowledge is not used in a positive way. Because we are holders of the entire traditional medicine. We know everything there is for things to develop. We know it. We are the guardians of all this. Only that they do not use it." (P29)*

Many local activists are frustrated about the divergence between the social identity and the self-conception of indigenous people with respect to their current and potential future role in the Brazilian society. They lament that most people – including leading politicians – do not make the effort to familiarize themselves with the indigenous culture and lifestyle (P45). The social identity of native ethnic groups reduces them to their outward appearance and the entertainment value of their ancient rites, while neglecting substantial aspects of their culture and social order (P29). Just like the social group of fishers, indigenous peoples perceive the social identity they are being ascribed by members of the out-group to be partial, to focus on subordinate attributes, and to limit them in expressing their identities.

However, there are also positive examples of non-indigenous people who do not only demonstrate and promote respect for indigenous peoples but who also make an effort to build bridges between the ethnic groups.

"They are different people. And we respect them in their otherness. And we do not only respect them, we need to go even further. We love them. I have made this experience. I remember when I went to a community of the Kayapó, and I did not speak a word of Kayapó.[96] *Nothing. I said, 'I will never again set foot in this community without knowing Kayapó.' And I learned. I will not say that I speak it the way I speak Portuguese, but I learned it. And the second time I went there – you cannot imagine. Oh my God! The biggest and most friendly, most intimite smile; I would say, 'Now he is one of us, he speaks our language.' They know that we try hard, and through verbal communication we understand their world." (P45)*

5.2.3 Introduction to Collective Identity

In Chapter 2 collective identity was defined as the shared sense of belonging to a collectivity (we) in contrast to other actors (them). It is constructed through a continuous process of identity work – that is, the individual and collective activities that people engage in with the purpose of defining and expressing who they are and how they relate to others (Rucht 2002: 331; Snow 2001: 2216). In accordance with the literature (Klandermans 1997: 41; Snow 2001: 2215–2216), the analysis of collective identities in the Belo Monte conflict reveals that the sense of belonging to a collective is influenced by similarity in personal characteristics, by common fate, and shared experiences of collective action. Activists in Altamira and Belém resemble each other in (1) their awareness of social, cultural, political, and economic developments, (2) their identification with the collective through the Amazonian Identity, and (3) their common mobilization through the CEBs. These aspects contributed substantially to the development of a collective identity, and continue to be a point of reference for members of the social movement in Altamira and Belém – despite its fragmentation.

Members of the diverse social groups that participate in the social movement against Belo Monte engage in identity work by de-emphasizing the differ-

96 The Kayapó is an indigenous people populating the states of Mato Grosso and Pará. According to data provided by the Health Information System for Indigenous Peoples (Sistema de Informação da Atenção à Saúde Indígena, SIASI) and the Special Secretariat for Indigenous Health Care (Secretaria Especial de Saúde Indígena, SESAI) this ethnic group, which is divided into various subgroups, comprised 11 675 individuals in 2014 (Instituto Socioambiental n.d.c). Some Kayapó communities participate in the collective action against Belo Monte.

ences between them. Instead, they stress that the inhabitants of the region are affected in very similar ways by the Belo Monte Dam (P25).

> *"For this people, the river represents life. The survival, the fishing. Everything there is. The people live close to the river. So it is the river that unites them. It unites. The waters of the Xingu River are what unites this people. So even if they live in different circumstances, the circumstances of the Xingu are the same: to survive on fishing, to survive based on the water." (P27)*

Interviewees frequently allude to the people's regional identification and their living conditions, which depend on the natural environment but at the same time define people as inhabitants of this socio-environmental space and as members of a specific social group. I call this collective identity the Amazonian Identity[97] and propose that it is characterized by

1. a geographical component;
2. a strong personal connection to the natural environment, which serves as a reference point for the personal identity;
3. an interdependence between the people and the environment;
4. the appreciation of diversity in terms of cultures and lifestyles; and
5. the acknowledgment that Amazonia and its inhabitants constitute a fragile living organism.

Hence, the Amazonian Identity is characterized by the people's living conditions and their natural environment. This confirms existing research about the influence of structural factors on the process of collective identity construction (cf. Flesher Fominaya 2010b: 398). The following statement illustrates the Amazonian Identity concept and alludes to its value for the local population.

> *"And the other thing that I consider fundamental was that we created this feeling of Amazonia, that we are Amazonia, regardless of where I am. [...] As we are the Amazon and we are a fragile biome, what happens there in Belo Monte affects my life here in Belém, it affects the lives of those who are in Rondônia, it affects the lives of those in Acre. This was another very positive feeling, this relief of feeling to be Amazonia, to arrive here in the city and say, 'I am a son of the Amazon rainforest. Even though I live in a big city, I feel part of the forest.' That feeling is also permeating the group. People also feel- they identify with*

97 The term Amazonian Identity is mainly used in cultural studies (cf. Chapter 6).

> *this [...] Even though we live here, we are indigenous, mestizos, riverine people.*[98] *We want this. This is important, this identification." (P1)*

As a collective identity, the Amazonian Identity complements the personal identities of people. It enables them to identify with a larger collective and to develop shared beliefs and interests. On the one hand, the Amazonian Identity allows forest people to reconcile their personal identities with a modern lifestyle and residence in the city. The interviewee's speaking of a relief in this context, indicates that forest people who live in the city encounter difficulties in terms of their identity. Whether these arise from the expectations and ascriptions of other people or from people's self-concepts and their own expectations of themselves remains unclear. On the other hand, the Amazonian Identity enables groups that did not feel involved in the Belo Monte conflict in the past to identify with the collective and participate in the social movement (P1). Local activists consider it their task to inform the urban population of the conflict, and they deliberately use the Amazonian Identity to establish the link between the lives and realities of the urban and rural population.

> *"And the Metropolitan Committee was established for the purpose of strengthening the Xingu Forever Alive Movement and to give visibility to this fight, because we are in the state capital and it was necessary to explain to the peoples, to the people here in the metropolitan area, that this fight is not only a fight of the people of the Xingu River; it is a fight of the entire Amazonian population. It is a struggle of those people who defend the environment and who defend the Amazon." (P3)*

According to interviewees, the Amazonian Identity was deliberately created through the interaction of people. As an important internal factor promoting movement cohesion, it will be discussed again in detail in Section 5.4.

5.2.4 Motivation for Collective Action

People have multiple identities that are organized hierarchically and become salient in different situations (cf. Chapter 2). The personal, social, and collective identities of local movement participants discussed in the sections above interact with each other and influence the person's interests and actions – including his or her motivation to fight against the construction of hydropower plants at the Xingu River. For example, religious interviewees claim that it is their vocation

98 Mestizos are people of mixed-race origin. Definition derived from the online dictionary *Michaelis Moderno Dicionário da Língua Portuguesa*, author's translation (UOL 2009b).

to preserve live and nature and to show solidarity with marginalized people. In a similar vein, activists who identify strongly with a particular social group explain that a lack of rights motivates them to fight for better living conditions. I have classified the motives that induce local activists to participate in the collective action against Belo Monte into the following four categories:

1. disapproval of the political and economic system,
2. a lack of rights in Amazonia,
3. distrust of authorities, and
4. a sense of moral obligation.

While the separation between people's character traits and their motivation for collective action may seem artificial, it serves the analytical purpose of tracing how people come to join a social movement and identify with a collective identity. In the following sections, I discuss the motives described by interviewees in detail.

5.2.4.1 Disapproval of the Political and Economic System

Many of the interviewed participants in the social movement against Belo Monte in Altamira and Belém originally decided to participate in collective action because they felt outrage about the political and economic system of their country. Over the years, these activists have participated in different struggles, and they perceive the Belo Monte conflict as a specific case in the realm of these struggles (P3, P37, P55). The fight for societal change and "a different Brazil" (P45) is a common motive among interviewees (P3, P9, P29, P35, P41, P55).

> *"The principle of the movement, if we were to consider it – that is, the strategy of the movement – is in fact this quest for the fundamental transformation of society. To transform the structure of society. So, all the movements that have this objective, that dream of this reality, and that develop their methodology and their action with a view to this big objective, these are movements that generally cooperate." (P49)*

Interviewees emphasize that they work on pressing issues and seek to contribute concrete proposals for the future development of the country (P9). Special attention is paid to the development of Amazonia in general, and the region of the Trans-Amazon Highway and Xingu in particular.

The local activists' perception of the political and economic system and the current development concept figures prominently in the collective action frame of the social movement and will be discussed in detail in Section 5.3.

5.2.4.2 *Lack of Rights in Amazonia*

The fight for societal change refers to a number of economic, social, political, cultural, and environmental attributes that local activists either fight to obtain because they are not guaranteed at the moment (for example, enforcement of rights), or defend from destruction because they are threatened by the current political and economic system (for example, indigenous cultures). A central issue is the fight for rights and their enforcement throughout the Brazilian Amazon (P9, P16, P31, P37). Local activists define their fundamental rights as to include "the right to a healthy life, to a decent life" (P1; also see P9), "a life with respect, especially on the part of the government", and peace instead of violence (P31). They take efforts to learn about their rights and to develop awareness of the observance and infringement of their rights by other people and the authorities (P29). Moreover, interviewees report to work in various contexts and with different allies towards the observance of their rights in everyday life (P9, P13) and in the context of Belo Monte (P29). They focus on marginalized, disadvantaged, and socially excluded people; among them native ethnic groups, *quilombolas*, and people in extreme poverty (P19, P27, P31, P43). Some interviewees also claim that women are especially affected by infringements of their rights and by infrastructure projects like Belo Monte (P35).

Interviewees frequently connect the defense of human, economic, social, cultural, and environmental rights to the defense of Amazonia, which indicates that these rights are particularly threatened in this region (P3). Indeed, the defense of nature, life, and traditional ways of life constitute another group of motives behind collective action. Given the persistent exploitation of the regions' natural resources and the destruction of the natural environment throughout Brazil, many activists fight for the preservation of the natural environment and for socio-environmental justice (P9, P13, P23, P27, P31, P53).[99] As nature is a source of life, a defining part of identity, and a provider of food and shelter, defending nature from destruction effectively means to defend life (P23). Religious activists emphasize that the defense of life derives directly from the gospel (P16) and that God placed men on earth with the mission to defend his Creation (P16, P53). Others claim that the defense of life is a universal value of mankind (P31).

99 Many interviewees explicitly mention the defense of the river, to which they attach a high value (P23, P27, P29). The notion of the Xingu River will be discussed further below.

> *"What also becomes a common interest is the concern for life in the environment, and this is a fight that any population that feels threatened anywhere in the world, in any part of the planet, will wage." (P31)*

The struggle for life in Amazonia includes a struggle for the preservation of the lifestyles and cultures of indigenous communities and other minority ethnic groups that live as hunter-gatherers or shifting cultivators. These groups have been threatened by attempts to effectively integrate the Brazilian Amazon into the national territory, by resource exploitation, and by the influx of foreigners. Local activists seek to defend the "way of life of the Amazon populations" (P1) and the socio-environmental diversity of the region, as they consider them patrimonies of humanity and thus worthy of protection (P37).

While the motives to defend nature, life, and traditional lifestyles were separated analytically during data analysis, they determine each other in the collective action. Water and land constitute necessary conditions of life; especially for forest peoples whose necessities of life are not readily available. Local activists oppose Belo Monte because they perceive it as a threat to the prerequisites of life.

> *"So, our personal struggle is this: to defend the river, to defend the land, to defend our land where we live today. And by defending the river and by defending the land, we are defending life." (P23)*

The fight for human, economic, social, cultural, and environmental rights, and the defense of life are important motives for local activists as the infringement of these rights and the impunity of crimes are persistent problems in Amazonia in general, and in the Belo Monte project in particular. Their pre-existing motivation is further reinforced by the particular local context, and more precisely by people's interpretation of the context. Therefore, I repeatedly refer to the motives of local activists throughout Section 5.3, where I discuss the framing of the Belo Monte conflict and the SMOs' different ways of confronting it.

5.2.4.3 Distrust of Authorities

Another common motive for collective action among interviewees is the general belief that civil society should monitor the authorities (P19, P41).

> *"This government is there because we also helped to place it there. It has to learn. I believe that society has this role, to make the government understand that it is responsible for everything." (P29)*

With respect to the economic, political, social, and environmental challenges of the Volta Grande, interviewees demand that policymakers acknowledge the situation, direct their attention to the region, and take the necessary steps towards its sustainable development (P31). To this end, activists from Altamira have repeatedly traveled to Belém and Brasília to pressure the state and federal governments to improve public services in the areas of health, education, infrastructure, financial services, etc. (P9). In the specific case of the Belo Monte project, the protest SMOs focus on pressuring the government to renounce the entire undertaking, to hear the Brazilian people, and to effectively include the society in the energy planning for the country (P9).

> *"The movement has the role of developing intelligent ways of making demands. It is not just about demanding for the sake of demanding or for the sake of saying, 'We are being compensated'. Rather, it means to demand that the role of the government be fulfilled in a way- because all this is their right, regardless of Belo Monte." (P19)*

In contrast, the monitoring SMOs continue what they call the "social control" of the government; yet, with a view to ensuring Norte Energia's compliance with the conditions of the preliminary license, the mitigation measures, and the development plans (P41).

The skepticism of local activists towards the authorities is said to be based on and reinforced by bad experiences of the past. Interviewees repeatedly refer to big infrastructure projects – among them the hydropower plants Balbina, Tucuruí, and Curuá-Una – that were implemented in Amazonia without due consideration of their social and environmental consequence. Interviewees recall that these projects did not create any benefits for the local population; instead, they caused the displacement of thousands of people and the disruption of social structures. Violence, prostitution, and drug trafficking increased, and only a small minority benefited from these projects (P1, P16, P27, P31, P53). Interviewees also complain that the energy produced in these dams is not used to supply the local population; instead it is channeled to other regions of Brazil (P16).

> *„Also with a view to the impacts caused by the Tucuruí hydropower plant that were not remedied until today. Many communities still have lawsuits pending, demanding compensation for losses – and this was 20 years ago or more. In addition, the government planned another hydropower plant in the Amazon called Balbina, which is bankrupt. Balbina, a failed project." (P51)*

Local activists expect that „history will repeat itself" (P23), and that the people affected by the Belo Monte project will experience the same abandonment on the part of the government as the other regions once the project is completed (P13, P51).

5.2.4.4 *Moral Obligation*

The social movement against Belo Monte is further strengthened by its participants' moral considerations. Interviewees claim that it is their moral obligation to fight for social change in general, and against the Belo Monte Dam – which they perceive as a symbol of the current political and economic model – in particular.[100] Yet, they state different reasons for why they hold this belief. In line with the central attributes of their personal identities, some activists say that it is part of their Christian mission to defend God's Creation (P16), while others emphasize that fighting Belo Monte is a question of honor and a matter of conscience (P29). Some interviewees commit themselves to the fight for rights and justice, which they believe is a struggle that every men and women should join (P27, P55). From their point of view, it is a general obligation for society to demonstrate, to denounce malpractice and misguided developments, and to organize for collective action. "Silence means consent", these interviewees proclaim (P9).

The moral obligation is reinforced by the long duration of the Belo Monte conflict and the involvement of several generations in the collective action. For example, a fisher who fights for recognition and rights that their ancestors did not have – like the registration of fishers in the realm of fishers' colonies,[101] the payment of the fishing closure allowance, and equal rights for female fishers (P25) – explicitly dedicates their efforts to the memory of their ancestors. Likewise, an indigenous activist fighting for indigenous rights, the preservation of their culture, and the demarcation of their ancestral lands claims to be continuing a historical struggle that was passed down generations (P29, P37).

> *"My grandmother told me the entire history of what we experienced until today. I sat down with my grandmother, and she told me everything we suffered [...] And what my grandmother passed on to me, I grew up with the knowledge of our history, of all the suffering. And this will grow a spirit of revolt, a will to change this process, in us as well. When my*

100 The symbolic meaning of Belo Monte is discussed in detail in Section 5.3.

101 Fishers' colonies are legally recognized institutions of the workers in the sector of artisan fishing.

grandmother died I said, [...] 'Grandma, I promise I will never stop this battle. Everything that you could not do for us, I will do.' So, whenever I think of stopping the fighting, I remember what I promised my grandmother, and I will not stop fighting. For all that she did not achieve, for all that she lost. She lost her family, she lost much of her culture in search of freedom. All this is very much alive." (P29)

Interviewees report that the elders of indigenous communities, who have been dedicated to the fight against Belo Monte for many years, urge the younger generation to continue this fight. Calling upon their conscientiousness, they demand that the young subordinate their individual interests to the collective interest and the intergenerational struggle (P37). The elders argue that the forest with its abundant resources and the indigenous society with its specific culture are the wealth of their peoples. They were passed down for generations and should continue to be passed down to future generations (P37).

The moral obligation is also strong in those participants in the social movement who have lost comrades in the struggle for social change, and who feel obliged to honor their memories by continuing the work they have done.

"To retreat, that is to say, to leave this very important struggle- [respondent sobs, I.P.] To leave this very important struggle means to kill the dreams. (...) It means to kill the dreams and the struggle of so many people who gave their lives for this, and for us to continue this fight. So many- Dorothy, our union members here, Brasília, Bartolomeu, Dema. And now this couple that was murdered, José and Maria." (P9)

As the quotes above illustrate, many local activists dedicate their work to other people who did not enjoy the recognition and the rights that activists are struggling for nowadays (P25), and who gave their lives in the struggle for social change. Interviewees – regardless of their origin – claim, that ceasing the struggle for rights and justice would mean betrayal of their social group, their ancestors, or individual comrades (P29).

5.2.5 *Repercussions of the Conflict on Local Activists*

The personal accounts of interviewees show that more than two decades of fighting against hydropower plants at the Xingu River have taken their toll on movement participants and their families. Interviewees claim that they have grown old in the struggle (P35), and that some have become "more or less addicted to it" (P1). The constant involvement in the conflict, which requires activists to dedicate a lot of time and energy, wears them out until they realize that they have been leaving other people and interests behind (P27, P29).

> *"Until I stopped for a while because I was seeing that it really wears us out. The entire battery. It discharges. It wears us out in a really terrible way, and you look back and say, "Wow, I am neglecting my personal life, I left everything behind for the sake of this fight." (P29)*

Interviewees admit that the movement may seem tired and fragile, but they assert that this is only the outward appearance (P19). Some local activists lament that they neglected their children because they were fully occupied with the collective action against the hydropower project (P25, P35). Over time, some activists chose to balance their commitment with their private life and personal interests, while others continue to prioritize the collective action against Belo Monte (P35).

Many interviewees report that the conflict over Belo Monte creates pressure and emotional stress. While some movement participants keep a low profile in order not to lose their jobs or experience other negative effects (P13), others are more outspoken about their believes and risk being stigmatized and labeled as troublemakers (P25, P27).

> *"But we are paying a high price for this, for doing- for being on this side. We [...] were often massacred [sic] for defending this other project, this other model of development, which is not one of big constructions. We have been ridiculed a lot in this city." (P35)*

As a result, local activists avoid to stage demonstrations in areas where they do not have the support of the majority (P25). Nonetheless, experiences of repudiation cause frustration and disappointment. The protest SMOs try hard to get through to other people and mobilize bystanders for their cause, but are sometimes confronted with disinterest and a lack of support (cf. Section 5.1). As the issue is complex and the government and Norte Energia are suspected to deceive the population, activists place importance on educating the population about the project. The experience of being misunderstood and failing to convey the organizations' understanding of the conflict – that is, their collective action frame – creates feelings of ineffectiveness among activists. One activist describes the challenges of convincing their community as follows:

> *"Will they believe in my theory that goes 'This is ours. You have to fight for the project.'?[102] They will not. They will not believe in it. This is what*

102 In this statement, project does not refer to the Belo Monte project but to a community project initiated by the activist.

> *the problem is. And these things are things that hurt me. I suffered a lot from this whole situation when I realized that my talk was different from that of the community." (P29)*

Unwilling to change their opinion about how to confront the Belo Monte conflict, this activist did no longer feel legitimized to represent the community and eventually withdrew from the leadership (P29). Other activists who perceive their activities as a "huge challenge" and "a very difficult situation" seek support from other organizations and individuals (P9).

While the participation in the social movement is frequently perceived as to include a number of sacrifices and risks, interviewees are quick to qualify their complaints by acknowledging that any activity involves risks and that their activism is worth the effort (P1, P25).

> *"I believe this is a fight worth fighting. It is worth fighting, because at least we are fighting for a just cause, for justice, for the future not only of our region; for the future of our country, the future of the very planet, because it involves all this; and the people are blind, they are deaf. When they open their eyes, it will be late. And that is what is happening. (..) Belo Monte has no reason to be." (P29)*

The positive experiences that local activists make with their participation in the social movement against Belo Monte motivate them to keep up their commitment (P29). Many interviewees describe their activities to be fulfilling and meaningful (P13), and they feel rewarded when they see that their struggle is effecting changes in people's lives (P25).

> *"However, there is nothing more satisfactory for me than seeing that the rights of the people are guaranteed. This is the greatest miracle there is, to see that the rights of a person are guaranteed. And you see the joy of a couple of people who have been living from fishing for 40 years and never had any rights, and for the first time they receive the fishing closure allowance." (P25)*

Nonetheless, the risks that activists in Altamira and Belém are willing to take are substantial. Some participants in the social movement have been confronted with criminal complaints by the CCBM for alleged instigation of the workforce and interference in the construction (P27, P55).

> *„One can afford to say a lot of things, but one cannot afford to say 'no' to the dam. If you say 'no,' you will either be ignored or you will be isolated – and there have been situations like this – or you will be sued or criminalized, so this is about the situation we are in." (P49)*

The struggle for a differentiated development and against the exploitation of the Brazilian Amazon has already claimed the lives of several activists (P9, P13, P25, P41). The most prominent examples include the murders of Ademir Alfeu Federicci, coordinator of MDTX and known as Dema, in 2001 (P9), and Sister Dorothy Stang, member of the Congregation of the Sisters of Notre Dame de Namur, in 2005 (P47). One interviewee recounts a conversation with Dorothy Stang who spoke in tears about being persecuted and threatened – two weeks before she was found shot to death (P13). Erwin Kräutler, the former bishop, has been receiving death threats for about thirty years because of his activism on behalf of indigenous peoples and his participation in the social movement against Belo Monte (P31, P45). The hostility suffered by former and current activists creates psychological pressure and emotional stress (P29). Some interviewees burst into tears while talking about their own activism and the violent death of friends and comrades, which shows that the emotional stress also affects activists who have not been threatened directly (P9, P29). Yet, interviewees claim that the challenges they confront also strengthen and brace them for the conflict. By confronting persecution, violence, and death, activists develop strategies of coping with difficult situations (P13, P23).

In view of the harassment and persecution, local activists in Altamira and Belém have developed a certain resilience to the pressure and emotional stress (P1, P3, P25). Many of them claim that hope and their faith in God are the main motives behind their continuous struggle against all odds (P23, P29, P31). Moreover, local activists draw a line in terms of how much they are prepared to risk in the fight against Belo Monte, claiming that they "do not want to die in this either" (P35). Some have resigned from leadership positions or taken a break from their activism,[103] in order to protect themselves and to take care of personal matters (P1, P27, P29, P35). As one interviewee admits,

> *"I stopped for a while, because I had personal problems and even problems outside the family, so I decided to stay there more often, because there are times when it is better that we protect ourselves and withdraw a little bit." (P25)*

Local activists emphasize that their retreat is temporary, as "the good combatant does not stop, he takes some time off" (P25).

103 While some SMOs are hierarchically structured and appoint official leaders, other SMOs claim not to have any leaders. The issue merits a separate discussion in Section 5.4 and in Chapter 6.

In general, movement participants in Altamira and Belém are characterized by a strong adherence to their principles and convictions (P29).[104] They appreciate the attempts of the local population to make demands on the Norte Energia consortium and the government in order to have their rights recognized (P13, P51). They take pride in the obstinacy of some communities (P16) and their refusal to allow studies and inspections of their territory (P23). And they try to keep up their daily routines and economic activities (P23), even declining job offers with Norte Energia in order to remain independent in their thought and action (P25). Local activists and parts of the local population demonstrate their independence, for example, at the ballot by making their vote contingent on the political candidates' opposition to hydropower dams at the Xingu (P25). Interviewees report that the population's susceptibility to manipulation by candidates has declined in recent years (P45). They take pride in having contribution to this development by raising people's awareness and by encouraging their political participation (P45).

5.2.6 *Preliminary Conclusion*

The analysis of personal and social identities in this section has shown that movement participants in Altamira and Belém share a number of characteristics, including a strong sense of volunteerism and a true dedication to the cause. Their general predisposition for participation in social movements arises from attributes that are particularly salient in the personal identities of these activists, namely (1) a regional identification, (2) a religious faith and lifestyle, (3) a sense of organic intellectualism, or (4) a sense of political resistance. Female activists are considered to possess additional attributes and capabilities that they bring into the struggle against Belo Monte. These include their power to create life, their close connection to nature, and their long-term perspective.

In terms of social identities, I have pointed out the special characteristics and lifestyles of the peoples inhabiting the Amazonian state of Pará. Their social identities have a strong geographical and time component, in that they make reference to the unique Amazon region and to the centuries-old history of indigenous and traditional peoples in the area. The analysis of social identities further reveals discrepancies between self-perception and perception by others.

104 Interestingly, interviewees across both factions of the social movement claim to follow their convictions; yet, the protest SMOs accuse the monitoring SMOs of having betrayed the social movement. This is an important aspect of the fragmentation of the social movement, which will be discussed in detail in Section 5.4.

While interviewees from the ranks of the fishers, the riverine people, and the native ethnic groups value their cultures and lifestyles, they perceive to be neglected, depreciated, and discriminated against by the majority population and the authorities.

The Amazonian Identity was deliberately created as a collective identity that complements the personal and social identities of activists and bystanders, and enables them to develop shared believes and interests with a larger collective. I propose that it is characterized by a geographical component, a strong personal connection to the natural environment, the interdependence between people and environment, the appreciation of diversity, and the fragility of the living space.

The analysis of typical motives behind the collective action has shown that movement participants in Altamira and Belém are driven by a general disapproval of the political and economic system, a lack of rights in Amazonia, distrust of the authorities, and a sense of moral obligation to shape social life. Their predisposition for collective action is further strengthened by the additional threats they expect from the Belo Monte project. However, the conflict also has severe repercussions on local activists in the form of threat, repression, stigmatization, exclusion, and health problems. In order to cope with the various challenges, interviewees have developed a certain resilience to pressure and emotional stress. The principle of hope, faith in God, and a responsible use of their own physical and emotional resources help activists to keep up their activism.

To this point, the argument I am building runs as follows: The personal, social, and collective identities of local movement participants, their predisposition and motivation for collective action in general, and in the conflict over the Belo Monte project in particular, interact in such a way that already existing forms of activism are intensified and directed towards the struggle against Belo Monte. In the next section (5.3), I elaborate in detail on the social movement's collective action fame for the purpose of explaining how local activists perceive of the Belo Monte project and its interaction with the region, and how they define their own role and activities in the conflict. As I have argued up to now, identity work and framing processes are central dynamics impacting upon cohesion and fragmentation in the social movement. Based on the detailed analysis of identities (in this sections) and frames (in the following), Section 5.4 will examine the internal and external factors that promote cohesion and fragmentation in the social movement. The section aims to demonstrate how the election and coming into office of the Workers' Party altered the context conditions for civil society in Brazil and contributed to the fragmentation of the social movement against Belo Monte.

5.3 Collective Action Frames

As discussed in Chapter 2, the framing process includes three core tasks – namely (1) the identification of a problem in social life that needs alteration, (2) the proposal of a solution to this problem, and (3) a rationale for and an appeal to engage in collective action (Benford and Snow 2000: 615–618; Snow and Benford 1988: 199). The interviews with local activists posed questions on the commonly perceived problem that arises from the Belo Monte project (diagnostic framing), and on the proffered solutions to this problem (prognostic framing), which I classified into short-term and long-term solutions, based on the interviewee's accounts.

This section starts with a detailed discussion of the Belo Monte diagnostic frame, which is shared in large parts by the two factions of the social movement. The diagnostic frame alludes to the characteristics and meaning of the Belo Monte project, the regional context conditions, the consequences of the undertaking, and the controversial implementation procedure. The regional context, and more specifically the close connection between people and nature, is a central aspect of the diagnostic frame. As the natural environment constitutes an important point of reference for people's identities, it influences their motives to participate in collective action. In the second part of this section, I analyze the controversies in the collective action frame that developed in the course of the Belo Monte project. The advancement of the project brought some activists to reassess the entire situation and to renegotiate its meaning. This process resulted in the definition of divergent diagnostic and prognostic frames, and in the separation of the MDTX into the Xingu Vivo Movement and the Foundation. Subsequently, the two factions engaged in separate framing activities and developed their own strategies and tactics for confronting the Belo Monte conflict. However, both factions continue to promote their common long-term solution to the region's development problems. After discussing the differentiated development concept proposed by local activists across SMOs, I elaborate on their different strategies and tactics to achieving this type of development. The section closes with a preliminary conclusion about the role of framing in the social movement. I propose that framing processes play a particularly important role in the fragmentation of the movement. This discussion is resumed in Section 5.4.

5.3.1 *The Belo Monte Diagnostic Frame*

"What does Belo Monte really mean for the people in this region?" was the first question I asked interviewees in Altamira and Belém. This question sought to induce people to talk about the conflict from their perspective and to emphasize those aspects that they considered important – rather than reproducing standard and desirable answers. Most interviewees referred to Belo Monte as a representative of something larger or a symbol of a certain kind of thinking. This assessment was usually connected with a critique and/or the expression of disagreement. I have grouped the responses to the first interview question into the following four categories:

1. Belo Monte is a symbol of an ideological dispute. According to this group of interviewees, the debate goes well beyond the conflict over Belo Monte (P21). The project demonstrates that there exist different views of Amazonia, different perspectives for the region's development, as well as different ideologies regarding the development of Brazil and its society (P3, P2, P9, P41, P53, P55). These interviewees consider hydropower projects like Belo Monte as representatives of an outdated development model (P37).
2. Belo Monte is a symbol of domination. These interviewees claim that Belo Monte constitutes a violation of their (constitutional) rights and poses a threat to their traditional livelihoods (P16, P19, P25, P29, P35, P49). The critique has to be seen in light of the regional context conditions of Belo Monte – for example, the exploitation of the region, the disrespect for traditional lifestyles, etc.
3. Belo Monte is a representative of the prevalent economic model. According to this group of interviewees, Belo Monte represents and promotes the neoliberal economic policies that have been embraced by Brazilian governments since the 1990s. They criticize this model for over-emphasizing economic interests and promoting development at any price, often to the detriment of people and the environment, and without considering viable alternatives (P13, P27, P47, P51).
4. Belo Monte is a "door opener". This group of interviewees claim that Belo Monte is paving the way for further hydropower projects in Amazonia. The critique of hydropower is implicit in these statements and is being explicated during the course of the interviews. The interviewees' focus is on emphasizing the need to resist the beginnings of a detrimental development (P1, P43).

Moreover, interviewees emphasize that Belo Monte is embedded in unique context conditions that should be considered in the planning and implementation of a large infrastructure project (P31, P39). While the majority of activists allude to the complexity of the issue and seek to place the hydropower plant in a larger context of meaning in their opening statements, only one interviewee summarizes the symbolic meaning of Belo Monte in a single word: destruction (P23). This view is widely shared among local activists as the further analysis of the data shows (P1, P9, P29, P37, P53).

> *"The dam is destruction. A dam destroys, a dam kills. A dam pulls the people out of their houses; it pulls the people off their lands. The dam causes harm, because all it does is to enrich a small group to the detriment of a larger group that will lose its land, its origin, its cemeteries, its cultures, its gods; and we do not need this." (P1)*

As the classification of opening statements shows, the Belo Monte diagnostic frame involves a variety of aspects that are interlinked with other concepts that could broadly be described as context conditions to the Belo Monte conflict. The hydropower plant – while a contentious project in itself – interacts with its surrounding area because it affects and is likewise affected by the natural environment and the political, economic, and social dynamics of the region. Therefore, activists interpret Belo Monte in terms of their existing beliefs and ideas. However, many statements about the meaning of Belo Monte were made in passing, and sometimes interviewees assumed that the meaning of certain aspects was obvious. This indicates that the connection of the Belo Monte diagnostic frame to existing beliefs and ideas is a largely unconscious process. Throughout the interviews, activists allude to a variety of issues that add up to a consistent story about Belo Monte within its temporal and spatial context. From an analytical point of view, their statements can be classified into four categories:

1. the characteristics and general meaning of Belo Monte,
2. the regional context of Belo Monte,
3. the consequences of Belo Monte, and
4. the controversial implementation procedure.

The content of the individual categories will be discussed in detail in the following sections in order to reconstruct the Belo Monte diagnostic frame. Acknowledgment of the meaning that activists attribute to Belo Monte is necessary for understanding the central dynamics of this movement: the development of movement cohesion on the basis of collective identities and collective action frames, and the subsequent fragmentation of the social movement caused by internal and external factors leading to a divergence of the collective action frame and an identity crises among activists.

5.3.1.1 *Characteristics and General Meaning of Belo Monte*

The meaning of Belo Monte is multilayered in that it draws from various debates and alludes to a large variety of aspects. For activists who live and act in Altamira, in its adjacent municipalities, and in Belém the different themes are inherently connected. Therefore, interviewees speak of Belo Monte in a holistic fashion and make frequent references to individual aspects and implications of meaning that need to be disclosed and interpreted in the analysis. The general meaning of Belo Monte comprises various aspects, the key issue being a critique of the prevalent development model, which manifests itself in Belo Monte. However, interviewees also allude to the historic development, characteristics, and economic viability of the project. As these aspects are intrinsically linked, their separation is somewhat artificial but helpful in understanding the meaning of Belo Monte from the perspective of local activists.

The Brazilian Development Model and its Manifestation in Belo Monte

At the start of the new millennium, Brazil experienced a rapid economic development that was paralleled by a large increase in energy consumption. Local activists in Altamira and Belém frequently refer to this scenario when elaborating on the meaning of a hydropower plant at the Xingu River. Given the country's political and economic aspirations, the project assumes a symbolic meaning beyond the generation of electricity.

> *"So whenever we start talking about Belo Monte, we remember that talking about Belo Monte is not just talking about a hydropower plant that the government wants to build in the middle of the Amazon forest. Belo Monte is like a symbol of an entire development model that has historically been implemented in this region." (P21)*

Many interviewees strongly oppose this development model given its neglect of the human being and its ignorance of development aspects that are not directly related to economic progress. As one interviewee said,

> *"it's a vision of progress that is being questioned. It is not a question of having one river more or one river less. In the name of progress we are ready to invest everything. The most important element is not the life of the people. The most important element is to produce energy, no matter*

> *what the cost. The cultural cost, the ecological, the environmental, etc. For me this is the major question that is at the center, in the bulge of the Belo Monte question." (P47)*

The symbolic meaning of Belo Monte is a recurrent issue in most of the interviews, and it refers to a number of issues.

First of all, Belo Monte is seen as representative of the prevalent economic model, which many activists criticize. They condemn the superior position of economic issues and the excessive pursuit of profit (P16, P23, P27, P29, P35, P51, P55), which frequently involves corruption (P31), the exploitation of Brazil and other countries' resources (P13), and a particular mindset of "thinking that they own the world" (P23). From the activists' point of view, the population is subordinated to economic interests (P35, P49).

> *"The government does not think much about what we commonly mean by progress in terms of human dignity and human rights, public health, education, public safety, transport, housing, and sanitation, and other things." (P43).*

The statement illustrates the struggle over meaning that is strong in the debate about the region's future development. Local activists criticize the authorities for failing to maintain an equilibrium between the economic, social, political, cultural, and environmental spheres of life (P3, P21, P47). They claim that the PT government is still supporting the narrow view of development, that was prevalent under the military regime (P37, P43, P45, P53). Interviewees are particularly frustrated at the ruthless enforcement of the government's development model, that sacrifices environmental integrity, indigenous cultures, and traditional lifestyles to the generation of electricity (P47). A recurrent (rhetorical) question asks for the purpose and the beneficiaries of this development model.

> *"So the government acted in a truculent way by enforcing this project against the society, and the society will bear the burden. And this burden is already occurring [...]. So this is the first aspect that makes us oppose the project, because it also aims for a development model that the government tries to sell through its discourse, saying that Amazonia needs energy, needs development. But we wonder: development for what and for whom? And of course, this question is not relevant in the economic model of the mighty and in the invasion of the Amazon for the extraction of its wealth, which needs electrical energy." (P51)*

Questions like "The progress is for whom?" and "This is progress?" are raised repeatedly by the interviewees (P1, P3, P29, P31) and are associated with the question as to what price the society is willing to pay for supposed development

(P55). The exclusion of local people from benefits creates an "illusion of progress" (P16, P27) and the feeling that the government's concern for development is not sincere (P1, P16). Interviewees claim that the authorities' attempts to develop the region have repeatedly caused environmental destruction and the decimation of indigenous peoples in the name of progress (P1, P29).

> *"The government has always given incentives for destruction and continues giving them. Hence, you have a discourse of sustainable development but in reality you have a practice of environmental and cultural degradation in this region." (P37)*

Interviewees question the intentions of the authorities because they do not believe in the alleged necessity of hydropower plants in Amazonia (P51). The demand of the local population could be accommodated if already existing plants like Tucuruí Dam were repowered and properly maintained (P51, P55). Hence, interviewees conclude that the construction of a hydropower plant at the Xingu River serves other purposes, such as the exploitation of mineral resources in the riverbed (P13, P29, P51). Moreover, local activists expect that the implementation of Belo Monte will gain symbolic meaning and pave the way for additional dams along the Xingu River and other hydropower projects throughout Brazil (P1, P43, P47, P51). The social movement's purpose is to resist the beginnings of this development. From their point of view, the collective action against Belo Monte symbolizes the defense of rivers, peoples, and life in general (P31). By contrast, the successful realization of the project would represent the "fall of resistance to the construction of dams" (P1).

Besides questioning the real intentions behind the Belo Monte project, local activists denounce the manner in which the authorities seeks to address the problems of the region. While one local activist criticizes the mitigation projects as an attempt to "quench the centenary hunger with popcorn" (P13), another interviewee complains about dams being presented as the only path to development (P29). Consequently, local activists frequently propose the elaboration of alternative sources of electricity (P1, P3) and the improvement of existing facilities (P13, P55).

> *"And a country that has a coastline like ours, that has sun like ours all year, that has biomass and everything, and that still complies with the construction of dams is a country that is bound to be left far behind, considering that other countries such as European countries, or Germany indeed, now produce more solar and wind power than Brazil – that is a shame." (P1)*

Interviewees assume that the federal government promotes hydroelectricity in an attempt to privilege multinational corporations that benefit from large infrastructure projects (P23, P23).[105] Their reference to "so-called development" (P9, P9) emphasizes their discontent about the discourse.

To sum up, local activists consider the Belo Monte Dam a typical project within the Brazilian development model that mirrors the government's narrow understanding of development as economic progress, its excessive pursuit of profit, and its neglect of social, political, cultural, and environmental aspects.

Development, Attributes, and Assessment of Belo Monte

Besides this general critique of Brazil's development path and the authorities' intentions behind the Belo Monte project, some interviewees offer a technical and economic assessment of the venture, which is intimately connected with its historical development. As outlined in Chapter 4, the original plans for the exploitation of the Xingu River's hydroelectric potential date back to the 1970s. Originally, the project was designed by the military government in line with its strategy to foster economic growth through increased industrial production, which required a growing energy supply (P9, P55). After the World Bank withdrew its financial support in 1989 the dam project was put off until major blackouts in July 2001 and September 2002 caused a sense of crisis in the Brazilian population and forced the federal government to take action (P3, P55). The newly elected president, Lula, ordered the revision of the plans at the beginning of his first mandate (P21, P37, P39).

From the movement's point of view, the "supposedly left-wing" Workers' Party took a decisive step by "taking the project out of the drawer" (P55).[106] The technical modifications that are reflected in the change of name from Kararaô Dam to Belo Monte Dam figure prominently in the diagnostic frame. While the supporters of Belo Monte claim that significant adjustments were made in order to reduce the social and environmental impact of the project (P19, P37), opponents of Belo Monte reflect critically upon the preconditions and consequences of these modifications (P19, P29). Their arguments are based on the mandatory Environmental Impact Assessment (P37) and additional scholarly research (P45). Based on experiences, interviewees warn against repeating mistakes of the past

105 The discussion of the project's beneficiaries is resumed further below.

106 As will be discussed in detail in Section 5.4, the implementation of the hydropower project at the Xingu River significantly altered the relationship between the Workers' Party and civil society, especially in Altamira.

(P23, P43) and claim that any hydropower project in the Xingu River basin is unfeasible in social, environmental, and economic terms.

> *"All the recommendations of these scholars who carried out the environmental impact studies – or almost all their recommendations – remained on paper, they were not adopted. Because many of them said: 'Look, it is not feasible to do the construction.' If you read the full environmental impact study - it is a thing of over 20 000 pages – first, it is a mess; second, most people who read it conclude that it is not viable, neither environmentally nor socially, and to a much lesser extent economically." (P37)*

Therefore, the most prominent argument of local activists in Altamira and Belém refers to the technical deficits of Belo Monte, which render the project economically unviable (P19, P29, P45). The economic unfeasibility of the hydropower plant is a particularly controversial issue, as it is financed to a large extent with public resources provided by the Brazilian National Bank for Economic and Social Development (Banco Nacional de Desenvolvimento Econômico e Social, BNDES) (P1, P9). Referencing scholarly research, interviewees argue that due to seasonal variation in the water level the flow of water will not be sufficient to exploit the full potential of the electric power generating station (11 000 MW) during most of the year (P43). Expecting the power plant to be idle for six months and under-utilized for another three months of the year, they claim that Belo Monte will neither guarantee self-sufficiency nor stability in the country's energy production (P1). Hence, local activists suppose that the authorities are covertly planning to build additional dams along the Xingu River in order to channel more water to the power house (P1, P43). The official denial of such plans and irregularities in the procedure add to the local people's suspicion that the responsible authorities and involved enterprises are deceiving the population (P9, P19).

Summing up, participants in the social movement against Belo Monte are highly skeptical of the modifications in the projected hydropower plant at the Xingu River. First, they oppose the exploitation of the river's hydroelectric potential in general. Second, they are not convinced that the technical modifications will substantially reduce the negative consequences of the project. By contrast, they consider the revision an illusion that is supposed to conceal the project's detrimental effects and the authorities' true intentions (P29). Based on these arguments, interviewees conclude that hydropower plants are an outdated technology that should be replaced by more efficient alternatives (P31).

5.3.1.2 *Regional Dynamics and their Interaction with Belo Monte*

Amazonia is characterized by an extensive and diverse territory with abundant natural resources, a rich biodiversity, and a variety of ethnicities and cultures. Being home to *quilombolas*, riverine people, indigenous communities, hunter gatherers, and other forest peoples, the region is perceived to be multifaceted, indeed to be "various Amazonias" at once (P55). Some local people also call it "Planet Amazonia" (P16). However, the views of Amazonia held by the local population, the authorities, and the Brazilian majority society are diverse, even antagonistic, and therefore a source of continuous conflict.

In order to assess the influence of the local context on the implementation of the Belo Monte Dam and on the mobilization of the population for collective action, one needs to understand the social and economic structures that developed when Amazonia was colonized. The historical background, that is summarized and explained in this chapter, constitutes an important part of the Belo Monte diagnostic frame.

Settlement and Development in the Volta Grande

According to local activists, settlement and development along the Trans-Amazon Highway and the Xingu River basin have always occurred in cycles, starting with the Portuguese colonization since the year 1500 (P1, P29) and continuing with the periodic creation of settlements throughout the centuries (P55). Many people came to the Xingu in search of a livelihood (P13). Others were deliberately settled there by the authorities in an attempt to integrate the region into the Brazilian nation state (P21, P55). Interviewees believe that the constant inflow of people from all over Brazil contributed to the development of a unique social structure (P41). Over time, the settlers developed a subsistence economy based on family agriculture (P41). However, many of them never obtained ownership of the land they occupied, and the settlements were not consolidated through consistent regional planning (P39). With the Belo Monte project, these formal issues become relevant to affected settlers, as a lack of ownership calls into question their eligibility for compensation (P13).

Interviewees explain that the cyclical pattern of settlement has been accompanied by periodic surges in government attention and attempts to promote the economic development and integration of the region. Yet, the attitudes and strategies of the various administrations in implementing socioeconomic policies in the region indicate a persistent power asymmetry between the developed South and the underdeveloped North and Northeast of Brazil.

> *"Because all our life, we were educated to serve, to obey. It was like this during the cycle of the chestnut, it was like this during the cycle when they gathered animal skins, it was like this during the rubber boom, the lumber boom, and now with the cycle of Belo Monte; the people come from outside and impose their wills upon our wills, they impose their truths upon our truths, and we feel helpless because we are – as we say ourselves – we are the weakest part." (P25; also see P1 and P27).*

According to local activists, the authorities' strategy is linked with a conception of the natural environment that completely contradicts the local population's perception. This conflict over meaning is at the core of the Belo Monte conflict. Many people in the rural surroundings of Altamira – be they fishers, indigenous or riverine people – live off the natural resources provided by the land (P23) and the river. The Xingu River is home ("our house") to many people (P27) as more than 20 indigenous peoples and innumerous riverine communities are said to live in its basin (P35). Its waters are perceived as a public good (P16), and used for bathing, washing, cooking, drinking, fishing (P23), and transport (P29). Due to its perceived cultural value, its beauty (P35) and mystical meaning (P45), interviewees frequently describe the Xingu River as a natural heritage (P35). They also value the particular dynamic of the river, the way it disperses, and the biodiversity it sustains (P49, P55). By contrast, the authorities' conceptualization of the river is said to be based exclusively on economic considerations. Local activists criticize the state and the construction industry for assigning the river an "exchange value" and a "market price" (P3). Organizations like the Movement of Dam Affected People ceaselessly insist that water is not a commodity (P49). Local activists claim that an extensive damming of the Amazon rivers would constitute a de facto privatization, ending liberty and the right of people to their ancestral land (P31).

The conflict over the meaning of land and water is but one example of the contradictory conceptualizations of natural resources and the different views of development that are prevalent in Amazonia. Consequently, interviewees consider the implementation of a hydropower project at the Xingu River as a major affront, especially to the indigenous peoples of the region.

> *"For some peoples the Xingu River is where God lives. Therefore, building a dam at the Xingu River would be the same as building a nuclear power plant in the Vatican. Do you know? The meaning for Catholics would be the same. It is a major offense, it is very serious because you are directly affecting an entire history, an entire culture, an entire tradition, an entire array of signs and meanings that the river has. It is not the river, for the*

> *sake of the river. It is the river for the meaning that is carries for these peoples." (P1)*

The construction of a hydropower plant at the Xingu River does not only impact upon the socioeconomic conditions of life but also upon the cultural integrity of indigenous peoples (P55).

> *"The Xingu River is our home, there is a very spiritual connection. In cultural terms, for us [name of tribe] the sky is under the water. Therefore, all our spirits go under the water. It is all this strength; this historical issue. This is everything. It is culture itself. It is <u>our</u> culture. It is our life that is in the Xingu River. If the Xingu River ends, it means the end of all our strength; as it is ending." (P29)*

The persistent pressure on indigenous territories creates a particular threat to their cultures and their survival as distinct ethnic groups. Beyond the conflict over different conceptualizations of natural resources like land and water, the authorities' ignorance of indigenous identities, cultures, and knowledge, and its antiquated view of native ethnic groups being subject to the state's tutelage strain the relationship between the state and the native populations of Brazil.

In general terms, the lack of public policies towards the region has resulted in serious underdevelopment and a number of problems that are aggravated in the process of the Belo Monte project. One of the region's most pressing concerns, which is highly relevant with regard to Belo Monte, is the question of land rights (P53). The settlement of the region was generally not accompanied by land use regulations and socioeconomic policies. The following quote illustrates the consequences of this governmental neglect.

> *"Here in Amazonia we customarily say: [...] There is not a hand's width of land in Amazonia that is not disputed by the most diverse actors. Be they possessors, land grabbers, be it a company engaged in land speculation, or someone else. So, if you build a hydropower plant it means that you take away a good part of the territory of someone else – always. Whether this territory is legal or not, whether it is lawful or not, that is another question." (P55)*

Local activists criticize that the responsible authorities have never offered solutions for the conflict over land and property rights, and they do not consider the implications of the already existing disputes for the Belo Monte project. Interviewees complain that 40 years after the latest wave of colonization, 50% of the settlers in the region have not yet received a title to their land, and the authorities have not been able to implement an adequate land use planning scheme for the region (P39). Given that in this region "everything is already based on land"

(P23), participants in the social movement against Belo Monte question how the authorities want to compensate and relocate the people who are now affected by the construction of the Belo Monte Dam.

Socioeconomic Characteristics of the Region

Another persistent problem in the Xingu River region is the small number of employment opportunities. In Altamira, only the retail trade and a limited number of private institutions offer regular jobs (P31). In the municipality of Sousel, the public administration is the only regular employer next to some clandestine logging companies (P25). Local activists claim that insufficient public investments result in a lack of employment opportunities, thus forcing people to sustain their livelihoods through subsistence agriculture and fishery. From their point of view, the federal government thinks of Amazonia as a region without development perspectives (P55) and subordinates regional development to national interests (P1, P3, P35, P55). The persistent exploitation of the natural resources, which was particularly strong during colonial times and during the military era (P21, P55), contributes to the socioeconomic deprivation of the region and hampers its development despite its wealth in biodiversity (P45). Interviewees believe that a different development of the region would have been possible, if the state had invested in the region's trade capacities (P39) and a specific education tailored to the agricultural lifestyle of the settlers (P41) at an early stage of the frontier development. Yet, the lack of public support for sustainable economic activities in the region creates incentives for the continuation of unsustainable practices (P37).

> *"If you don't [...] [invest, I.P.], it continues the way it has always been, and the way it has always been, has been a degrading way. The way people know how to survive here is by destroying. So, I am not blaming, saying, 'Oh, these farmers!' – blaming the loggers, the farmers. Quite the opposite. They always had an incentive to do this. If they had an incentive to preserve the forest, they would be preserving. The people who are here, who live here, who survive of the things that are here, often pursue what is possible." (P37)*

Interviewees emphasize that social and environmental questions are inherently linked (P37) as people, suffering from insufficient investments and public policies, exploit nature to make a living. Among the most pressing socioeconomic problems are the poor public infrastructure – including water, wastewater, and electrical power supply – and inadequate public services in the areas of health and education (P41). Many households are not connected to the national grid and can only make limited use of home appliances and communications technology by using diesel generators. Yet, local people are not only frustrated about the insufficient infrastructure. They are particularly upset that these deficits are used to portray the population as underdeveloped and backwardly (P1) and to justify economic activities that will supposedly foster the region's development (P1).

Among the many deficits in the provision of public goods, the lack of public safety, the persistent violence, the infringement of human and civil rights, and the impunity of these crimes are frequently mentioned as influential context conditions (P9, P21). While these grievances initiated the emergence of an active civil society in Altamira (cf. Section 5.1), they constrain social movement activities and discourage participation. The Catholic Church denounces these deficits on a regular basis. With reference to a meeting with the Secretary for Human Rights, an interviewee reports,

> *"there we pointed out to her many things that we see here in Amazonia, especially the violation of human rights in the realm of the sexual exploitation of children and adolescents, the trafficking of persons and drugs, the trafficking of arms, the slave labor. We pointed out the violation of human rights. And there is also the death threats towards human rights defenders." (P16)*

The struggle for a differentiated development and against the exploitation of Amazonia has claimed the lives of many activists in the region (cf. Section 5.2). Therefore, violence and insufficient law enforcement constitute important context conditions for the Belo Monte project and the collective action against it.

To sum up, the historical background of settlement and development along the Trans-Amazon Highway and the Xingu River has important implications for current events. The authorities' failure to implement a consistent land use planning scheme and social policies with the arrival of settlers in the 1960s and 1970s, the lack of employment opportunities, the insufficient investments in infrastructure, and the lack of public safety are key indicators of the region's underdevelopment. They explain the authorities' interest in implementing the Belo Monte project, the local population's aversion to the project, and the conditions under which collective action in Pará takes place.

5.3.1.3 Consequences of Belo Monte

Local activists in Altamira and Belém are well informed about the effects of Belo Monte. They expect impacts on all aspect of people's lives (P9, P39, P43) and threats to future generations (P31). Hence, their assessment of costs and benefits constitutes an important part of the Belo Monte diagnostic frame.

The consequences of a hydropower plant at the Xingu River have been evaluated in a number of studies, including the mandatory EIA and independent research by distinguished scholars (cf. Fearnside 2006; Filho 2005; Hernández and Magalhães 2011; Sousa Júnior et al. 2006, among others). Interviewees frequently refer to these works in an attempt to substantiate their personal observations with scientific facts. Nonetheless, the local population faces many uncertainties (P55). The authorities and Norte Energia are criticized for failing to identify potential problems and to provide definite answers to the people's questions (P25, P29, P31). Local activists believe that the authorities are acting irresponsibly towards the people and the environment by launching an irreversible project with significant consequences and high uncertainty.

> *"The result, as I was saying, is unpredictable, and even worse, it is irreversible because, once it is concluded, we cannot say: 'We ended in failure, we made a mistake, let's fix it.' In this case there is no repair. This is lost." (P43)*

This section outlines the environmental and socioeconomic consequences that are discussed in the realm of the diagnostic frame as well as the distribution of advantages and disadvantages of the project.

Environmental consequences

According to local activists, the detriments of the Belo Monte Dam are omnipresent and affect people in all areas of life. The environmental damages include an array of aspects, as the following statement illustrates.

> *"The society of Amazonians – several entities organized here – is against this project because it will destroy the environment and the large reserve of natural resources, of biodiversity, fish, animals and the forest. And, above all, it will impact the course of the waters in the Volta Grande of the Xingu River." (P51)*

While the Belo Monte Dam is perceived as a symbol of environmental destruction in general terms (P1, P3, P23), local activists place particular emphasis on the remarkable biodiversity of Amazonia. They lament that hitherto unexplored species will be lost past recovery (P1, P9, P23) and that society will be deprived of valuable natural resources (P9). The extensive logging and clearing of forest vegetation is expected to increase the risk of erosion and landslide (P23, P27, P37). Local people are also concerned about the pollution of the river water (P9, P23), and the decline of the water level, which will have adverse effects on the river's biodiversity and on the traditional populations who live off the river. They fear the extinction of various fish species and aquatic animals (P3, P23, P47, P49) that account for a substantial share of the indigenous and riverine peoples' diet (P25, P43).

> *"If you block off the river, you dry-up the Volta Grande. The indigenous people living here receive 80% of their protein from fish. If you dry-up the Volta Grande there will be no fish left. Where are these people going to eat? Where can they go? They will have to be removed." (P55)*

As the Xingu River is linked to a large network of rivers and streams forming the Amazon basin, local activists are concerned that the Belo Monte Dam will modify the course and water levels downstream and in the *igarapés*. This would have a significant impact on the environmental and cultural dynamics of fishers, indigenous, and riverine peoples (P39, P53). Scientists and local activists expect that the diversion of the river will alter the hydrology in the Xingu River basin, which could lead to changes in the weather and the global climate (P13). Moreover, the decay of organic material in the river and the reservoir is expected to produce methane, a potent greenhouse gas found to promote climate change (P9, P43, P53).[107] Interviewees are concerned about health hazards arising from the emission of gases (P31), the proliferation of dengue and malaria (P43), and the silting of wells and leakage of sewage pits (P13).

Many local activists caution that the "messing around" with nature involves unpredictable risks for the region and the entire planet (P9, P19, P21). Some interviewees believe that God and nature will take revenge by repelling the human actors at some point in time (P23).

> *"She [nature, I.P.] responds in her own way, but she responds. Time may pass, she will come and she will come with all her force. And man is wanting to be more than God, pulling the river from here and putting it there, and nature will respond. I fear- I believe it is like this, I want her to*

107 Interviewees frequently refer to Philip Fearnside, research professor in the Department of Ecology at the National Institute for Research in the Amazon (Instituto Nacional de Pesquisas da Amazônia, INPA) in Manaus, Brazil, who has published extensively on the social and environmental consequences of infrastructure projects including hydropower plants in the Amazon region (see, for example, Fearnside 1999, 2006, 2008, 2012).

> *respond. If only she responded directly, immediately, because we want it fast." (P27)*

While the environmental consequences remain unpredictable, the reaction of God and nature is considered a chance to draw public attention to the destruction caused by mankind. As discussed in Section 5.2, religious faith and a strong bond to nature are important sources of hope, and they motivate local activists to participate in the collective action (P23, P31).

Socioeconomic consequences

The social consequences of Belo Monte refer primarily to the alteration of customary structures and dynamics within families and the local society at large. Many interviewees complain about the increasing chaos in the city of Altamira (P9, P16, P37, P49), which refers to insufficient health care, education, housing, sanitation, safety and transportation (P45). Immigration is perceived as a major strain (P9, P23, P27, P35, P53), as it creates a number of psychological and material prejudices for the local population. Some interviewees are afraid of foreign infiltration (P23), others perceive a growing competition for resources (P37). They claim that prices for real estate and rented property have risen due to increased demand, gentrification, and speculation (P23, P25, P27, P41); so have food prices (P23) and living expenses in general (P51). The public infrastructure is judged to be insufficient to accommodate the demands of the local population and the increasing numbers of immigrants (P16, P55). Especially the public facilities for education and health services, which were already insufficient before the start of the Belo Monte project, are now completely overloaded (P23, P27, P37), as are the road network and the public transport system (P27, P35, P51). Local activists also name the rapid population growth as a reason for the increased number of crimes (P13), the sexual exploitation of children and adolescents (P1, P9, P27), and the proliferation of violence, drugs, and prostitution (P9, P23, P27, P53).

Another important aspect is the damage to societal and family structures. From past experiences and current observations, local activists know that when affected people are forced off their land, families and neighborhood structures tend to break apart, which causes emotional stress and sorrow (P16). One interviewee living on the banks of the Xingu River describes their personal situation at length.

> *"This is going to change my life. The change at home will arise from the separation inside our family, because we have different goals. I plan to*

continue working. As my work is in the municipal area, I have to stay within the municipality. My brother wants to buy land property, so we will separate because I will not live with them. My father still does not know what he will do, because we are five siblings and he says there will be nothing left. He is 65 years old already, so he now intends to split up between us. According to him, he will live in the house of one child for a few months, and then in the house of another child, and he will move back and forth. What will this be like? This is already an inconvenience. Because as long as he has his house, he has his things, and there is no need to move from one side to the other; because he does not have a wife anymore, he is a widower. So this will cause inconvenience. Yet, I will be concerned about where he will live, because I am the one who cares for him. He does not want to live with me permanently, because he has this issue, 'If I stay with one, the others will be jealous' – they will be disappointed thinking that he does not want to stay with them anymore. So he will feel divided as well. And this is where the psychological, emotional conflict starts. For us- I have been suffering from this since the registration and I keep trying to organize my life and organize their lives. How are we going to keep our family together? Because we are very close as a family." (P23)

The expulsion of people from their land is considered one of the severest consequences of large infrastructure projects, especially for elderly people who have developed strong emotional ties to the land that they have been cultivating for decades (P23, P27, P29, P31, P39, P51, P55). Several interviewees confirm that the disappropriation and expulsion of people from their territories create uncertainty (P25, P27, P37, P55) and "a feeling of impotence" (P25).

In addition, Belo Monte is perceived as a threat to the livelihoods of diverse social groups who stand to lose both their source of income and their distinct identity. Many social groups define themselves, and are defined by others, based on their economic activities and their lifestyles, which represent important elements of their culture and social identity (cf. Section 5.2). Hence, impairments of a certain way of living and earning a livelihood are perceived as threats to the cultural dynamics of the region's traditional populations (P31, P53). Many interviewees emphasize the fate of the indigenous and express concern about the possible destruction of their cultures.

"We have to make a distinction: there is a physical death and there is a cultural death. And here at the Xingu River, because of Belo Monte, both of them may occur. The cultural death, because it wrests from them the

chance to survive in a given space, which is very meaningful for them because it is the ground of their myths, their rites, it is where they buried their ancestors. If you wrest this from the indigenous people, you cut their umbilical cord with the earth. We need to understand that they have another relationship with the earth, different from ours." (P45)

Given the indigenous peoples' strong ties to their ancestral land and their dependence on an intact nature for survival, some interviewees consider the implementation of Belo Monte as genocide against the indigenous (P9). Activists lament that many indigenous people have come into contact with alcohol, prostitution, nontraditional foodstuff and pharmaceuticals (P29, P35, P39), and argue that their increased encounters with people of other ethnicities promote conflict (P39). Another major problem that is said to result from recent developments is the growing alienation of indigenous children and adolescents from their communities and cultures. As young indigenous people get in contact with the white majority society, they lose interest in ancient traditions and religious rituals.

"For you to understand the soul and the heart of the elderly: What is happening is the apocalypse. They simply do not understand anymore. Automatically, the young people do no longer relate to the elderly as they did before [...] The youth no longer have these ideals of their distinct organization." (P43)

Local activists fear that the intergenerational conflict in the indigenous communities is fueled by the conflicts associated with the Belo Monte project in general, and by the authorities and Norte Energia's course of action in dealing with the indigenous communities in particular (cf. Section 5.4).

Distribution of Advantages and Disadvantages

The assessment of the project's advantages and disadvantages is intrinsically connected to questions about which individuals and groups are affected by the construction works and the finished hydropower plant. This is a particularly relevant and at the same time controversial issue between the supporters and opponents of the project.

Interviewees report that from the authorities' point of view, only the inundation of indigenous territories justifies resettlement programs and financial compensation. Hence, an important aspect in the modification of the original Kararaô project was the reduction of the inundated area for the purpose of reducing the impact on indigenous territories. Communities – regardless of ethnicity – that are effectively cut off from the water through the diversion of the river are not officially recognized as being affected by the hydropower plant (P43, P55). From the social movement's point of view, this narrow understanding of the project's social, economic, and environmental impacts does not acknowledge the lifestyle, interests, and demands of the rural population. They offer an alternative definition that includes various social groups and a variety of direct and indirect impacts within and beyond the region (P43, P51). Local activists argue that the townspeople are indirectly affected for the reasons discussed above, and that the detrimental consequences of Belo Monte will take effect over long distances because of the socio-environmental interdependency (P51; also see P1). Particularly severe impacts are expected on indigenous communities who stand to loose their ancestral lands (P47, P51). The following statement illustrates that the state and the local population have very different perceptions of the project's impacts.

> *"For the government, the affected region is not the region that will suffer the consequences of the dam, that will dry up. Only those regions that will be inundated are considered to be affected. However, the regions that will be affected include those regions that will dry up, because there will be too little water, there will be too little fish, there will be no more living spaces for the animals, and especially, especially for the indigenous peoples; so the evaluation of the government is quite different from [our] evaluation of how much the indigenous peoples will suffer." (P47)*

While local activists claim that changes in the course of the river and the water level will affect people in the distributary rivers and streams of the Xingu River (P39, P47), the Norte Energia consortium refuses to compensate the people living downstream of the hydropower plant (P47, P49).

Despite the negative consequences – some of which were identified in the EIA and addressed in the conditions issued with the preliminary license in 2010 – the federal government and the Norte Energia consortium maintain that the positive development effects predominate. Interviewees, however, challenge this rhetoric. Despite temporary benefits like increased tax revenues in the port of Vitória do Xingu (P47), they have made the experience that the authorities and the enterprises involved do generally not fulfill their obligations in large infrastructure projects (P35). Hence, they expect that the Belo Monte Dam will not create a sustainable local development (P1, P3, P16). With respect to power supply, they expect that the electricity produced in Belo Monte will not be allocated to the local population, but to the commercial and industrial centers in the South of Brazil and to foreign countries (P1, P16, P21, P23, P27, P47,

P49, P53, P55). Regarding the alleged benefit of employment opportunities, local activists criticize the low wages (P41), long working hours, and restrictive vacation regulations (P47). They consider the job creation to be shallow, as dam projects tend to create financially precarious, physically dangerous, and slave-like working conditions, rather than sustainable employment in respectable and dignified jobs (P9, P53). Alluding to the center-periphery divide identified above, local activists claim that the local population is considered a cheap labor force, while high-skilled employees like engineers and entrepreneurs are recruited outside the region (P16).

> *"So, we do not have a development policy containing projects that formalize work, that provide a retirement scheme, because this issue of employment in hydropower is a temporary issue. It is temporary. Many people are employed only while the construction is underway; afterwards they are dismissed. Hence, this policy is a policy of death." (P31; also see P41 and P53).*

Given that local activists do not expect sustainable local benefits, who are the beneficiaries of the Belo Monte project? While most interviewees remain vague in naming the individuals and enterprises gaining from the project, some interviewees single out large industrial enterprises (P21, P23) and energy intensive mining companies that benefit from cheap electricity (P1, P13, P51, P55). Moreover, a number of international enterprises providing the necessary equipment and material for the construction of the hydropower projects are named as beneficiaries of the construction (P9, P13, P31, P55). In more general terms, local activists allude to "a group that has political and economic interests and that is even financed by the government" (P1). They call it an open secret that Lula entered into an agreement with "strong economic sectors", as the following statement illustrates.

> *"What we perceive is that there was a kind of agreement between a government that called itself left and progressive – namely the Lula government – with highly conservative sectors of Brazilian politics and very strong economic sectors, which are the big donors for [electoral, I.P.] campaigns. [...] It is a very clear fact that when you take the accountability reports of Dilma and Lula's campaigns, those who donated most for their elections were the enterprises that are constructing the dams." (P1)*

While this perception is widely shared among interviewees (P9, P21, P27, P51, P53), some claim that the decision to build Belo Monte was really taken by the construction industry (P49), which forced the federal government into granting licenses and concessions to the enterprises (P27, P51).

Summing up, interviewees complain that the positive effects of the Belo Monte project are privatized to the benefit of a small group, while the negative effects are socialized to the detriment of the large majority (P1). They further claim that the federal government ignores scientific research and acts to the detriment of the people and the environment for the purpose of promoting the interests of the economy (P31, P51). The Belo Monte diagnostic frame deliberately addresses the project's advantages and disadvantages as well as questions about who is affected and who stands to benefit from the construction works and the finished hydropower plant. The project's symbolic meaning and implications are used to raise the awareness of seemingly unaffected people and to forge alliances with organizations throughout Amazonia (P1). By reaching out to the population and appealing to their believes the social movement broadens the basis of potential activists.[108]

5.3.1.4 Controversial Implementation of Belo Monte

Another important aspect of the Belo Monte diagnostic frame is the course of action followed by the authorities and Norte Energia in implementing the project. Local activists claim that "the government is conducting a crime against the entire population" (P9) and against the environment (P29). Some interviewees go so far as to call the political system a "civilian dictatorship" (P45). The most frequently mentioned points of criticism include,

1. the attitude and behavior of the authorities and Norte Energia towards the social movement and the local population;
2. the federal government's interpretation of national and international laws and the perceived pressure on the judiciary; and
3. Norte Energia's course of action regarding the fulfillment of the conditions stipulated in the preliminary license, the compensation of dam affected people, and the implementation of additional mitigation projects in the realm of the PDRS Xingu (that is, the Regional Sustainable Development Plan) and the PBA (that is, the Basic Environmental Plan).

Interestingly, the opinions of local activists regarding the conditions and the mitigation measures diverge. As will be shown below, their different evaluations of these instruments resulted in the development of different collective action frames and the fragmentation of the social movement against Belo Monte.

108 The mechanisms by which people align their goals and activities with the preferences of the social movement are discussed in Section 5.4.

Therefore, the different understandings of these matters will be discussed in detail further below.

Attitude and Behavior Towards Social Movement and Population

According to interviewees, the attitude and behavior of the authorities and Norte Energia towards the population are characterized by ignorance and disrespect. The Belo Monte Dam is said to be "pushed down the throat, without listening to the populations that should be heard" (P19). Local activists are frustrated about the authorities' lack of responsiveness as well as their failure to include the general public in the planning process and conduct effective consultations with the indigenous. Although many obligations rest with the consortium of operating companies, local activists generally address their claims to the federal government, arguing that it is ignoring their questions, concerns, and opinions (P13, P16, P29, P43). The hydropower plant itself is perceived as a foreign object that generates many problems due to a lack of fit with its area of location (P55).

> *"This is what is important, because here inside [Amazonia, I.P.] we are not being heard by the federal government. The government is making decisions alone and it is not taking into consideration anything that is being said here." (P1)*

The statement emphasizes the geographical and ideological divide between the center and the periphery of Brazil. Local activists criticize that the project was developed and decisions were made far away in Brasília without considering the demands and interests (P27) as well as the living conditions of the native populations who depend on the river for their survival (P19, P27, P51). Politicians and the Brazilian majority society are criticized for ignoring the natives' specific knowledge of the regional environment and climate (P13, P27), and for failing to inform themselves comprehensively about the region and its inhabitants (P45).

> *"There is no clear perception of the people, of these entities, of valuing the culture of the population, of valuing the natives, of hearing the people, of asking for participation. All this is denied." (P16)*

Interviewees acknowledge that the authorities and Norte Energia conducted meetings with the local population in some places. Yet, they criticize that only few meetings took place in the remote villages with few participants (P45), and that attendants were allowed to ask questions but did not have the right to a response (P25). One interviewee recounts an information meeting about the management of conservation areas,

> *"where the Municipal Secretary for the Environment came and imposed his idea, and the people signed the minutes of the meeting because this is the habit of the population" (P25).*

Local activists claim that the authorities merely seek to fulfill the formalities of the licensing process rather than engaging in a dialogue with the population (P49, P55). The federal government rejects all criticism.

> *"There is no discussion. Dilma refuses any discussion. You do not get there. If you have an agenda to discuss with the government- If in this agenda Belo Monte is one issue among others they immediately dismiss the Belo Monte issue because it is not up for discussion. That is very clear." (P43)*

According to interviewees, the authorities have developed a discourse strategy that promotes the Belo Monte project and repudiates the collective action against it. The information provided by the authorities is said to be incomplete, inconsistent and/or misleading. The authorities are criticized for making false promises (P27, P49, P49), omitting information (P19, P21, P23), and lying deliberately about the costs, benefits, and circumstances of the construction (P23, P29, P43, P47).

Another strand of the public discourse is to ridicule and criminalize the social movement, to blame its members as opponents of progress (P43), and to threaten activists with repression and persecution. The following statement illustrates the strained relationship between the state and the social movement.

> *"Many will fight the government, it will be a cold war, but who will lose is the one who opposes the government, because the government does not want to back off. The government talks like this: 'I am the government. And it goes as follows: You have to accept, because if you do not accept, we will send the police, we will send lawyers, we will criminalize you'." (P31)*

As a consequence, interviewees classify the struggle as an "unequal" encounter (P1, P29) between "a Goliath and a David" (P31). They compare the authorities' hostile attitude towards the social movement with the practices of the military government, which originally developed the project (P1, P9, P37). The repeated attempts of both military and civil governments to enforce the construction of a hydropower plant at the Xingu River are perceived as authoritarian (P9, P45). Interestingly, local activists believe that it is impossible to implement such a large infrastructure project in a democratic way, given the plant's significant impact on the region (P1, P21).

Legal Irregularities

In line with their criticism of the authoritarian course of action, local activists regularly denounce legal irregularities occurring in the implementation of the Belo Monte project. At the time of the field research, 13 public civil actions of the Federal Public Ministry were pending in the Brazilian federal legal system for several years without final judgment (P55).[109] Interviewees suggest that the authorities take advantage of deferments in the court proceedings and press ahead with the project while judicial review is still pending (P9, P41, P43). The objective of this tactic is to reach a point of no return where the abandonment and dismantling of the work will have become unfeasible (P1). A particularly controversial act, frequently mentioned in the interviews, is the granting of the preliminary license in 2010 (P51). Local activists question the quality of the EIA, which is a prerequisite for the authorization of large infrastructure projects, and criticize that the authorities did neither consider the results nor implement the recommendations of the RIMA (P37). From their point of view, the environmental law and the legislation for the licensing of large infrastructure projects were violated, which makes the granting of the preliminary license an illegal act (P1, P3, P37, P41, P45). Interviewees further denounce the federal government's refusal to attend a hearing by the Inter-American Commission on Human Rights (IACHR) about the situation of human rights, and particularly indigenous rights, in the case of Belo Monte (P55).

As regards the compliance with existing laws and regulations, interviewees denounce a discrepancy between the written law and its enforcement (P37), and a general disregard of human, social, cultural, economic, and environmental rights (P9). They claim that the authorities have violated the Brazilian Constitution – which is pointed out as the highest law of the country (P29) – and the Convention 169 of the International Labour Organization (ILO) by failing to conduct proper consultations in the indigenous communities (P1, P16, P29, P51).[110] While the authorities claim to have complied with the relevant regula-

109 Interviewees disagree about the exact number of legal actions currently pending in the Brazilian legal system. According to Bermann (2013), the Federal Public Ministry filed 13 Public Civil Actions and two Actions for Misconduct between May 2001 and June 2013 regarding violations of the country's social and environmental legislation.

110 The ILO Convention 169 is a legally binding international instrument concerned with the rights of indigenous and tribal peoples. Article 6 (1) of the convention stipulates that governments should "consult the peoples concerned, through appropriate procedures and in particular through their representative institutions, whenever consideration is being given to legislative or administrative measures which may affect them directly" (ILO 1989). The convention was adopted on 17 June 1989 and entered into force on 5 September 1991. It was ratified by Brazil

tions, activists criticize that the consultations with affected indigenous communities were deficient or lacking completely (P19, P29, P49). According to interviewees the meetings did not allow for a clarification of questions and an exchange of opinions (P29, P43, P45, P47), and they were hampered by language problems and cultural differences (P29).

In addition to the dispute about the consultation of native ethnic groups, local activists denounce infringements of human and civil rights granted in the Constitution (P9, P29, P47, P51). Their examples include the erosion of the right to demonstrate (P27), the denial of an adequate compensation for dam affected people (P51), and the destruction of autonomous cultures and lifestyles (P53, P55). In more general terms, local activists consider the authorities' course of action as a strategy to circumvent legal constraints and to facilitate the smooth implementation of the project. The following statement illustrates the consternation of a local activist about the procedures.

> *"The other day IBAMA fined them. It fined the Norte Energia consortium.*[111] *But what happened? The director was fired. Do you know? Because he fined them. So, it is like this, it is a game. A big game. It is not easy." (P35)*

Given the legal irregularities, interviewees are concerned about a potential damage to the Brazilian democracy. They question whether Brazil is and will remain a democratic country (P27), given the federal government's strained relationship with the Supreme Court (P31) and the way it neglects people's constitutional rights in relation to the Belo Monte project (P45).

Noncompliance with the Conditions and Neglect of Social Factors

The third major point of criticism is closely related to the granting of the preliminary license as it refers to the noncompliance of Norte Energia with the conditions specified therein. Interviewees criticize the delay in civil works stipulated to prepare the region for the Belo Monte project and the consortium's course of action in compensating dam affected people. As the analysis shows, the implementation is a central issue in the Belo Monte conflict (P16) and an important aspect of the diagnostic frame.

The conditions for the implementation of the hydropower plant at the Xingu River were originally established in order to prepare the region for the ar-

in 2002 (ILO 2012).

111 The purpose of the fine was to punish Norte Energia for noncompliance with the conditions.

rival of migrant laborers seeking employment at the construction sites and settlers hoping to benefit from the expected economic development (P37). The inclusion of the conditions in the preliminary license raised the population's hopes for local benefits (P19, P27).

> *"This also raised the question of society, which started to talk in favor of Belo Monte – part of the society – because of these conditions, thinking that their neighborhood would improve, that their neighborhood would get a square, that their neighborhood would get a school, a modern health post, service and everything. So now, one realizes that none of this was done, but it was there in the conditions." (P19)*

Until today most expectations remain unfulfilled, as the Norte Energia consortium fails to comply with the conditions stipulated in the preliminary license (P27, P37) and the city does not thrive as predicted by business people (P23, P43, P55). As discussed above, interviewees criticize the insufficient investments in health services, education and transport, and the long delay in the projects (P27, P35, P37, P41). Medical services that were originally sufficient for the population of Altamira are increasingly overloaded, because the additional facilities required in the conditions were not built in time (P23, P27). Local activists criticize the lack of planning (P27) and the insufficient preparation of the city for the project (P16, P41). They are concerned that the situation will deteriorate with the advancement of the hydropower project (P51).

Beyond investments in infrastructure and public services, the conditions include financial compensation and support for people who live in the vicinity of the construction site and have to leave their property. According to local activists, affected people can chose between different forms of compensation. Yet, they criticize that the compensation process is lacking transparency and reliability.

> *"The Brazilian state simply declared that area a public utility. When the state does this, it leads to the redemption of land by the state. Then the company becomes responsible – so to speak – for removing the people and it will pay an indemnity. It will negotiate. There are three different proposals for compensation. That means, there is no equality, there is no caution with this." (P55)*

Local activists monitoring the compensation process report that may families opt for the direct payment (P39) but encounter many problems that arise from the specific living conditions of the local population. As many people lack official land titles or share land with other family members, they are not eligible for a full compensation (P23). This creates a number of social and economic problems for affected families. First, the persistent conflict over land discussed above makes it difficult for people to find purchasable land property in the first place (P23, P55); much less within reach of the city, equipped with infrastructure and access to water (P23). Second, property prices have soared with the start of the construction works, forcing family members to combine their compensation or to rent accommodation in Altamira (P23). Especially extended families have difficulties in obtaining land property that is large enough to house and sustain the livelihood of all family members (P23, P31). Third, many families are inexperienced with the management of large amounts of money and therefore run into financial problems.

> *"Everything became more expensive. The money that one is receiving is not enough, and not to mention that there are already families that were compensated not even a year ago and they do not have a cent anymore, not even to buy food. There is nothing left. Because they did not know how to invest it. And in their studies they say the following: that they were going to appoint a social worker to accompany these families in investing the money, in order to avoid what happened in other dam projects, that families were incapable of investing the money; they spent it all, and then were left with nothing. This is already happening." (P23)*

The fourth problem arising from the compensation of affected people, is social strain within families and communities. Inside families, conflicts have emerged about the unequal compensation of family members, about where to move, and how to restructure family life (P23). Within the communities, individuals have complained about disparities in the amounts they have received compared to other people in comparable situations (P39). Hence, several factors interact to produce social and economic problems for people who are forced to leave their homes, including the disruption of relationships between neighbors, friends, and family members (P16, P23).

> *"The company pays what it wants to pay; then the guy leaves.[112] When he leaves, he is used to living in that place. He takes the money – let us assume one million reais – and buys another land property. He does not know if he is buying good land or not. Ultimately, the money is used up and he does not have a social network, which he had in the place where he was before. And the company is not doing resettlements. In practice, it is not providing the option to find a good place that the farmers agree upon, and to place them there with the same neighborhood structure;*

112 The interviewee refers to the compensated person.

> *because it is not only a question of land. It is a question of all the relationships that you have in a particular region; neighbors, kinship, friendship. This is being disrupted." (P37)*

According to local activists, social structures are as important as the financial compensation, because family and friends are a central source of support. Yet, affected people do not get the chance to choose a suitable mode of compensation as the statement above illustrates. Interviewees accuse Norte Energia of practically expelling the people from their land without permitting negotiations about the indemnity sum or offering alternative forms of compensation (P35). Moreover, as the consortium does not follow the announced schedules, affected people cannot plan ahead when to terminate their economic activities (for example, planting food crops) and when to leave their territory (P23). Hence, local activists complain that the Norte Energia consortium is taking advantage of its negotiating power and refusing to pay the legally guaranteed indemnity sums (P51).

5.3.1.5 Summary of the Belo Monte Diagnostic Frame

As the analysis shows, it is necessary to acknowledge the meaning that activists attribute to the Belo Monte project in order to understand the central dynamics of the social movement – that is, the development of movement cohesion on the basis of a collective identity and a collective action frame, and the subsequent fragmentation of the social movement as a result of a divergence of the collective action frame and an identity crises among activists. Both processes will be discussed in detail in Section 5.4.

The analysis of the Belo Monte diagnostic frame has shown, that local activists from both factions of the movement frequently refer to a variety of issues when asked about the "real meaning" of Belo Monte. From an analytical point of view, these aspects can be classified into four categories that add up to a consistent story about Belo Monte within its temporal and spatial context:

1. the characteristics and general meaning of Belo Monte,
2. the regional context of Belo Monte,
3. the consequences of Belo Monte, and
4. the controversial implementation procedure.

The meaning of Belo Monte is complex and alludes to the strained relationship of the local population with their authorities on various levels and their estrangement from the rest of the country. The frame further captures their sensation of being exploited in a colonial fashion, their skepticism about the prevalent development model, and their questions about who benefits and who pays the price of what the authorities present as development. The following statement captures the various dimensions that local activists mention with reference to the Belo Monte project.

> *"And there is still a politician who, with the greatest poker face, affirms that this is the price to pay for progress. The truth is that neither he nor his family pay for it. It is the state of Pará which continues to be treated as a colony, exploited and debased, condemned to pay in environmental terms and in terms of prejudices to its people; an exorbitant price for the progress of the rest of Brazil." (P45)*

The frequent discussion of the historic background and current context conditions raises the question if the conflict really centers on the Belo Monte Dam or if the project is merely a symbol of a larger dispute. As the analysis shows, the struggle is frequently embedded into discourses about good life, forms of society, and alternative development paths. Interestingly, the Belo Monte diagnostic frame includes general questions of power asymmetry that are addressed in terms of traditional cleavages like center vs. periphery and urban vs. rural. Questions arise about whether the concept of cleavages contributes to understanding the framing process in the Belo Monte conflict and, in more general terms, the differences between social movements in Western and non-Western countries. These questions will be discussed in more detail in Chapter 6.

5.3.2 *Controversies in the Collective Action Frame*

The analysis and reconstruction of the Belo Monte diagnostic frame presented above produced a coherent picture of the conflict from the perspective of the interviewees. It demonstrates that local activists from both factions of the movement share a general understanding of the contentious issue. Their interpretations and beliefs are consistent with respect to the symbolic meaning of a hydropower plant at the Xingu River, the relevance of the historic and current regional context, the social and environmental consequences of the project, and its cost-benefit ratio. This is not surprising, given that the local activists have a common history of social struggle for sustainable development in the region.[113] Over many years they engaged in a common framing process – that is, recurrent

113 I argue that a common history of social struggle is an important factor promoting movement cohesion. This discussion will be resumed in Section 5.4.

negotiations over the meaning of development and the advantages and disadvantages of a hydropower plant at the Xingu River.

However, with the authorization and advancement of the construction, local activists started to argue about the likelihood of their being able to prevent the Belo Monte project, and about the role and responsibilities of the social movement. Their reassessment of the situation resulted in a divergence of the collective action frame, and in the fragmentation of the movement. Two factions emerged from the separation of the MDTX into the Xingu Vivo Movement and the Foundation. I call them the protest SMOs and the monitoring SMOs. Despite their shared opposition to the Belo Monte project, these organizations have different opinions on

1. the status of Belo Monte,
2. the social movement's role and influence in the conflict, and
3. the advantages and disadvantages of the mitigation measures.

These controversies are discussed in detail in the following sections.

5.3.2.1 The Status of Belo Monte: An Accomplished Fact?

In the process of diagnostic framing, the status and future development of Belo Monte are particularly controversial issues. Since the beginning of the inventory studies in the Xingu River basin in the 1970s, hydropower projects have been perceived as a potential threat. With the start of the construction in the summer of 2011 the threat became a reality (P23). However, this does not mean that Belo Monte itself is commonly considered a reality or, as local people say, a "fato consumado" – that is, an accomplished fact. Indeed, the two factions within the social movement against Belo Monte diverge primarily in terms of their perceptions and evaluations of this issue.[114] A classification of interviewees according to their attitudes towards this question reveals that all of them disapprove of Belo Monte (P41). However, given that licenses were granted and the construction is underway, opinions on how to act toward Belo Monte, the authorities, and the involved enterprises differ substantially.

The protest SMOs oppose the project rigorously. They claim that Belo Monte is not (yet) an accomplished fact (P21, P31, P37, P45, P51) and seek the prohibition of the project and the abandonment of any plans for the exploitation of the hydroelectric potential of the Xingu River (P51). By contrast, the

114 The following analysis refers to the interviewee's perception of the issue at the time of the field research (May to June 2012).

monitoring SMOs claim to disapprove of Belo Monte, but have come to accept the project as something that cannot be prevented anymore (P35). A comparison of interviewee's opinions about the status of Belo Monte and the advantages and disadvantages of the mitigation measures shows that local activists who rigorously oppose the project are organized in the Xingu Vivo Movement in Altamira, the Metropolitan Committee in Belém, and the grassroots organizations affiliated with these organizations. Moreover, the Catholic Church and most notably the former Bishop of Xingu, Erwin Kräutler, share the view of these organizations and support their activities. I refer to these organizations as the protest SMOs, as their strategy aims to prevent the construction of the Belo Monte Dam.[115] By contrast, local activists who have accepted the Belo Monte Dam as a fact are organized in the Foundation, ISA, MAB, and the grassroots organizations affiliated with the Foundation. I refer to these organizations as the monitoring SMOs, as they focus on the rapid and accurate implementation of the mitigation measures and monitor these processes closely. Interviewees form the ranks of the monitoring SMOs agree that the Belo Monte project has detrimental effects on the people and the local population. However, they are skeptical as to whether a social movement with its limited means and even the judiciary will be able to stop it (P35). This faction of the social movement focuses on negotiating with the authorities about development initiatives in the realm of the Belo Monte project.[116]

5.3.2.2 *The Social Movement's Role and Influence in the Conflict*

Beyond disagreement about Belo Monte's current status, movement cohesion is challenged by the interviewees' different perceptions and evaluations of the various interests in the project. According to the monitoring SMOs, the Belo Monte Dam is one issue among others within a general dispute between state and society. In this dispute, both parties have interests that need to be balanced by means of negotiations.

> *"This government attempts to negotiate in some way with the society in order to find out – based on a legal basis, which is the Brazilian legislation, the Brazilian Environmental Law – what would be the instruments that arise from the hydropower plant; that for us would perhaps be the most interesting part, less the hydropower plant." (P41)*

115 The strategy of the protest SMOs, which interviewees call Plan A, is discussed further below.

116 The strategy of the monitoring SMOs, which interviewees call Plan B, is discussed further below.

Hence, the monitoring SMOs consider the struggle over Belo Monte as a negotiation process that involves the balancing of the oppositional interests of the involved parties, which they describe as follows. The primary interest of the federal government is the construction of the Belo Monte Dam, which is part of the PAC and derives from a comprehensive national and international perspective of development processes (P41). By contrast, the primary interest of the local population is a differentiated sustainable development of the region that is tailored to the environmental conditions and lifestyles of the local population. This includes, for example, the sustainable use of natural resources, the development of a processing industry, which increases the share of value creation inside the country and reduces the export of raw materials, as well as the local population's participation in development processes (P41).

Interviewees affiliated with the monitoring SMOs explain their particular understanding of the Belo Monte conflict with reference to the attempted implementation of its predecessor, the Kararaô Dam: The military government's attempts at implementing the hydropower complex without any mitigation measures and accompanying development projects provoked severe and lasting resistance by local activists (P41). From their point of view, the social movement's early resistance achieved the modification of the project, the realization of scientific studies, and the definition of criteria upon which the project was eventually conditioned (P41). In addition, its request for public participation opened a window of opportunity for negotiations with the authorities. In order to achieve the best possible results in terms of the region's development, the monitoring SMOs demand the fulfillment of the conditions, the provision of public policies, and the implementations of sustainable development projects in return for the acceptance of Belo Monte (P41).

By contrast, the protest SMOs are not willing to negotiate about the implementation of a hydropower plant at the Xingu River at all. They criticize that the provision of public goods is made contingent on the local population's acceptance of Belo Monte.

5.3.2.3 *The Advantages and Disadvantages of the Mitigation Measures*

As discussed in Chapter 4, the preliminary license for the construction of the Belo Monte Dam included 40 conditions with the objective of preparing the region for the arrival of migrant workers and settlers. Moreover, as a prerequisite to the granting of the installation license the Norte Energia consortium was obliged to develop a PBA in order to mitigate the negative consequences of the hydropower project through investments in infrastructure and services (P39).

In light of the significant investments into the region and the consortium's non-compliance with the conditions stipulated in the preliminary license, the monitoring SMOs focus on providing information and support to the local population, monitoring the fulfillment of the conditions, and participating in the steering committee of the PDRS Xingu. Despite their general critique of and opposition towards the Belo Monte project, they believe that Belo Monte might develop differently from other hydropower projects because of the mitigation measures (P39, P41).

> *"If we judge by other regions where large projects like Tucuruí were built, here in the state of Pará, the outlook you get is that of a disaster at sight. But then, on the other hand, the fact is that in other projects that were implemented in the state of Pará, both hydroelectric and other large projects like mining, the government was not so cautious as to create a package of measures around them in order to respond to the detriments caused by the project. And Belo Monte is different. The Lula administration made an effort to [...] reduce as much as possible the damages, the environmental ones as well as the social and economic ones."* (P39)

The monitoring SMOs' general approval of the mitigation measures and development plans does, however, not blind them to their shortcomings (P35). Interviewees claim that the volume of the PDRS Xingu is too limited to resolve the problems of the region (P35), and that the sustainable forest management stipulated by the PDRS Xingu is unfeasible due to the previous unregulated logging activities that have damaged large areas of tropical rainforest past recovery (P39). Nonetheless, they consider the PDRS Xingu an important instrument that requires more time to be implemented (P39, P41).

By contrast, the protest SMOs disapprove of the mitigation measures and development plans, as they consider them attempts at bribing the local population into acceptance and quiescence (P9). From their point of view, the allocation of resources to short-lived items like computers, boats, and vehicles does not improve the population's quality of life, which is actually limited by deficits in health care, education, and sanitation (P9). They consider the steering committee of the PDRS Xingu an ineffective body that fails to generate definitions of and measures for regional development and that merely creates conflict between CSOs who seek to maximize their own benefits (P9). As a consequence, the protest SMOs refuse any cooperation with the authorities and the Norte Energia consortium.

Notwithstanding their distinct evaluations of the mitigation measures and development plans, interviewees from both factions of the social movement harshly criticize the authorities and Norte Energia for their attitude and behavior vis-à-vis the indigenous communities. According to movement participants, the government ordered Norte Energia to provide significant amounts of money, staple food, boats, vehicles, and fuel to indigenous communities (P16, P23, P29, P37, P47). While these activities are promoted as an emergency plan, interviewees consider this course of action a deliberate strategy to disorganize and destabilize indigenous communities (P37).

> *"Goodness! You kill the indigenous structure. Because it is not even structuring, because you do not tackle questions of health, education, protection of indigenous lands, food safety. So, it is a destructuring plan. You put money there in an arbitrary way, and you have a small group of leaders, who are the leaders who speak Portuguese, who relate to the city and end up managing the money; some even in good faith, but then you start having extreme pressure on the communities: 'Ah, now we have discretionary income. Ah, then I want this, I want that, I want another.' So, the thing is going completely random and arbitrary." (P37)*

In addition, the protest SMOs suggest that the authorities are deliberately using mitigation measures to retreat from their obligations. They question the legitimacy of the conditions, claiming that what is being presented to them as conditions of the Belo Monte project are actually their legal rights (P29). These should be fulfilled independent of any infrastructure project (P19, P29).

> *"This means a lot of damage to the Brazilian nation. These are negations of public policies concerning health and education, housing, sanitation; because in all these hydropower projects the government makes the rights of the population contingent on the population's acceptance of the construction [...]" (P9)*

The perceived bribery of the population, particularly of the indigenous population, has been identified in this study as one factor that promoted the fragmentation of the social movement. It will be discussed in more detail in Section 5.4.

The movement participants' controversy about the advantages and disadvantages of the mitigation measures is the third aspect – next to their disagreement about the status of Belo Monte, and about the social movement's role and influence in the conflict – that has led to the fragmentation of the movement and to the development of diverging prognostic frames.

5.3.3 *Prognostic Frames*

According to the literature, collective action frames are "action-oriented sets of beliefs and meanings that inspire and legitimate the activities and campaigns of a social movement organization" (Benford and Snow 2000: 614). The collective action frame of the social movement against Belo Monte (1) demands a differentiated development for the region, which is tailored to the region's characteristics and requirements. It (2) claims that Belo Monte is not the solution to the region's problems – thus objecting the official government discourse – and (3) requires the participation of the population and the appreciation of traditional and indigenous knowledge and competences in the decision making. Activists from both factions of the movement identify with this part of the collective action frame. Yet, their perceptions of (1) the status of Belo Monte, (2) the SMOs' role and influence in the conflict, and (3) the advantages and disadvantages of the mitigation measures diverge.

As a consequence, the two factions of the movement developed separate prognostic frames that propose different solutions, possible activities, and strategies for tackling the problem of underdevelopment in the region. While both factions demand a differentiated development concept for the region, their short-term strategies and tactics to achieving this type of development differ. The protest SMOs seek to prevent Belo Monte in order to repel the government's development model (Plan A), while the monitoring SMOs seek to promote their own development concept through negotiations with the authorities (Plan B). This section discusses the activists' shared concept of a differentiated development (long-term solution), before turning to the factions' respective plans for confronting the Belo Monte conflict (short-term solution).

5.3.3.1 *Development as a Long-Term Solution*

One of the most prominent arguments in favor of the Belo Monte Dam is the region's underdevelopment. Local activists across SMOs agree that the municipalities along the Trans-Amazon Highway and the Xingu need development assistance. However, their concept of development differs significantly from that of the federal government; first, in how development is defined and, second, in how it is pursued.

> *"At the national level you have, for example, a socialist project and a developmentalist project. You have a project that thinks of agribusiness and another project that values agroecology, family farming, and the whole matter of the forest, the extractivism. On that other side there is*

another mode of thought, which is to take away the possible maximum of timber for this – for them this is development. On our side, we think that you have to preserve the RESEX and build up an economy based on extractivism.[117] *These are different views." (P41)*

As the statement shows, local activists have precise ideas about the kind of development that they aspire for the region. They acknowledge that the local population would welcome economic progress and a certain degree of comfort (P16, P55). However, they strongly reject the idea that development requires a hydropower dam, mining, or the cultivation of soy. From their point of view, the abundant natural resources of the region offer alternative development paths (P1). Moreover, interviewees suggest that the local population has a different standard of comfort than the majority population in the South of the country (P1, P55). As one interviewee claims, "development is not something that is so essential for life" (P55).

A particularly critical aspect of development is the persistent exploitation of natural resources in the name of economic progress. In opposition to this way of thinking, interviewees emphasize that development cannot be limited to economic indicators but has to take into account the population's quality of life and well-being, an interaction between urban and rural lifestyles, human dignity, civil rights, an social values.[118] The acronym DHESCA is frequently used in this context, as it implies the equilibrium of human, economic, social, cultural, and environmental rights (P3).[119] Local activists argue that a development concept for Amazonia should focus on the sustainable use of renewable raw materials (P47), the preservation of natural resources and traditional peoples (P3, P37), and the actual needs of the local population (P47).

Based on their criticism of the current development model and their understanding of the Amazon region and its development potential, local activists in Altamira and Belém promote the following development concept.

"Development, for us, has to include two things: it has to be solidary and sustainable. And solidary and sustainable means a broad relationship

117 RESEX refers to extractive reserves (Reservas Extrativistas). These are areas set aside for the sustainable exploitation and conservation of renewable natural resources by traditional populations. The aim of RESEX is to balance ecological interests with social interests by allowing sustainable economic activities that improve the lives of the local inhabitants (Instituto Socioambiental n.d.d).

118 These aspects should be considered against the background of underdevelopment, insufficient employment opportunities, poor housing conditions, persistent violence, infringement of human and civil rights, impunity, etc. as discussed above.

119 DHESCA is the acronym for Direitos Humanos, Econômicos, Sociais, Culturais e Ambientais.

> *between the human beings and the environment. [...] Development is related to a number of things that should lead to the well-being of the population. And this does not only include to possess things. It includes community relations, it includes the use of time, it includes respect for the environment, it includes a series of things that the current vision of the government does not- it is contrary." (P53; also see P31)*

Given that local activists seek to balance social, environmental, and economic factors (P21), they are highly skeptical of what is presented to them as sustainable development – especially with respect to supposedly climate-friendly hydropower plants (P1, P55).[120] Whereas in industrialized economies the term sustainability has become a bussword in recent years, the local population of Altamira and Belém has developed its own concept of a sustainable regional development that aims to preserve the diversity and productivity of biological systems.[121]

Another claim made by local activists in the debate about development in Amazonia concerns the need for tangible results for the local population. Economic indicators are only of limited interest and relevance to ordinary people, if they do not feel improvements in their daily lives (P55). For the local population, key indicators of development include the provision of public safety, public transport, housing, education, basic sanitation, medical assistance, and other services that contribute to human dignity and a good life (P16, P43). However, local activists also request that the providers of these services acknowledge the traditional knowledge and practices of the local population and existing institutions. In this context, activists claim that the local population's traditional medical knowledge and methods of treatment should receive more attention and appreciation (P1) and that traditional regional knowledge should be included in the curriculum.

> *"Do we want our schools to be equipped with computers, with internet access? We do. But we can do this using solar cells and learning to speak the language of the Munduruku, too.[122] To speak the language of the Kayapó that- Why am I forced to learn English, while I cannot learn to speak Kayapó?" (P1)*

---

120 As discussed in Chapter 4, the environmental friendliness of hydropower plants is disputed.

121 Possible differences in the conceptualization of sustainability in Western and non-Western societies are discussed in Chapter 6.

122 The Munduruku is an indigenous people populating the states of Amazonas, Mato Grosso, and Pará. According to data provided by SIASI and SESAI, they comprised 13 755 individuals in 2014 (Instituto Socioambiental n.d.e).

From the local activists' point of view, there should be a differentiated approach to education that focuses on the integration of traditional knowledge, educational services for the entire population (P35), and specific educational programs for adults that meet the demands and interests of the local population (P35, P39).

A differentiated development concept for Amazonia should also tackle inequality, promote the extension of collective rights – for example, indigenous territories – and improve the inclusion of marginalized groups. Solidarity, companionship, collectivism, and respect for diversity should guide the social development of the region and the interaction between people and nature (P3, P9, P37). The relationship between people and their natural environment is a central aspect of the differentiated development concept for Amazonia, as it is essential for the people's very survival (P53). As a consequence, any intervention in the natural environment will have repercussions for its inhabitants – both in beneficial and detrimental ways.

> *"Worse than destroying and clearing the forest is that you finish with the culture of a particular community, a particular people. This is the greatest environmental devastation you can create. The environment, in this case, is in the sense of man being included therein." (P55)*

As the local population's concept of environment includes the human being as an integral part of it, the close relationship between people and nature – which impacts upon people's identities and self-concepts as shown in Section 5.2 – is an important aspect of the development concept.

To sum up, the differentiated development concept promoted by local activists aims for a preservative development that reconciles social, economic, and environmental factors. This development model renounces large scale industrialization in favor of small scale solutions that are tailored to the climatic and geographical context, the lifestyle, abilities, and demands of the local population, and the socioeconomic requirements of the region.

Measures to arrive at a developed Amazonia

Questions remain about what measures ought to be taken to implement the development concept designed by local activists, and how to achieve the anticipated benefits. Local activists emphasize that after years of abandonment the region requires higher and more reliable state investments. They claim that incentive structures, policies, and funding lines are needed in order to "direct the local development onto a different path" (P37; also see P35 and P41). Most importantly, interviewees call for policymakers and the population to stop and think – that is, to reassess the current development model, to learn from successful regional experiences, and to consider alternative views (P55). This step includes that policymakers and local activists engage in an open-minded exchange, appreciate the opinion and arguments of the other side, and seek to create a common basis for their discussions (P13). It also requires some policymakers and parts of the population to reconsider their notion of Amazonia and its development potentials (P1).

Local activists believe that the actual implementation of a differentiated development concept ought to start at the community level by focusing on its particular requirements, transferring ownership to the community members (P29), and acknowledging the expertise and capacities of civil society organizations (P9). For example, interviewees suggest that the transport and sale of fish should be organized by the fishers themselves, in order that they take responsibility for the processes and enjoy the benefits of entrepreneurship (P13). The claim for more participation is based on the belief that the local people do have precise ideas about what is needed for their medium- and long-term development, but lack the resources and structures to implement their ideas (P13).

Another important aspect is the active participation of society and academia in energy planning in general, and with respect to the Belo Monte Dam in particular. Local activists demand a strengthening of participatory mechanisms,

> *"so that the society has possibilities – together with the scientific communities of our country – to mount a sustainable energy planning, truly sustainable, with the alternatives that we have, many alternatives that we have in our country, that range from solar energy to biomass, and so many others." (P9)*

The lack of participation and ownership of the local population in development projects is a recurrent theme that is frequently connected to historic power asymmetries and questions of respect and acknowledgement. Local activists claim that the enterprises involved in the construction of the Belo Monte Dam have much more political influence than the local population (P1).

Divergence of short-term strategies and tactics

While all interviewees promote a consistent concept for the long-term development of their region, the short term strategies and tactics for dealing with the current challenges associated with the construction of the Belo Monte Dam differ significantly across social movement organizations. Based on different understandings of the status and potential outcome of the project, of the organizations' role and influence in the process, and of the advantages and disadvantages of the mitigation measures, the social movement split into the protest SMOs and the monitoring SMOs. They have officially stopped their cooperation and follow different strategies and tactics in their collective action against Belo Monte. Interviewees clearly differentiate these strategies as different plans. While Plan A seeks to prevent the Belo Monte Dam, Plan B aims to improve the impact mitigation.

Figure 4 illustrates the rationale behind the Belo Monte conflict. It summarizes the different perceptions of Amazonia held by the authorities and local activists, as well as their corresponding development concepts. According to interviewees, the Brazilian authorities perceive of Amazonia as a region with abundant natural resources but without any development perspectives. The local inhabitants are considered backward and underdeveloped, and the resources are perceived to be underutilized. As a consequence, the authorities focus on exploiting Amazonia for the purpose of fostering economic growth in the South of the country, while at the same time disregarding the interest of the population in the Brazilian Amazon. This mindset and attitude of the authorities translate into a top-down implementation of the hydropower project at the Xingu River. By contrast, local activists oppose the project unanimously based on their common perception of Amazonia and their common development concept for the region. They value the abundant natural resources as well as the social, cultural, and ecological diversity, which form the basis for the personal and social identities of the Amazon peoples. Consequently, their development concept for the region seeks to balance the human, economic, social, cultural, and environmental aspects of life with a view to sustaining livelihoods in Amazonia. Despite common long-term objectives and shared opposition to hydropower projects at the Xingu, the social movement eventually split as the result of a divergence of the collective action frame and an identity crisis. Henceforth, the protest SMOs pursue Plan A and enter into open conflict with the authorities. The monitoring SMOs follow Plan B and negotiate with the authorities. Both plans are discussed in detail in the following sections.

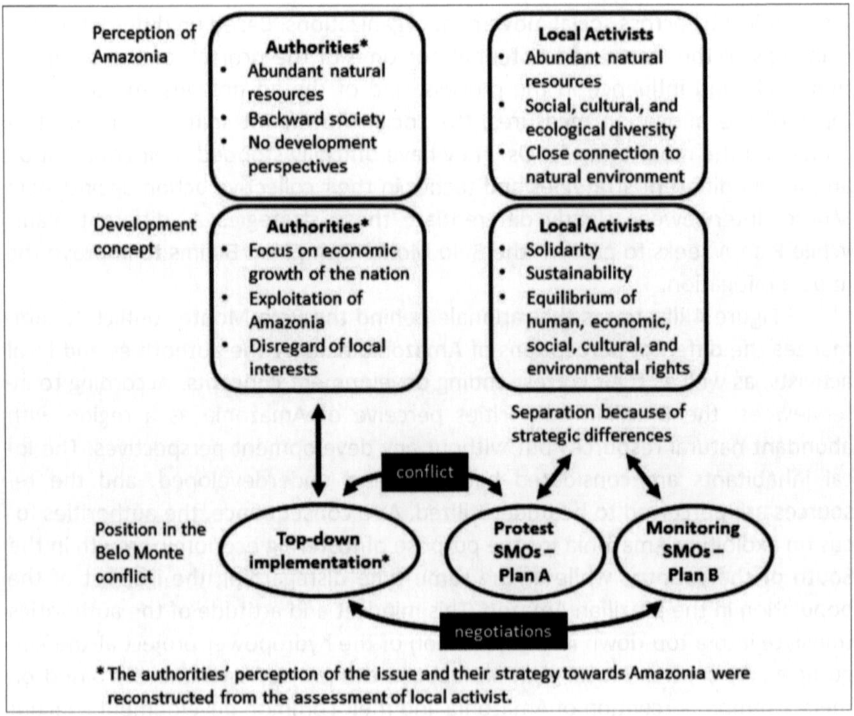

Figure 4: Rationale of the Belo Monte Conflict

5.3.3.2 *Plan A: The Unconditional Fight*

The faction that seeks to prevent the Belo Monte Dam at all cost consists of the Xingu Vivo Movement and its member organizations, the Metropolitan Committee, and various organizations affiliated with the Catholic Church. In order to substantiate their outright opposition to the project, these organizations refuse any negotiation with the authorities and enterprises involved in the Belo Monte project. In the words of one interviewee,

> *"there is a group that says: 'No. Stop! Stop! Stop! That is the end of the discussion.' If you say: 'But...' – 'That is the end of the discussion! We have made up our minds. We have formed our opinion. Come with whatever ideas you may have – there is no more discussion.' This is Plan A." (P43)*

The goal of these organizations, whom I call the protest SMOs, is to prevent the construction of any hydropower plant at the Xingu River – regardless of compensation schemes, mitigation measures, etc. In order to achieve this goal, protest SMOs engage in individual and collective activities, which are facilitated by the forums that Xingu Vivo and the Metropolitan Committee provide (P21).

The strategy of the protest SMOs includes different areas of activity that one interviewee classifies as (1) the scientific front, (2) the legal front, (3) the communication front, and (4) the political front (P21). These four fronts interact as follows.

> *"The front of political articulation [...] has a function that runs through the others. [...] So the political front discusses with the legal front and takes the information that the legal front provides; it takes the information from the scientific front, which refers to the problems of the Belo Monte project, the unsustainability of the project – that is, in the economic field, in the social, cultural, environmental, and even political field – and defines an action [...]" (P21)*

Local activists across SMOs frequently emphasize that their opposition against Belo Monte is based on the economic, ecological, and legal problems of the project (P1). In order to substantiate this claim, the protest SMOs focus on providing proof and communicating to the general public that a hydropower plant a the Xingu River is economically unviable, and ecologically and socially unsustainable.

Scientific Research

Protest SMOs cooperate closely with researchers at universities and other research facilities in Brazil and abroad (P1, P31) for the purpose of compiling scientific expertise about the impacts of hydropower plants in general, and the Belo Monte Dam in particular. The studies they refer to assess the economic viability and cost-benefit-ratio of the project, the technical features and alternatives of hydroelectricity (P31), and the ecological consequences of large hydropower plants (P43). The most important scientific assessment of the Belo Monte project commissioned by the protest SMOs is the report by the Panel of Experts published in 2009 (Painel de Especialistas 2009) (cf. Chapter 4). The following statement illustrates the high credibility of the panel and its appreciation by local activists.

> *"And we know that the Panel of Experts is a <u>serious</u> panel of researchers of the highest degree of integrity and technical competence, who are*

partners of the entities, who are partners of the indigenous communities in the sense that they provide with a great scientific capacity hard, real, and irrefutable data to contradict the Belo Monte project." (P51)

Based on the data provided by the Panel of Experts and other researchers, local activists seek to provide pragmatic, scientific, and legal arguments with a special focus on the quality of the information they disseminate (P55).

Legal Actions

In connection with the scientific analysis of the Belo Monte Dam, legal actions against unlawful procedures in the planning, licensing, and implementation of the project have gained in importance as a collective action strategy since 2001 (P3, P37, P41). The Federal Public Ministry is perceived as a powerful partner who supports the social movement not only in the enforcement of the environmental legislation, but also in guaranteeing the rights of activists in the face of threats and prosecution (P3, P23, P37). However, local activists also report that the support of the Public Ministry depends on the personality of the respective prosecutor. While the public prosecutor of the MPF in Belém is an outspoken opponent of the Belo Monte Dam and a reliable ally of the social movement against Belo Monte (P9, P31, P51), the relationship of the social movement with the public prosecutors of the Public Ministry of the State of Pará, which is located in Altamira, is strained (P19). The MPF engages in a continuous supervision of the process in order to react to misguided developments in a timely fashion (P41). However, the legal actions initiated so far have not produced the expected results. Local activists claim that the deferment is a deliberate strategy that enables the federal government to press ahead with the construction and create facts (P1).

"I think we are experiencing times of a very bad government, of a judiciary that is being knocked over; no one is able to achieve correct judgments of the lawsuits, and there are several actions that – if they were judged – could stop Belo Monte." (P37)

Another important ally on the so-called legal front is the Pará Society for the Defense of Human Rights (Sociedade Paraense de Defesa dos Direitos Humanos, SDDH). It provides legal advice and assistance to activists in case of criminal prosecution (P55) and supported the denunciation of the Belo Monte project before the IACHR (P55; also see IACHR 2011: 77–78).

Communication and Political Action

Protest SMOs attach great importance to the assessment and dissemination of relevant and reliable information based on scientific assessments and legal counseling. Given the vastness and remoteness of Amazonia, media coverage is an important aspect of their communication strategy. However, the protest SMOs perceive a bias in favor of Belo Monte in media reports (P37, P49, P51); hence, they seek to include marginalized people and eyewitnesses into the debate (P1).

With regard to the local population, the protest SMOs focus on education and awareness-raising (*conscientização*) and the spreading of information through a variety of activities (P49, P51, P53).[123] These range from street theater and other artistic activities, to the development of digital information material, to seminars and debates, to street protest, and to the occupation of buildings and construction sites (P1, P3, P16, P21, P49). The purpose is to demonstrate how the Belo Monte conflict affects the lives of seemingly noninvolved people (P51). Moreover, the protest SMOs seek to promote the dialogue between different social groups in order that they develop common objectives that strengthen the collective action.

> *"So, this articulation, this joint discussion between the peoples of the Xingu region, between fishers, riverine communities, farmers,* quilombolas, *gatherers, and townspeople as well is very important in order that everyone can understand the process in a broader way. And this discussion has not yet been the way we would have liked it to be, it is still initial, but it is important that this articulation between the peoples continues, because their goals are changing. While initially their goals were more on a personal level, they are becoming- There is a possibility that they will become more collective goals." (P21)*

The communication activities also include the writing of manifestos, protest letters, and reports to international banks (P51), government agencies, and the judicial authorities – including the judges of the Supreme Court – in order to raise their awareness of the contentious issue (P21, P21, P27). At the beginning of the conflict, members of the social movement also engaged in meetings with government officials, including high-ranking personnel like former President Lula (P45, P53).

123 SMOs within the social movement against Belo Monte are free to choose their preferred activities. Their autonomy is one of the movement's working principles and contributes to movement cohesion (cf. Section 5.4).

The communication strategy further involves international advocacy as an important and effective instruments of collective action (P3). Local activists appreciate the political and financial support and the visibility they gain from international cooperation (P3). They claim that international pressure can have a decisive impact on government decisions (P3, P49). However, interviewees acknowledge that nowadays Brazil is able to implement the hydropower project without international financial aid, and that the international pressure will therefore be less influential than in 1989 when the project was prevented by the withdrawal of the main financier, the World Bank (P1).

Summing up, the purpose of the so-called Plan A is to prevent the construction of the Belo Monte Dam. In order to achieve this, the protest SMOs focus on (1) the dissemination of information in order to create public pressure on policymakers, and (2) court proceedings in order to arrive at a legal judgment about the lawfulness of the Belo Monte project. Interviewees are proud to report that many people have become aware of the problems associated with Belo Monte and have joined the movement (P51). They claim that – as a consequence of their efforts – it has already become impossible to implement a hydropower plant at the Xingu River without resistance (P31).

5.3.3.3 *Plan B: The Struggle for Impact Mitigation*

The second faction of the social movement against Belo Monte – whom I call the monitoring SMOs – comprises the Foundation, its member organizations, ISA, and MAB. As discussed above, the monitoring SMOs oppose the exploitation of the hydroelectric potential of the Xingu River and have fought against the project alongside the protest SMOs for a long time. Yet, with the advancement of the construction, this group of activists came to believe that the project cannot be stopped anymore (P41). As a consequence, the monitoring SMOs started to incorporate the Belo Monte Dam into their planning. They claim that a complete analysis of the situation requires them to acknowledge its existence (P39, P41) and to consider its various impacts in their strategic planning (P39, P41). However, interviewees make sure to emphasize that they disapprove of hydropower plants at the Xingu River.

> *"Belo Monte will never be a work of ours and we will never defend Belo Monte, because Belo Monte is a work of the government, of the strategy of the government and not of civil society. What civil society did was to participate in public hearings with lots of firmness, with much criticism, with great determination, and it continues participating until today in the process of monitoring, of uncovering, of enforcing." (P41)*

Local activists affiliated with the monitoring SMOs believe that the interests of both parties – that is, state and economy on the one hand, and local population and SMOs on the other hand – ought to be balanced by means of negotiations. Given the historic exploitation, underdevelopment, and abandonment of the region, these SMOs demand the reparation of the historic debt that the governments incurred in the region as well as the solution of problems that the local population has been dealing with for decades (P39, P41). The goal of the monitoring SMOs is to avoid that the project passes the region without creating lasting benefits for the population (P39). In order to achieve this goal, they (1) negotiate with the authorities and Norte Energia, (2) participate in the steering committees of various development projects, (3) monitor the fulfillment of the conditions stipulated in the preliminary license, and (4) counsel the affected people.

Negotiations

The negotiations of the monitoring SMOs with the authorities and the Norte Energia consortium are based on a particular understanding of the Belo Monte conflict. After years of abandonment, the federal government has started to invest in the region and take on responsibility for the provision of public goods. However, as one interviewee says, "nothing comes for free. Everything has a price, and the price is this: Belo Monte" (P39). In view of the serious socioeconomic, environmental, and legal problems of the region and their historic roots, even the activists affiliated with the monitoring SMOs believe that the acceptance of Belo Monte is a high price to pay for government attention and the prospect of development (P39). Hence, they monitor the entire process closely,

> *"discuss the integration of our agenda into this project, so that the federal government cannot abort the project or leave it unfinished and leave an entire sea of problems here for us to drown in after the construction of this project." (P39).*

The central strategy of the monitoring SMOs is to balance their own development agenda with that of the federal government in order to work towards the realization of their differentiated development concept (P39). In doing so, they built on the collective action of the past two decades, claiming that the struggle has produced some important results. These include the modification of the hydropower project, the definition of the conditions in the preliminary license, the thorough revision of the EIA/RIMA, and the establishment of the PBA and the PDRS Xingu (P41). However, their negotiations with the authorities are hampered by the latter's alleged noncompliance with the national and international legislation(see above).

Participation

One major point of criticism of the Belo Monte project that is shared by activists across SMOs concerns the lack of public participation in the planning and implementation of the project. Interviewees from the ranks of the monitoring SMOs emphasize that their participation in steering committees, forums, and conferences is an important instrument for claiming the rights of the local population and for influencing the implementation of the development projects (P35, P41, P53). For example, the Federation of Agricultural Workers (Federação dos Trabalhadores na Agricultura, FETAGRI), which is one of the organizations affiliated with the Foundation, holds a seat in the steering committee of the PDRS Xingu. It this realm, FETAGRI applies for the funding of development projects that foster small-scale production with a focus on food products (P39). From the monitoring SMOs' point of view, the PDRS Xingu is a funding opportunity for the development projects that they have been wanting to realize (P39).

> *"For example, here in the PDRS we present a proposal, a project to promote the production and to farm areas with technical equipment in another municipality. First, to work with 100 families in each municipality in the area of food production. So, our role is to accompany step by step the implementation of this project by monitoring and guiding it, etc." (P39).*

However, the monitoring SMOs also acknowledge the constraints of the PDRS Xingu and other development instruments, which are just starting to gain functionality (P41).

Monitoring and Counseling

Interviewees affiliated with the monitoring SMOs attach great importance to the conditions of the preliminary license, the mitigation measures, and the development plans (P39). Yet, they are convinced that the federal government and the companies involved in the Belo Monte project will try to keep the cost of public services and compensation to a minimum (P41, P51). Therefore, the monitoring of the various processes connected to the implementation of the Belo Monte project is an important part of their strategy (P37).

> *"What is the challenge now? It is to ensure – through the forum of social monitoring – that every action of these becomes real. I still think that the challenge is clearly on that issue right now." (P41)*

Similar to the protest SMOs, the monitoring SMOs attach great importance to the dissemination of information. However, their focus is on educating the local population about their rights and advising them on how to behave in case of conflict over their properties (P39, P49). Activists keep in contact with representatives of Norte Energia and the CCBM, the Federal Public Ministry, and government agencies in order to resolve conflicts. The compensation of affected people is a particularly controversial issue, as Norte Energia does not seem to treat people equally when it comes to the estimation of the property value and the payment of compensation (P41). Moreover, the information provided by Norte Energia and the CCBM is considered unreliable; hence, the monitoring SMOs take care in advising affected people on their rights.

> *"If we have information, we can advise an affected person on the rights he has. The CCBM works with the notion of 'I will give you a house. You will receive a nice house.' [...] But if I, as a social movement, know the PBA, the Basic Environmental Plan, I will say: 'Look, beyond the house, you will have to receive here by your house a recreational area for the community, a school of good quality, and all that'." (P41)*

The observations of the monitoring SMOs regarding the compensation of affected people, the fulfillment of the conditions, and the implementation of the development projects are also an important source of information for the MPF, which takes legal action in cases of misdemeanor (P41).

To sum up, the monitoring SMOs believe, that the Belo Monte project is inevitable and that the social movement should focus on negotiating the best possible solutions for the region's development. Moreover, interviewees emphasize that their struggle for the fulfillment of the conditions and the implementation of public policies is "a kind of manifestation" (P41). This perception of and strategy towards dealing with the conflict is a characteristic of the monitoring SMOs, which distinguishes them from the protest SMOs.

5.3.3.4 The Relationship Between Plan A and Plan B

Social movement organizations in Altamira and Belém agree that the long-term solution for the region's problems cannot be a hydropower plant at the Xingu

River as suggested by the federal government. Instead, local activists propose a differentiated development that provides an equilibrium of social, environmental, and economic factors, that acknowledges and promotes the given economic focus on small-scale agriculture, forest economy, livestock farming, fishing, and extractivism, and that invests in education, infrastructure, and sustainable tourism. The short-term strategies and tactics of dealing with the region's underdevelopment and the advancement of the Belo Monte Dam differ between protest and monitoring SMOs.

Interestingly, interviewees have different views on the relationship between the two plans. One interviewee claims that activists of protest and monitoring SMOs can participate in joint events but that the strategies themselves cannot be reconciled.

> *"Now, in the Xingu+23, I think they will go together, but not in terms of their philosophy. [...] There is no way. Because this is the most ordinary logic: If you fight for Plan B, you accept the hydropower plant." (P43)*

Another interviewee who believes that Belo Monte is not yet an accomplished fact claims to be prepared to do both: to stop the dam and to support affected people in claiming their rights.

> *And it may be that this work gets stuck in the middle, because the disaster to come is not yet completed. It is better to avoid the disaster than to have the total disaster. So, if tomorrow we had the means to stop this dam – they can count on me. Now, if the fishers complain that they are not receiving compensation they can count on me as well, if they want." (P47)*

Yet another interviewee who participates in the monitoring SMOs describes Plan A and Plan B as two directions of a common form of action.

> *"We show that this licensing process is completely wrong, that it is disrespecting the law. At the same time we are fighting for it to be obeyed, and for the rights of the population to be provided for, and we- Like, we are helping the social movement to have information and to have fuel for fighting against [Belo Monte, I.P.]. To say: 'Stop it all! This is all wrong. Stop!' You give more information to this movement." (P37)*

While interviewees agree that the two factions of the social movement against Belo Monte follow different strategies, they disagree about the implications of this divergence for the cohesion of the social movement and the relationship between organizations and activists. Some interviewees, like the first one cited in this section, draw a clear line between the two factions. By contrast, the second and third interviewee imply that it is legitimate to combine both goals. The perceived relationship between Plan A and Plan B has implications for the boundary-making between the two factions, which will be discussed in Section 5.4.

5.3.4 *Preliminary Conclusion*

The analysis of the collective action frame has shown that the Belo Monte project has a strong symbolic meaning for local activists in Altamira and Belém. Interviewees associate the hydropower project with

1. an ideological dispute about development
2. the domination of Amazonia by external authorities
3. the manifestation of the neoliberal economic system, and
4. the launch of further hydropower projects in Amazonia.

From the local population's point of view, hydropower plants are a major threat to their socio-environmental living space and, accordingly, to their cultures and lifestyles. They do not oppose Belo Monte for the purpose of hampering the economic development of Brazil, as the federal government, the construction industry, and parts of the Brazilian majority population claim. Instead, local activists base their criticism of the neoliberal development model in general, and of the Belo Monte project in particular, on the historical exploitation and political abandonment of the region, which have resulted in social, political, and economic underdevelopment. Civil society organizations in Altamira and Belém seek to reconcile socio-environmental protection with socioeconomic advancement. Despite the separation of the social movement in the course of the Belo Monte conflict, activists across SMOs continue to promote a common development concept that builds upon their historic struggle for development along the Trans-Amazon Highway and the Xingu. This concept demands that the traditional lifestyles of indigenous communities and forest peoples be acknowledged, assured, and supported. Moreover, it requires state investments and technological aid to carry out specific projects that promote small scale agriculture and livestock farming, which are believed to promote the sustainable use of resources, create lasting benefits for the local population, and reduce the dependence on imported foodstuff.

While both factions of the social movement promote the differentiated development concept as a long-term solution to the region's underdevelopment, they have developed different understandings of and strategies for confronting the current conflict over the Belo Monte project. The analysis of the collective action frame reveals controversies over

1. the current status of Belo Monte,
2. the social movement's role and influence in the conflict, and
3. the advantages and disadvantages of the mitigation measures.

The protest SMOs believe that the Belo Monte project can still be prevented. Hence, they continue fighting it with all possible means and reject any negotiations with the authorities, claiming that negotiations would imply consent with the hydropower project. In contrast, the monitoring SMOs are convinced that the project will be finalized. As a consequence, they follow a negotiation strategy with the authorities and focus on development projects and mitigation measures with the objective of achieving the best possible results for the region's development.

To this point, the analysis shows that both the identities of local activists and the collective action frame are heavily influenced by context conditions. Interviewees show a strong identification with the region and its unique characteristics. On the one hand, they value and seek to maintain their socio-environmental living space. On the other hand, they also aspire to a sustainable development that improves the living conditions of the local population, while at the same time preserving the diversity and productivity of biological systems. The Belo Monte project is seen as an additional factor entering into the existing dynamics of collective action in Altamira. In this section, I have already alluded to the impact of the Belo Monte project on the movement dynamics – specifically, identity work and framing processes. The following section analyzes these dynamics in detail, focusing on the factors that promote cohesion and fragmentation in the social movement.

5.4 Movement Dynamics

The authorization of the Belo Monte project by Legislative Decree No. 788 of 13 July 2005 and the actual start of the construction works in July 2011 initiated severe changes in the civil society of Altamira and in the social movement against the Belo Monte Dam. Local activists who had been affiliated with the newly elected Workers' Party and had been fighting Belo Monte for almost 20 years fell between two stools. They had to decide whether they wanted to remain loyal with the Workers' Party or with the social movement against Belo Monte. Activists who had been working together for decades started to eye each other suspiciously, and conflicts over loyalty and trust started to strain their personal and professional relationships. Moreover, the visible advancement of the construction works caused disagreement among local activists about the status and future development of the Belo Monte project, and about the organizations' roles and responsibilities in the conflict. The way interviewees talk about the struggle and its implications for civil society and individual activists in Altamira today indicates that the experiences have been traumatic for some individuals.

> *"Like, the social movement is locally shattered. [...] Imagine yourself fighting for 30 years for something not to happen, and then seeing the thing happen. There are very severe trauma, open and complicated wounds that need to be cured, the alliances need to be re-established." (P37)*

While interviewees lament the weakening of the social movement and the rupture of activists' relationships, they also indicate that wounds can be healed and alliances can be re-established – thereby implying a positive future for collective action in Altamira.

In this section, I analyze the processes of cohesion and fragmentation in the social movement against Belo Monte that the interviewee alludes to in the statement above and that form the central arguement of this chapter. While this study initially intended to explain the persistence of the collective action and the apparent cohesion of the social movement against Belo Monte, I found that the movement has been suffering from fragmentation as a result of changing context conditions. In this section, I propose that the factors promoting the cohesion or the fragmentation of the social movement against Belo Monte can be divided into internal factors (that is, factors arising from internal movement dynamics that can be instrumentalized by activists) and external factors (that is, factors arising outside the social movement). The first part of this section focuses on the processes of cohesion in the social movement against Belo Monte. I argue that identity work, a number of working principles, leadership, framing processes, and a founding myth are the most important internal factors that contribute to the development and maintenance of movement cohesion. A common destiny and a common enemy are the most important external factors promoting cohesion. The existence of a common purpose, which would further contribute to movement cohesion, is ambiguous in the social movement against Belo Monte. Hence, I analyze the interviewees' statements about the existence and meaning of a common purpose in this section and resume the discussion in Chapter 6, where I evaluate the implications of a common purpose or a lack thereof for movement cohesion and fragmentation. The second part of this section focuses on the process of fragmentation, which was not originally included in the theoretical framework and emerged from the original data as an in-vivo code. I start with a brief excursus for the purpose of defining the concept and outlining existing research on factionalism in social movements. Then I analyze the internal and external factors that contributed to the fragmentation of the social movement against Belo Monte. I propose that a divergence of the collective action frame is the most important internal factor, while the election and coming into office of the Workers' Party and its alleged strategy of bribing and creating discord among the local population are among the external factors that contributed to the movement's fragmentation. Towards the end of this section, I assess the relationship between the two factions of the social movement and the movement's boundaries towards outside agents.

5.4.1 *Cohesion in the Social Movement*

As discussed in Chapter 2, social movement scholars argue that a sense of cohesion is fundamental for the development of collective action (Flesher Fominaya 2010b; Hunt and Benford 2004; Polletta and Jasper 2001; Teune 2008). According to Pearlman, cohesion is "the cooperation among individuals that enables unified action" (Pearlman 2011: 9). The cooperation of civil society organizations in Altamira has a long history and relies on personal relationships between activists. In the 1980s, the existing organizational structures and growing awareness of social, political, and economic problems facilitated the emergence of collective action against hydropower plants in the Xingu River basin (cf. Section 5.1). The development and maintenance of movement cohesion was promoted by internal and external factors until changing context conditions and the start of the construction works initiated a process of fragmentation.

5.4.1.1 *Internal Factors Promoting Cohesion*

Identity work, a number of working principles, leadership, framing processes, and a founding myth are the most important internal factors that contribute to the development and maintenance of cohesion in the social movement against Belo Monte.

Identity work

As discussed in Section 5.2, the social movement against Belo Monte deliberately created a collective identity – with I termed Amazonian Identity – to facilitate the identification of the population and potential activists with the social movement. The establishment of Xingu Vivo and the Metropolitan Committee as forums for cooperation and exchange are considered decisive steps towards creating a common space (P21). Both organizations enable the inclusion of individuals who are not affiliated with a social movement organization and promote the interaction of people and organizations, thus uniting the formerly scattered activities (P3, P19, P21). For example, the Metropolitan Committee has established a methodology that regulates its decision making process with the objective of taking unanimous decisions (P3, P21, P43).

> *"So, methodologically, it means the development of a process of debating in search of consensus. Even if it is a partial consensus, but this has been our proposal and our action. And it has been an experience, I believe, a learning experience for other struggles, for other organizations, for other situations that offer this possibility to meet, to dialogue, and to arrive at collective actions, in whatever field this may be." (P21)*

Local activists are particularly proud that Xingu Vivo and the Metropolitan Committee avoid confrontation between activists, and instead focus on the common purpose and the development of collective activities that all activists can identify with. They claim that two factors are particularly important for sustaining cooperation between SMOs – that is, analytically speaking, for maintaining movement cohesion. The first aspect is the participants' acknowledgment that the struggle against the Belo Monte Dam is larger than their individual understandings, truths, and wishes, and much more than a struggle against a hydropower plant (P21). The second aspect is the organizations' ability "to dialogue, to overcome conflicts, and – following that – to articulate unity" (P21; also see P55). Hence, movement participants actively engage in identity work, which requires them to abstract from their individual experiences, interests, and concerns, and to seek dialog with other activists and affected people.

Interestingly, some activists claim that it is the task of the leadership to set a good example and work toward a collective identity by promoting a continuous dialog and elaborating common agendas and joint activities (P49). The demonstration of the leadership's unity towards the rank and file members promotes a sense of unity in the movement, which can then be passed on to society in order to raise awareness for the conflict and mobilize the public (P49).[124]

124 The role of leaders in the social movement against Belo Monte will be discussed further below.

Working Principles

Organizations and individuals in the social movement against Belo Monte base their interaction on a number of working principles that reflect the unique characteristics of the social movement. The strong heterogeneity of the movement demands commitment and patience from local activists as they define their collective identity and collective action frame.

The analysis of working principles shows that openness and the appreciation of diversity are particularly important in the social movement against Belo Monte. The political and ideological orientation, ethnicity, and religion of movement participants are considered irrelevant (P9, P16), while respect plays an important role (P1, P49). In order to show this diversity and the broad range of people and organizations that oppose Belo Monte, its members take turns in representing the social movement, participating in activities, and appearing in public. The mobilization of young people in Belém is considered an important improvement that was made possible by the creation of the Metropolitan Committee. Especially the university students are said to strengthen and accelerate the movement (P1).

> *"And what we have here in Belém is this group of young people, people from the universities, that do fantastic things, things you cannot imagine, and they take it up, and go, and do it; and they know, they organize, they debate in the schools, they go to the squares, to the streets and they do it. When we look up, things are already happening. This is very cool. I think this is cool." (P1)*

Emphasis is placed on autonomy, both within the movement (internal autonomy) and vis-à-vis third parties (external autonomy). Internal autonomy refers to the principle that every group can address its audience in the preferred form and with emphasis on those aspects of the collective action frame that are particularly relevant for their members and followers (P1) – as long as they subscribe to the common purpose of the movement (P3). Accordingly, there is little control of the SMOs' activities.

> *"I do not need to be there to supervise it and say: 'Look, you have to do this.' Everyone picks up the information, sets up his product, goes there, and does it. I think this is what is cool, because you create ramifications in all segments [...]" (P1)*

Xingu Vivo and the Metropolitan Committee, in their function as forums of the social movement, consolidate the different discourses and activities, and they facilitate cooperation between SMOs, while at the same time ensuring their internal autonomy (P21, P37). This way, the social movement organizations "maintain unity in diversity" (P16).

External autonomy refers primarily to the social movement's financial independence from third parties, including the state (P1, P19). In particular, the acceptance of financial resources from companies that benefit from hydropower is considered to be inconsistent with the movement's beliefs and objectives (P1). External autonomy further refers to an ideological and organizational differentiation from the state and the economy. Interviewees draw a clear line between the political sphere and the apolitical sphere of civil society, emphasizing their adherence to the ideals of civil society and their efforts to remain "clean" – a term that makes reference to corruption and nepotism in the political sphere (P41).[125] Nonetheless, national and international partners – for example, International Rivers and Amazon Watch, among others (P19, P41) – play an important role. They do not only provide financial support; they also raise awareness of the issue, provide and disseminate information, and exert political pressure on decision makers (P3, P16, P27, P35).

While openness and internal autonomy enable the participation of a broad range of people and organizations, they also require a significant level of trust among social movement participants, which – according to interviewees – is very strong in the social movement against Belo Monte.

> *"You can talk to anyone, you can go there and talk to anyone. Everyone can speak, everyone who is part of the group can speak, is cognizant; we have confidence in everyone, we have a very good relationship of trust between the groups, although a group belongs to a party, another one belongs to another party, another one belongs to a union, another one to another." (P1)*

Interviewees admit that the cooperation between SMOs is intermittent in the sense that organizations are not involved in all activities at all times (P21). Still, openness and respect for otherness, autonomy of SMOs within the movement, and trust in the loyalty and capacity of fellow activists enable cooperation between groups that would disagree in other contexts.

125 Members of the protest SMOs claim that the monitoring SMOs are no longer independent civil society organizations as they participate in the administration of the government funds that are allocated to the region through the PBA and PDRS Xingu.

Leadership

The existence of leaders in the social movement against Belo Monte is a controversial issue. Interviewees prefer to talk about the movement as a collectivity. Being asked about possible leaders or representatives of the movement, they react in many different ways. Their understandings of leadership are not only diverse, but also inconsistent in themselves.

In this section, I categorize the interviewees' statements about leadership for the purpose of systematizing their diffuse beliefs about leadership in general, and their perception of leadership in the social movement against Belo Monte in particular.[126] The in-depth analysis of the data shows that interviewees have different opinions about whether or not leadership in a social movement is generally desirable, and how leadership is actually practiced in the social movement against Belo Monte. Some activists believe that a social movement like the one against Belo Monte should not have selected leaders. They argue that a social movement is a collective and that it is characterized by a decentralized network structure (P1). Moreover, they claim that the shared responsibility protects activists – to a certain extent – from harassment and persecution.

> *"The protest does not bear the face of a single person, it bears the face of the Metropolitan Committee and of the Movement. So, the responsibility for the protest rests with all of us. It is collective. This is important, also for reasons of security, so that there are no leaders who could be identified and arrested. This is why we do not appoint leaders." (P21)*

The argument also alludes to the internal autonomy mentioned above, which allows any activist to contribute to the collective action, take responsibility for certain activities, and express leadership in the social movement (P1, P3, P21).[127]

Another group of interviewees claim that leadership is important in social movements – including in the social movement against Belo Monte. They believe that it is necessary for a social movement to train and develop its leaders (P27) and to pass on the leadership from one generation to the next (P27,

126 Throughout this section, I use the term leadership in accordance with the working definition given on page 53 – that is, "the process of persuasion or example by which an individual (or leadership team) induces a group to pursue objectives held by the leader or shared by the leader and his or her followers" (Gardner 1993: 1). However, the purpose of this section is to identify the attributes that local activists associate with leadership. Their leadership concept will be further elaborated in Chapter 6.

127 Interviewees suggest that every participant in the social movement can "act out leadership" (P3:480). This contradicts other statements and demonstrates the inconsistent use of terms and the diffuse leadership concept.

P41). Moreover, the burden of collective action should be shared between several people in order to reduce the risk for the individual (P27). In accordance with their understanding of leadership, these interviewees believe that the social movement against Belo Monte has various leaders (P3, P13).

Regardless of the interviewees' opinion about the desirability of leadership in social movements in general, and their perception of the actual practice of leadership in the social movement against Belo Monte in particular – interviewees across SMOs acknowledge the existence of a few people that serve as "points of reference" within and outside the movement (P1, P25). These historic and contemporary leaders emerged over time; they were/are especially dedicated to the collective action and represent the fight in a particularly symbolic way (P1, P53). These individuals are perceived to represent the entire movement, and they share share a number of characteristics that I categorize as follows:

1. exceptional dedication (P1, P3, P21, P25, P35),
2. soft skills, in particular the ability to mobilize people and integrate the collective action (P1, P13, P25, P25, P49),
3. symbolic meaning and wide representation (P1, P3, P16, P19, P51, P53),
4. experience and historic legitimacy (P3, P21, P49, P53, P55),
5. integrity and courage (P1, P3, P13, P16, P25, P31, P51), and
6. intellectual capacity (P21, P49, P51).

While these attributes describe some key characteristics of the leaders in the social movement against Belo Monte, they do not represent the social movement's leadership concept. In fact, it is questionable whether the participants in the social movement would be able to agree on a common understanding of leadership. The current practice of leadership differs across SMOs. While some SMOs produce their own leadership (P21), only a small number of leaders are widely recognized.

Interestingly, the self-perception of these leaders differs slightly from their perception by others. They acknowledge that they fulfill certain roles within the movement – for example, the coordination of activities. Yet, they neither identify themselves as leaders, nor do they claim sole responsibility for the collective action (P1, P43). Instead, they emphasize that the coordination of the social movement is a collective effort (P1, P9) and that they merely motivate the affected population to take action (P49). While the leaders of the movement believe in the legitimacy and capacity of the people to make claims against their authorities, they have made the experience that the population needs a minimum of support and coordination (P49). Hence, they keep in contact and moderate meetings with the authorities but insist that the affected people are the protagonists in the conflict (P41).

> *"When I met with Lula, I insisted Lula agree to my bringing along representatives of the people. I was the one who talked least. Because I make the people talk." (P43)*

Thus, another important attribute of leaders in the social movement against Belo Monte is their modesty and focus on empowering the people, whom they consider the protagonists of the conflict.

To sum up, leadership is a controversial issue in the social movement against Belo Monte. Nonetheless, interviewees identify a few people who have authority across SMOs and represent the entire movement. These individuals share a number of characteristics. While they do not amount to a shared leadership concept, these attributes are informative for the theoretical debate about leadership in general, and in non-Western social movements in particular. I resume this discussion in Chapter 6.

Framing Processes

Social movement scholars frequently emphasize that framing is a process of recurrent negotiations over meaning (Benford and Snow 2000: 614; Herkenrath 2011: 47; McAdam et al. 1996: 6). According to Benford and Snow, social movement organizations trying to forge alliances with other organizations and to recruit activists employ frame bridging, frame amplification, frame extension, and/or frame transformation to align their collective action frames with those of other organizations or individuals (Benford and Snow 2000: 624–625). The analysis showed that frame bridging and frame extension play a particularly important role in the negotiations over the meaning of Belo Monte.[128]

In accordance with the literature (cf. Chapter 2), participants in the social movement against Belo Monte report that it is a challenge to create and maintain a feeling of belonging among movement participants. Yet, they consider their efforts worthwhile because they claim to be working towards a common purpose (P9).[129] Some interviewees give particularly detailed accounts of how individuals and organizations come to identify common interests and objectives, which allow them to develop a sense of we-ness with the social movement. Ac-

128 In methodological terms, I derived the concept from the literature; however, its subcategories emerged largely from the original data by means of constant comparison. Only in a second step did I compare the subcategories to the exemplary framing processes described by Benford and Snow.

cording to their statements, a similar understanding of the meaning of Belo Monte (diagnostic framing) is a prerequisite for cooperation. However, activists also need a forum where they can meet and exchange information face-to-face. This is a particular challenge in Amazonia, as the long distances, insufficient infrastructure, and lack of financial resources hamper regular meetings (cf. Section 5.1).

According to Benford and Snow, collective action frames have to resonate with the target audience – this means, they must be credible and salient – in order to gather public support and mobilize new activists (Benford and Snow 2000: 619). Local activists in Altamira and Belém are particularly proud of having created a comprehensive diagnostic frame that resonates with the most diverse organizations and individuals.

> *"So, the coolest thing was precisely this: that all of them were able to identify in the building of this dam the problem that they would bring to their followers. And that was cool because they all delve into this topic and when we talk, the things add up and they come together, and all this is Belo Monte. All this is a summary of what will be the evils that this dam will bring for all these segments within the community, within Amazonia." (P1)*

While the diagnostic frame identifies a large array of topics, it also provides thematic linkages between the individual aspects and ensures that these add up to a consistent picture of the Belo Monte conflict. From an analytical point of view, framing processes, in which an organization first recognizes that its collective action frame is congruent with that of another organization or movement and then establishes a link between the two frames, are called frame bridging. This process may also occur on the individual level when a person realizes that his or her grievances are shared by others. A noteworthy encounter, in which frame bridging took place, was the meeting of indigenous peoples and fishers in October 2011. During the occupation of the Belo Monte construction site the two groups organized a large assembly of their members.

> *"On that occasion they exchanged information about their problems. The fishers spoke a bit about their feelings, the indigenous people told the fishers about their experiences and they saw that the problems were sim-*

129 The discussion about the existence and meaning of a common purpose is resumed in Chapter 6, where I evaluate the implications of a common purpose or a lack thereof for movement cohesion and fragmentation.

ilar. And regarding those problems that were not similar, they understood that there are other problems beyond their own problems." (P21)

According to local activists, the personal exchange between the peoples of the Xingu, which was sporadic in the past, is essential for the collective action because it can turn individual objectives into a collective purpose (P21).

The second framing process, next to frame bridging, that is relevant in the collective action against Belo Monte is the extension of the diagnostic frame in order to mobilize hitherto unmobilized segments of society. Frame extension refers to the inclusion of aspects that extend beyond the SMO's primary interests but resonate with potential adherents (Benford and Snow 2000: 625). In order to appeal to people living in other municipalities or even other Amazon states, the social movement against Belo Monte extended its collective action frame. It offered a broader definition of who is affected and included the indirect effects on people in other regions of Amazonia and beyond into its diagnostic frame. Moreover, the movement worked towards defining a common purpose – namely, the prevention of the dam construction – that is relevant to all participants in the social movement, albeit for different motives (P1).

Moreover, a collective action frame has to be credible and salient. It has to be relevant for and consistent with the beliefs, values, and experiences of the population; and the person or organization disseminating the frame has to be credible (Benford and Snow 2000: 619–622). As this study shows, the framing processes can be challenged by the complexity of the issue and the delay of tangible effects. According to local activists, the start of the construction work and the immediate experience of negative effects raised the awareness of the local population (P51). Yet, like Thomas the Apostle, many people only believe in what they see (P41; also see P55). As a consequence, local activists are often frustrated by the shortsightedness of other community members (P29) and their preference for prompt rewards.

> *"In the theoretical debate, the people do not really believe in the theory, in you saying: 'Guys, this is not the right path.' 'Yes, but what is the right path? Which one is more immediate?' If I talk about projects, these will take years until they are realized. If Norte Energia offers staple food, it will be sent within a week to 15 days. What then? Will […] [the other community members, I.P.] believe in my theory, which says 'This is ours. You have to fight for the project.'? They will not. They will not believe this. This is what the problem is." (P29)*

While interviewees acknowledge the neediness of the people and their preference for the provision of basic consumer goods (P29), they also criticize their short-sightedness. Given their own ability to comprehend and anticipate long-term developments, activists expect the communities to think ahead and analyze the possible prejudices that may arise from the acceptance of material and financial resources (P29).

The activists' detailed descriptions of their negotiations over meaning shows that social movements have to accommodate different perceptions of reality. Processes of frame alignment have played a crucial role in the social movement against Belo Monte. They have contributed to a common understanding of the conflict and of the collective action and have thus promoted cohesion in the social movement.

Founding Myth

In addition to identity work and framing processes, I propose that a founding myth, which emerged from the combination of identity work and framing processes, contributed to cohesion in the social movement against Belo Monte.

The social movement against hydropower projects at the Xingu River emerged in the 1980s as a reaction to the military government's plans to exploit the river's hydroelectric potential. Until today, interviewees take pride in the events that led to the prevention of the original project, the Kararaô Dam, in 1989. They claim that the First Encounter of the Indigenous Nations of the Xingu taking place in Altamira in February of 1989 constitutes an important point of reference for the collective action against Belo Monte (P31, P35, P37, P43). The story of the indigenous female warrior Tuíra who placed her machete in the face of the then President of Eletronorte, José Antônio Muniz Lopes, became a founding myth of the social movement (P53). The picture, which traveled the world (P19, P37) and contributed to the prevention of the Kararaô Dam (P3), became a symbol of the collective action against hydropower plants at the Xingu River (P1, P31, P41).

> *"The Belo Monte project in '89, 1989, this is a fact that is frequently referred to, the image of the indigenous Tuíra with a machete in the face of the president at that time of Eletronorte. Back than she showed that-how much the indigenous peoples and the traditional populations disliked the project. It became the symbol of the indigenous people not wanting the project." (P55)*

The event turned Tuíra into a role model for activists, and especially female activists, in the region. Until the present day, interviewees acknowledge her courage and daringness in the struggle against hydropower projects at the Xingu

(P1). Yet, the event only became a point of reference for the start of the collective action because it was framed as such. Local activists across SMOs enjoy retelling the story, and by doing so they attribute meaning to the event. Moreover, they associate Tuíra's placing her machete in the face of Muniz Lopes with courage and daringness, instead of choosing other interpretations of her behavior.

The founding myth promotes cohesion in the social movement against Belo Monte by enabling current activists to identify with former activists and to build upon their actions and achievements. In this sense, the founding myth creates a sense of belonging that is effective over time and across generations, and thus contributes to the collective identity of the social movement. Moreover, the First Encounter of the Indigenous Nations of the Xingu of 1989 is repeatedly framed as a significant event. It is deliberately classified as a symbol of the local population's opposition to the project and of the strength and effectiveness of their collective action. Hence, identity work and framing processes interact in the definition and dissemination of a founding myth, and contribute to the establishment and maintenance of movement cohesion.

5.4.1.2 External Factors Promoting Cohesion

External factors promoting cohesion refers to dynamics that are induced by external circumstances or agents. I have identified a common destiny of the local population and a common enemy as external factors that promote cooperation among local activists and organizations. According to Pearlman, a common purpose further contributes to cohesion in a social movement (Pearlman 2011: 9). Yet, the existence of a common purpose in the social movement against Belo Monte is ambiguous. As local activists name different objectives as their supposedly "common" purpose, I argue that this debate actually constitutes a threat to movement cohesion. Therefore, the activists' different understandings of the movement's purpose merit a separate discussion (see below).

Common Destiny

The analysis of social identities in Section 5.2 has shown that the lifestyles of fishers, indigenous, and riverine peoples are very similar. They share a living space (P35) and rely on natural resources to make a living. Hence, they will be affected in equal measure by the effects of the dam (P25). Despite their different social identities, the peoples of the Xingu River basin have created a sense of unity and solidarity based on an issue that unites them: the river (P25, P27,

P51). Interviewees propose that the common dependence on the river and the shared understanding of being affected and threatened by the hydropower project create a sense of common destiny among the various peoples of the region.

> *"The only certainty they have is that their current way of life will no more be the same. So, maybe – and this is my hypothesis – maybe this enables them to speak out against the project in a more or less united way, although for many different reasons [...]." (P55)*

In this sense, uncertainty is an important factor that makes people recognize what they have in common and articulate their opposition to the project (P55.

Moreover, interviewees explain that large parts of the local population consider the Belo Monte project as something inevitable. As discussed in Section 5.3, the region along the Trans-Amazon Highway and the Xingu has experienced various cycles of development in the past. They were typically induced by outside agents – as opposed to local initiatives – and excluded the local population from influence and ownership. As a consequence, local people tend to feel that the socioeconomic development of their region – and ultimately their personal well-being – depends on others. This perception is shared by various peoples of the region and fosters their understanding of a common destiny.

Common Enemy

As discussed in Chapter 2, the sense of belonging to a collectivity (we) is constructed in contrast to other actors (them). Hence, it is important for the social movement to define who is inside the movement and who is outside, who is friend and who is foe. Local activists in Belém and Altamira claim that collective action against Belo Monte is made possible by the existence of a common enemy (P51). But who is this enemy?

> *"Our challenge is to convince the people who are on the other side, the rank and file of the PT, the ones at the grassroots of the parties, that the enemy is someone else, it is not us. The enemy are the companies. The enemy is this authoritarian attitude of the federal government. The enemy are the consequences that we are suffering because of this venture, which are building up, they are building up for those who are fighting for the truth, for justice, to stop Belo Monte, because the government is wrong." (P9)*

Local activists do not only identify the authorities and the construction industry as their enemies; they also talk of abstract antagonists like "the consequences" of Belo Monte. Moreover, they differentiate between the federal government and its authoritarian attitude (P9), thus distinguishing the actor from the actions. This differentiation gives members of the Workers' Party the opportunity to participate in the collective action without having to dissociate themselves from the party.

> *"INTERVIEWER: So, this also opens up a space for members of the PT to participate in the fight?*
>
> *RESPONDENT: Yes. It depends on them whether they accept this. And the challenge is that they convince themselves of this. Because there are many PT members who participate in the struggle in Belém and in other states. And they are PT members, but they are seeing that this is wrong. As you said, the enemy is not the government itself; it is the attitude of the Government." (P9)*

Hence, the social movement differentiates between, on the one hand, the PT government – or more precisely, the members of the Workers' Party, many of whom are (former) comrades of the social movement participants – and, on the other hand, the attitude of the PT government with respect to the Belo Monte Dam (P3). This allows individuals to retain internal consistency in their relationship with the Workers' Party.[130]

Moreover, the social movement exculpates the PT government to a certain extend by blaming the economy and the circumstances for the PT government's decision to revive the project.

> *"Perhaps the Lula government and the Dilma government are only agents of this state in order to build Belo Monte. It is part of an articulated project, several infrastructure programs aimed at facilitating the turnover of large ventures of mining, of agribusiness in the Amazon. So all this causes Belo Monte to be something strategic for the government of the Brazilian state." (P53; also see P27 and P31)*

This statement points again towards the larger meaning of the the Belo Monte Dam. Interviewees consider the project as a door opener that will pave the way for the increasing exploitation of the region. Interestingly, the strategic decisions of the federal government are dissociated from the Lula and Dilma administrations, which are seen as mere agents of the state. This implies the existence of

130 I propose that the resumption of the hydropower project by the Workers' Party caused cognitive dissonance among the party members at the grassroots level. I discuss this issue further below.

structures and dynamics that are independent of the staffing of the administration.

Summing up, the identification of a common enemy promotes the cohesion of the social movement against Belo Monte. Various SMOs support the collective action strategy and address their grievances and claims to the federal government and the consortium of operating companies Norte Energia, as they agree that these represent the common enemy of the local population.

5.4.1.3 Threats to Cohesion: Is There a Common Purpose?

Throughout this chapter, I have repeatedly alluded to a potential common purpose of the social movement against Belo Monte. According to the literature, a common purpose is an important factor that contributes to movement cohesion (cf. Pearlman 2011: 9). The analysis of the primary data shows that movement participants do not only disagree about the definition of a common purpose but even about its sheer existence.

> *"Look, today the protest against Belo Monte follows several lines. There are many voices but they follow different lines. Some voices call for compensation, to improve their compensation. Other voices call for a general recognition of people who are affected and should be compensated. And there are also the voices of those who fight against Belo Monte, those who indeed refuse to accept the construction of Belo Monte. So, there are various lines of action." (P19)*

Activists from the ranks of the protest SMOs claim that some organizations have ceased to represent the interests of the Xingu Vivo Movement (P19, P43). While some interviewees emphasize the divergence of the two factions (P13), others state in passing that the social movement has a common purpose – albeit without explicating what they mean by this (P3, P19, P41, P51). In terms of in-group/out-group differentiation, some interviewees downplay the differences between the two factions (P35), while others identify different objectives and strategies (P39). How can these different perceptions be explained?

The in-depth analysis of the interview data shows that an analytical differentiation between different types of objectives is useful for understanding what segments pursue a common purpose at what stages in the collective action. I propose that one should differentiate between the superior objective of the social movement and the instrumental goals that SMOs pursue throughout the process.

Interviewees who explicate what they perceive to be the common purpose of the social movement generally refer to objectives that can be classified as follows:[131]

1. to stop Belo Monte: This group of activists claim that the common purpose of the social movement is to achieve the abandonment of the project (P1, P3, P9, P19, P53). According to these interviewees the creation of Xingu Vivo and the Metropolitan Committee as forums contributed to the alignment of the collective action and to the definition of the common purpose (P3, P19).
2. to defend life: Another group of activists claim that the common purpose of the movement is to defend life and to defend the people (P16, P23, P25, P49). From their point of view, the struggle for human rights is an issue that unites organizations (P16).
3. to ensure rights: These activists claim that the interests of SMOs are diverse but overlapping with respect to the fight for rights (P37). This purpose has to be considered in the context of the persistent infringement of rights in the region (P48).
4. to achieve differentiated development: Referring to the original purpose of the MDTX, some interviewees claim that the differentiated development of the region continues to be the common purpose of the social movement against Belo Monte (P35).
5. to ensure the fulfillment of the conditions: A central activity of the monitoring SMOs is to control Norte Energia's compliance with the conditions (P19, P39). Some activists believe that only certain SMOs pursue this objective (P19). However, other interviewees claim that the fight for mitigation is a common purpose of the social movement (P35).

While some interviewees believe that SMOs within the movement pursue different objectives, others claim that there is a common purpose. However, even the latter group disagrees on the definition of the supposedly "common" purpose. I propose that this inconsistency does not imply that the social movement lacks a common purpose. Instead, the existence of diverse but supposedly shared objectives mirrors the strong heterogeneity of the movement and the thematic scope of the collective action frame. I propose that the objectives mentioned above are relevant in different contexts and with respect to different planning

131 It should be noted that the categories are not mutually exclusive, as local activists tend to support several of these objectives. Hence, the categorization represents an analytical separation that aims to show what objectives are presented as the single most important and, most notably, common objectives of the activists.

intervals. The movement shares a superior objective – that is, the long-term sustainable development of the region. However, the two factions have defined different instrumental goals, which they pursue throughout the process. As this argument goes beyond the analysis of the original interview material, I will resume the discussion in Chapter 6, where I take the empirical discussion to a higher level of abstraction and evaluate the fragmentation of the social movement against Belo Monte.

5.4.2 Fragmentation in the Social Movement

Throughout this chapter, I have gradually established the rationale for my central argument: I propose that the election and coming into office of the Workers' Party, which has a strong basis in Altamira, had severe repercussions for the social movement against Belo Monte. It induced a divergence of the collective action frame and an identity crisis among activists, which in turn resulted in the fragmentation of the social movement. This part of the section demonstrates how internal and external factors contributed to this development. I start with an excursus on factionalism in social movement studies. The concept was not originally included in the theoretical framework and emerged from the original data as an in-vivo code. Afterward, I discuss the process of fragmentation and identify the contentious issues that caused the controversies in the collective action frame. This is followed by an assessment of the movement's boundaries and the relationship between the two movement factions.

5.4.2.1 Excursus: Factionalism in Social Movement Studies

Since the late 1960s, social movement scholars have investigated factionalism in social movements (Gerlach and Hine 1970; Zald and Ash 1966). Shriver and Messer credit Gamson's seminal analysis (1975) for demonstrating that movement failure is often preceded and caused by factionalism (Shriver and Messer 2009: 163). Much of the social movement literature considers fragmentation to be a normal phase in the life cycle of a social movement. According to Mauss, the social movement life cycle consists of five stages: (1) incipiency, (2) coalescence, (3) institutionalization, (4) fragmentation, and (5) demise (Mauss 1975: 62–65). While Mauss identifies a "normal fragmentation" that results from the very success of the social movement (Mauss 1975: 64), conflict and pressure can cause the fragmentation of a social movement at any stage in its life cycle (Oberschall 1973: 143; Smelser 1962: 304–305). Social movement researchers have developed different explanations as to when and why fragmentation occurs. A review of their findings seems useful in the present study, as the "normal fragmentation" described by Mauss does not adequately reflect the dynamics in the social movement against Belo Monte.

Kretschmer (2013) provides a systematic overview of the research on factions and factionalism. She defines a faction as "a subgroup within a larger organization that is in conflict with other members of that organization" (Kretschmer 2013: 443). While Kretschmer refers to intra-organizational conflict, the term has also been used to denote inter-organizational conflict – that is, factions in a social movement. According to Kretschmer, movements split into factions when a subgroup develops a distinct collective identity that distinguishes it from the rest of the movement. Research typically focuses on the causes, evolvement, and consequences of factionalism, including its different stages (Kretschmer 2013: 443).[132]

Moreover, scholars have focused on internal factors (Gamson 1975; Zald and Ash 1966) and external factors that cause movements to break apart (Balser 1997; Shriver and Messer 2009). They have found that external factors may provoke fragmentation along hitherto irrelevant internal fault lines (Lau and Murnighan 1998; also see Hart and Van Vugt 2006; Stark and Bainbridge 1985). This finding is particularly interesting for the Belo Monte study. Kretschmer further claims that "[u]nderstanding which environmental conditions exacerbate factionalism and which conditions dampen internal organizational conflict can provide us with a better understanding of how social movement fields evolve over time" (Kretschmer 2013: 445).

The Belo Monte study is particularly well suited to contribute to this research strand, as it provides an insight into how changes in the context conditions resulted in the fragmentation of the social movement. Moreover, it broadens the geographical range of empirical studies, given that many existing studies focus on Western industrialized countries (Balser 1997; Breines 2006; Cable and Shriver 2010; Shriver and Messer 2009). According to Foweraker, the risk of fragmentation is inherent in social movements, and even more so in Brazil, where inequality in terms of socioeconomic conditions and access to public services make it difficult for social movements to construct alliances (Foweraker 1995: 46). A case study from the Brazilian Amazon can contribute to this strand of research and extend the range of known context conditions by some unique factors.

132 Examples include Dyck and Starke (1999), Pondy (1967), and Worchel et al. (1992).

5.4.2.2 *Internal Factors Promoting Fragmentation*

Local activists in the social movement against Belo Monte are well aware that fragmentation is an inherent risk in any social movement. While praising the movement's diversity and their own efforts at creating unity, they are well aware that the different lifestyles, perspectives, behaviors, and discourses constitute a natural threat to the movement's cohesion (P53). Interviewees recount that a small number of organizations and individuals left the movement voluntarily, either because they changed their mind about the Belo Monte project (P1, P3), or because they did not agree to the working principles of the social movement (P21). The withdrawal of some participants whose beliefs and behavior did not accord with those of the movement did not cause much harm. In contrast, a divergence of the collective action frame contributed significantly to the fragmentation of the social movement. While local activists across SMOs share a common understanding of the contentious issue, they have arrived at different evaluations of the project's recent development. During the Cardoso administration, the organizations that have come to constitute the monitoring SMOs still participated in the struggle against Belo Monte because "really the project was very different" back then (P41).[133] However, with the authorization and advancement of the construction under the Lula administration, some activists started to question the social movement's strategy and prospects of success. Based on a thorough reassessment of the situation they realized that their own beliefs and strategies did no longer align with those of the social movement.

In hindsight, some activists take a very critical stance on the movement's strategy before the fragmentation.

> *"So, all this was bad because- It was always like, 'There is no Belo Monte. There is no Belo Monte.' So, the scenario with Belo Monte – no one prepared for this. The movements did not prepare; thus, when we came here a year ago, and I saw the things as they were- [...] Goodness, everyone worked to prevent Belo Monte. Only that in the meantime Belo Monte was approved, and lots of things are about to happen." (P41)*

Conflict about the status and future development of the hydropower project led to the renegotiation of the collective action frame and the development of distinct strategies for collective action. Local activists that came to join the monitoring SMOs explain that they could not ignore Belo Monte in their strategic planning (P41) although they disapprove of the project on a personal level

133 Fernando Henrique Cardoso was President of Brazil from 1 January 1995 until 1 January 2003.

(P39). They recount that the renegotiation of the collective action frame started in early 2008, at a time when the federal government started to pay attention to and invest in the region. This offered opportunities for local organizations to promote their development projects and demand the reparation of the historic exploitation and abandonment of the region (P39). As a result of the changing context conditions and the prospect of regional development, these organizations shifted their strategic focus.

> *"Then there was a complete change. On the one side, there were the indigenous, all the national organizations, all the international organizations. Their objective was only this: to stop Belo Monte. From the moment when the government started to override the licensing process and proceed to carry out the project on any account against all this here, several organizations adopted different positions. As a result, the two groups of organizations that we talked about yesterday emerged." (P37)*

While the protest SMOs continue to focus on the prevention of Belo Monte (Plan A), the monitoring SMOs place particular emphasis on the monitoring of the various development projects, negotiations with the government, and the counseling of dam affected people (Plan B). They believe that the latter activity is a key task for local civil society organizations; but one that was neglected in the early phase of the project's implementation.

> *"Who is left outside is the local population that needs more precise, more truthful guidance because the guidance by the company is never truthful, as there is an economic interest behind it. [...] If we have the information, we can teach the affected person that he has other rights." (P41)*

Interviewees from the ranks of the monitoring SMOs lament that the movement's focus on preventing Belo Monte distracted them from creating neighborhood associations and moderating the dialog between the population and the authorities. As a result, the monitoring SMOs committed themselves to providing this service to the local population after changing their strategic focus. Interestingly, interviewees give different explanations for the renegotiation of the collective action frame and the change in strategy. They either claim

1. that the fight against Belo Monte had become futile (P41), or
2. that the movement had to diversify its strategies because confronting Belo Monte did not suffice anymore (P35), or
3. that some organizations withdrew for strategic reasons (P39).

The different motives (or rather, purported explanations) for the movement's separation are interesting because they result in different perceptions of the current relationship between protest and monitoring SMOs, which will be discussed further below. In more general terms, they demonstrate how different perceptions of changing context conditions can initiate the renegotiation of the collective action frame, the development of distinct strategies for collective action, and ultimately the fragmentation of a social movement. Based on the above analysis, I propose that a divergence of the collective action frame is the most important internal factor that promoted the fragmentation of the social movement against Belo Monte.

5.4.2.3 External Factors Promoting Fragmentation

External factors promoting fragmentation refers to dynamics that are induced by external circumstances or agents. The coming into office of the Workers' Party altered the context conditions for the social movement against Belo Monte and challenged its cohesion. In addition, the government's behavior towards the local population and its financial support for individuals and certain social groups – which is largely perceived as bribery – promoted the fragmentation of the movement.

Changing Alliances

The coming into office of PT leader and former President Lula in January 2003 initiated significant changes in the context conditions for civil society in Brazil. The political agenda that the PT government pursued in the following years came as a surprise to many activists and party members (P55).

> *"This struggle subsided precisely as a result of this party, because we thought that it would be the solution for our country, and then it turned out to be the betrayal of the party's very conscience." (P31)*

Interviewees explain that social movements in Brazil experienced great confusion when the PT came into government. Given that the party is solidly based in grassroots activism, many organizations struggled to maintain their identity as civil society organizations and to differentiate themselves from those actors that came to form the government (P53). The close relationships and multiple affiliations of activists and party members blurred the boundaries between civil society and politics. Moreover, CSOs experienced a significant loss of qualified personnel who changed from the sphere of civil society into politics (P3, P31, P53).

Interviewees attribute the fragmentation of social movements in Brazil to several factors. Some of them are directly related with the change of government – for example, the quarrel between the PT and civil society, and the co-optation of activists.[134] Other factors are external but happen to fall into the same time period – for example the lack of resources and the decline in international cooperation (P3, P53). Co-optation by the government is frequently mentioned as a central reason for the demobilization of civil society in Brazil (P3, P9, P13). Interviewees claim that the allocation of resources to foundations and NGOs, which increased under the Lula administration, tied their hands and prevented them from assuming a role of opposition to the government (P29).

The changing context conditions also impacted upon the collective action against the Belo Monte Dam in Altamira and, to a lesser degree, in Belém. On the one hand, Altamira had an active civil society with a strong collective identity (P55). On the other hand, it was susceptible to conflict with the Workers' Party. The majority of the organizations and activists that initiated the collective action against hydropower projects at the Xingu in the 1980s were affiliated with the PT. Unionism was particularly strong at that time, and local organizations and unions in Altamira were keen to establish ties with the newly founded Workers' Party (P31). Relations were still close when the PT came into power. When Lula visited Altamira on 22 June 2010, he was the most popular president of the country with a 90% approval rate that, according to interviewees, allowed him to go anywhere in Brazil and demand that things be done his way (P55).[135] However, during his visit to Altamira the social movement against Belo Monte organized a protest event that attracted much attention. The movement's hostility, a quarrel about the admission of spectators to the venue, and the protest against Belo Monte – which culminated in the burning of a Lula puppet – severely disrupted the event (P13, P23) and strained the relationships of local activists. Many participants in the social movement against Belo Monte were affiliated with the Workers' Party, and some of them refused to participate in the collective action on the day of the visit (P55).

> *"This visit caused a fracture. It caused a fracture in the social movement because many people who were against Belo Monte, well, they were not against Lula. So, 'I am against a government project, but I am not against the government'. Only that, well, Lula came here and ridiculed the move-*

134 Co-optation refers to "ameliorative gestures in the direction of meeting and neutralizing the movement's criticisms" (Mauss 1975: 60). It focuses on "diluting, demobilizing, depoliticizing, and disempowering" (Coy 2013: 281) the movement by formally including it into the authority system (Coy 2013: 280–281).

135 While this figure is reported by an interviewee, it is true that Lula left office with an approval rate of 87%. His approval in the North and central East of Brazil – that is, in the Amazon region – did indeed reach 90% towards the end of his second term (Campanerut 2010).

ment against Belo Monte. So, there are people whose sense of being petista[136] *and lulista*[137] *was stronger than their sense of being against Belo Monte. At that moment, completely contradictory issues came up, so this caused a divide in the movement, and at that moment the FVPP left the Xingu Forever Alive Movement." (P37)*

Lula's visit to Altamira forced party members, who were struggling with divided loyalties between the Workers' Party and the social movement against Belo Monte, to take a stance on the contentious issue. As a result, they developed different strategies for dealing with the new situation.

Some party members felt betrayed by Lula and the Workers' Party (P31, P43). Claiming that the party changed its position regarding Belo Monte, they decided that the PT did no longer represent their interests (P45) and resigned from their party membership (P1, P27). Especially activists in leadership positions felt impelled to deliberately choose between their party membership and the social movement (P35). According to local activists, some party members were even expelled because they opposed the party's official position (P31). Other activists in Altamira and Belém remained loyal to the Workers' Party. Those activists and organizations that came to form the monitoring SMOs modified their activism and now follow what has been described as Plan B (cf. Section 5.3). By contrast, there are some former activists who gained offices in the government or within the party (P3, P31, P37, P43). While some of these people remain quiet with respect to Belo Monte (P9), others have started to promote the project (P1, P53).

Conflicts over divided loyalties not only affected the social movement on the organizational level in that they induced the fragmentation into protest and monitoring SMOs. The fact that the Belo Monte project is being implemented by a supposedly left-wing government, which was expected to put social change into practice, also caused personal disappointment with the party and its leadership (P27, P55).

"So, Belo Monte represents two things: on the one hand, it represents a grievous blow against social movements, environmental movements, and indigenous peoples along the Xingu, who resisted for thirty years, and against a government that was elected with the votes of social movements and that called itself an ally of the people of the Xingu. So, the implementation of the hydropower project is a hefty blow because the peo-

136 A petista is a partisan of the Workers' Party (PT in its Portuguese abbreviation).

137 A lulista is a supporter of former President Lula.

ples of the Xingu voted for Lula because they believed he would not build the hydropower plant. So, this is a grievous blow." (P1)

Local activists lament that the PT of all parties was the one that reconsidered the implementation of hydropower projects – despite having fought the exploitation of the environment alongside civil society organizations during its early years (P31, P35, P45). Beyond their disillusion with the party's political U-turn, some activists feel betrayed by Lula on a personal level and claim that the former president deliberately lied to them (P45).

> *"Here [in Altamira, I.P.], the resistance against Belo Monte identified itself with the PT, or the PT identified itself with the resistance against Belo Monte. That was until Lula took office. When we found out that Lula had changed his mind, we were totally disillusioned. Oh my God, how could he do this?" (P45)*

Interviewees criticize that Lula of all people was the one who authorized the Belo Monte project, given that he had shown interest in environmental issues and defended the rights of workers in the past (P27). Interviewees describe Lula as a very charismatic person, a leader, and a symbol of the social struggle in Brazil (P35, P55). Several members of the social movement had the opportunity to meet him personally and to bring forward their criticism of Belo Monte. On these occasions, the former president promised to continue the dialogue, to compensate the affected people, to avoid past mistakes, and to only authorize the project if it was to everyone's advantage (P45). Yet, over time local activists realized that Lula was not going to keep his promises and that the government was not interested in any dialog with the population (P45).

To sum up, the coming into office of the Workers' Party had repercussions on the social movement against Belo Monte – both on the organizational and the individual level. When the PT changed its position regarding Belo Monte, local activists had to choose between their loyalty to the party and their opposition to the Belo Monte project. While many people toe the party line thinking that all questions are being answered (P45), the protest SMOs believe that the PT administration is fomenting conflict among activists and bribing the local population into acceptance.

Bribery and Discord

Local movement participants frequently denounce the efforts of the federal government and Norte Energia to create discord among the local people and particularly among the participants in the social movement. From their point of view, the financial support for the region and the employment opportunities offered by Norte Energia form part of the strategy to silence the opponents of Belo Monte – preferably those who are opinion leaders in their family or community (P25, P29, P31).

> *"And the proof of this is that now they caught some leaders and bought their plots for X thousand. Why? To shut the mouth of the population. It was the first- one of the first acts of strong arbitrariness [...] No government should buy the dignity of a people. So, by buying the dignity of that leadership, they were buying the dignity of the people whom that leadership represented. That way they managed to intrude into some communities, to manipulate them for peanuts." (P27)*

Some people who came to consider the project inevitable and were afraid of ending up "floating in the water" accepted the compensation and stopped fighting Belo Monte (P13). As local activists acknowledge, poor people often lack the capacities and the courage to participate in the struggle and resist the authorities (P25, P31, P47). Moreover, many traditional peoples and settlers in the rural areas around Altamira have made the experience that development follows a cyclical pattern, and consider the Belo Monte project yet another cycle that they have to endure.

> *"And for most fishers and farmers it is not interesting, because they have experienced everything that I told you about these cycles, and they managed to get through these cycles, so they think that they will also get through this one, but they still did not realize that this cycle is the worst of all that we have had [...]" (P25)*

Indeed, some people wait without taking any action for the authorities to fulfill their promises (P43). While activists are frustrated about the population's apathetic behavior and failure to take action (P35), they also understand that the people's focus on material benefits offered by the authorities is a direct result of the abandonment of the region (P13).

> *"We say: He changed sides and so on. But in fact it is a consequence of the project itself on the people. What can you say? The guy has always been hit hard, so to speak. When someone comes and offers something to him, will you take it from him? Do you understand? That is it, this is difficult. Very difficult. The indigenous peoples and some of the riverine people changed sides precisely because of the situation of extreme poverty, in which they live." (P55)*

The government's strategy of buying the population's consent affects various social groups; however, interviewees claim that the indigenous are hit particularly hard. From their point of view, the provision of staple food and other short-lived items to indigenous communities is a deliberate strategy to break their resistance (P16,P23, P37, P47).

> *"And today the indigenous peoples are being treated as puppets – that is, as marionettes – in the hands of the government. This means, they do what the government wants. They do not react. They are silent – because of what? They are being manipulated, they are being co-opted for the purpose of preventing that there be an active indigenous voice in the struggle against Belo Monte." (P19)*

Local activists assess that the federal government's co-optation strategy has created conflict between different social groups and played indigenous communities off against each other (P29, P35). Diverging beliefs and interests, on the one hand, and the rapid and uncomplicated provision of financial and material resources, on the other hand, have motivated individuals to found new communities for the purpose of receiving additional money and goods (P29, P35, P53). Some indigenous leaders are able to convince their fellows of the necessity to remain independent in their economic activities in general, and regarding food supply in particular. Yet, other leaders fall for the offers of Norte Energia and neglect investments in infrastructure and production (P29). This short-term orientation causes concern among indigenous and non-indigenous activists who fear that the dependence of entire communities upon provisions by Norte Energia creates a state of dependence that will ultimately destroy the native cultures and lifestyles beyond recovery (P29, P35, P55).

> *"There is a new way of defeating the indigenous peoples, the* auricide *in addition to genocide and ethnocide. It kills the culture and the community organization of the indigenous with money. And this assault may be worse, and more subtle, and unabashed because it kills the culture and the social organizations of the indigenous peoples under the pretence of solidarity, and under the cover of compensation to mitigate the impacts and negative effects of Belo Monte. I would never say that the indigenous are in favor of Belo Monte. After having lived at the margins of society, enduring hardship, and being rejected by the majority society for centuries, they are suddenly in the spotlight and presented with all kinds of presents and benefits. Who will advise them not to accept these benefits? Only that behind them, there is a system, a strategy to break the resistance of the indigenous peoples." (P45)*

According to local activists, many communities fail to understand the process and to trust in the intermediators because they are overwhelmed by the sudden provision of policies and resources (P37, P43). Hence, interviewees are concerned that by the time communities understand that they have been betrayed it will be too late to preserve their culture and lifestyle (P43).

In a nutshell, the coming into office of the Workers' Party promoted the fragmentation of the social movement against Belo Monte because it altered the context of its activities. Interviewees claim that the movement was challenged by changing alliances, co-optation, the loss of qualified personnel, bribery, discord, and resentments against the PT and its leadership because of the party's political U-turn. The changing context conditions are an external factor; however, their impact on the social movement resulted from framing processes or, more specifically, negotiations among SMOs about the meaning of these developments. Eventually, the changing context conditions contributed to the development of diverging frames and the fragmentation of the social movement.

5.4.2.4 Factions and Movement Boundaries

As discussed in Chapter 2, the delineation of movement boundaries is an integral part of collective identity and an important aspect of identity work. It aims to create internal cohesion and a sense of we-ness inside the movement while at the same time differentiating it from other groups (Rucht 2002: 331).

Movement participants in Altamira have different opinions about the fragmentation of the social movement against Belo Monte and about the current boundaries between the protest and monitoring SMOs, which emerged from this fragmentation. Interviewees from the ranks of the protest SMOs harshly criticize the negotiation strategy of the monitoring SMOs. From their point of view, the fight for mitigation, compensation, and the recognition of affected people is not consistent with the objectives of the Xingu Vivo Movement (P19) because it requires an organization to have accepted the construction of the Belo Monte Dam as a fact (P43). Although many activists that are nowadays affiliated with the monitoring SMOs are former participants in the social movement in Altamira, they are said to have abandoned the strict opposition to Belo Monte (P19, P51).

> *"So, many leaders – including leaders that were part of the Xingu Forever Alive Movement in the past – withdrew from the movement because they were commanded by the government. They were either given an office or*

a commission, or they were pressured by the government party." (P3; also see P31)

Members of the protest SMOs claim that several organizations and activists gave in to the pressure of the federal government (P1) or confirmed their loyalty to the PT because they were afraid of losing or missing out on potential benefits (P13). Interviewees are especially critical of former leaders of the social movement of whom they expect high moral integrity. From their point of view, there is no excuse and justification for activists and organizations that remain quiet in the face of injustice (P9). From the protest SMOs point of view, the Foundation has basically become a government agency (P19, P31) that supports the construction of the Belo Monte Dam (P27) and whose close relationship with the Workers' Party hampers its participation in the Xingu Vivo Movement (P37). As a consequence, members of the Xingu Vivo considered it necessary to dissociate themselves from the Foundation (P27).

Local activists who participate in the monitoring SMOs counter the above argument and claim that their change in strategy demonstrates their sense of reality and their responsibility for the local population. These activists emphasize that society has to control the government at all times and that the local people rely on their support and guidance (P41). While the protest SMOs refuse to participate in the steering committees, the monitoring SMOs believe that civil society organizations should accompany the implementation of Belo Monte.

"The dissent that we have takes the form of- One group thinks that we do not have to participate in anything, in the struggle for the conditions, in the struggle to monitor the whole situation. [...] I am one of those who believe that it is better to monitor it with our strong position against Belo Monte." (P35)

Interviewees from the ranks of the monitoring SMOs emphasize that they have done their part in the struggle against Belo Monte, and refuse to accept responsibility for the advancement of the project (P35).

Interestingly, the monitoring SMOs' assessment of the protest SMOs is much more positive than vice versa. While the monitoring SMOs claim that the Xingu Vivo Movement is a more radical actor that has a different perspective on the conflict (P41), they acknowledge that the fight against Belo Monte is valid and deserves respect (P39, P41). They further agree with the protest SMOs that public mobilization, protest, and denunciation of malpractice are important instruments for civil society to influence political decision making (P35). Activists from the monitoring SMOs believe that the revision of the EIA, the elaboration of the PDRS Xingu and the PBA, and the definition of conditions were direct results of the continuous resistance of the local movement (P41).

> *"There are still a range of organizations that bear the flag of opposition. And is this wrong? No. It is all right. It is because of this positioning that the consortium, Norte Energia itself, seeks to make corrections that may [...] reduce the social, cultural, environmental impacts." (P39)*

Nonetheless, interviewees from the ranks of the monitoring SMOs believe that the situation has changed with the advancement of the construction, and that it is no longer reasonable to fight for the prevention of the Belo Monte project (P41). From their point of view, the protest SMOs have lost influence in recent years because they were not wiling to adapt to "an existing reality" (P41).

Since the separation of the protest and the monitoring SMOs, the relationship between the members of both factions has been difficult. Given the long-term dedication of these activists to social struggles in Altamira and to the fight against Belo Monte, the emotional aspects of the fragmentation should not be neglected. Some interviewees denounce individual members of the Foundation as traitors because of their loyalty to the PT (P27). Other members of Xingu Vivo seek to keep up the dialog with the Foundation and the other monitoring SMOs despite the dispute (P31, P43). Some interviewees take conciliatory steps by claiming that the personal conviction of activists is more important that their affiliation with civil society organizations (P9).

Hence, cooperation – especially on the personal level – is not ruled out, and individual activists sometimes participate in the activities of other SMOs (P13, P53). Interviewees report that meetings across the two factions of the movement do take place in situations where their interests and objectives cross.

> *"So, depending on the issue there is a meeting of various groups for an activity, and in order to prepare this activity you have preliminary meetings, exchange of e-mails and so on to prepare this. So, I think this is wonderful on the one hand, and confusing on the other hand. It is wonderful that, depending on the issue you reunite various people and various organizations for a purpose; so, it is dispersed, it is very diffuse, and depending on the organizer, you reunite many people for a common activity; and this is complex, because every one has a different interest and these interests cross at times." (P37)*

While cooperation between activists and organizations across the factions of the social movement remains possible, diverging understandings of the current situation and different interests hamper the development of a common plan of the social movement against Belo Monte (P37).

To sum up, the protest SMOs claim that any person who disapproves of hydropower projects at the Xingu River has a moral obligation to publicly denounce Belo Monte. From their point of view, a person's decision to accept Belo Monte as a reality and to adopt a negotiation strategy with the government (Plan B) constitutes betrayal on the social movement in Altamira. In contrast, the monitoring SMOs claim that opposition to Belo Monte can also mean to critically evaluate and monitor the implementation process and to demand ameliorative measures. Hence, the two factions differ in their evaluation of the appropriateness and normative rightness of a person's decision to follow Plan B. The decision between loyalty to the PT and loyalty to the social movement against Belo Monte, which many local activists faced after the Lula administration took office, is by no means a pragmatic one, as it touches upon a person's self-conception as a party member and as a civil society activist. Questions arise about what behavior the two factions expect from the members of the social movement against Belo Monte. While the protest SMOs claim that silence means consent, the monitoring SMOs believe that their negotiation strategy constitutes a form of resistance. Hence, on an analytical level we can distinguish between an outspoken, public opposition and a silent opposition against Belo Monte, and between an outspoken, public support of Belo Monte, a silent support, and an indifferent stance connected to positive expectations about Belo Monte.

5.4.3 *Preliminary Conclusion*

The above analysis of movement dynamics has shown that internal and external factors play an important role in the development and maintenance of movement cohesion. The movement's efforts to create a collective identity and a comprehensive diagnostic frame that resonates with large segments of society contributed significantly to movement cohesion. This finding confirms the second sensitizing concept, which proposes that collective identities and collective action frames are central to the successful mobilization of actors and the maintenance of movement cohesion in the social movement against the Belo Monte Dam (cf. Chapter 3). The analysis confirms that local people were able to link their individual understandings of the conflict to the movement's collective action frame by abstracting from their individual experiences, interests, and concerns. Moreover, the movement established working principles that facilitate the cooperation between SMOs. Openness and internal autonomy create a sense of we-ness among the very heterogeneous members of the movement. External autonomy and independence from the state and the economy ensure the movement's differentiation from third parties. While formal leadership is a controversial issue, there are some leaders who are widely respected for their abilities and their moral and symbolic meaning. The analysis also shows that a founding myth can contribute to the collective identity of a social movement. However, it has to be deliberately created and defined as a significant and symbolic event through identity work and framing processes.

As regards the external factors, a common destiny and a common enemy further contribute to movement cohesion. Uncertainty about the future helps people recognize what they have in common. Moreover, activists across SMOs agree to address their claims to the authorities and the construction industry. Interestingly, interviewees claim that their enemy is not the PT government but its attitude with respect to the Belo Monte Dam. This differentiation allows individuals to maintain their party membership, while at the same time opposing the Belo Monte project. The existence of a common purpose is ambiguous in the social movement, and local activists name different objectives as their supposedly "common" purpose. I propose that these objectives are relevant in different contexts and with respect to different planning intervals, and do therefore not imply that the social movement lacks a common purpose. Rather, the existence of diverse but supposedly shared objectives mirrors the strong heterogeneity of the movement and the thematic scope of the collective action frame.

The fragmentation of the social movement was caused by a combination of internal and external factors. Inside the movement, a divergence of the collective action frame, which resulted from the advancement of the construction works, contributed to its fragmentation. Disagreement about the status and future development of Belo Monte induced the renegotiation of the collective action frame and the development of distinct strategies for collective action. As a result, the movement split into the protest SMOs, which seek to prevent the hydropower project (Plan A), and the monitoring SMOs, which monitor the various development projects and negotiate with the government (Plan B).

Regarding the external factors promoting fragmentation, the coming into office of the PT administration significantly altered the context conditions for collective action against Belo Monte. Activists across SMOs consider it a stab in the back that the PT of all parties decided to exploit the hydroelectric potential of the Xingu River. Interviewees affiliated with the protest SMOs feel betrayed, not only by the PT and former President Lula but also by those comrades who quit the struggle against Belo Monte in the pursuit of benefits and opportunities. The conflict over loyalties strained historic relationships between activists and severely damaged Altamira's civil society. Moreover, local activists denounce the authorities' strategy of creating discord among the local people and bribing the population into acceptance and quiescence. They are particularly upset about the so-called emergency plan for indigenous communities, which from their point of view threatens to destroy the native cultures and lifestyles beyond recovery.

As regards the relationship between the two factions and the boundaries of the social movement, relations between the protest and the monitoring SMOs are strained – both on the personal and the organizational level. The protest SMOs are highly critical of the monitoring SMOs, claiming that the latter have betrayed the social movement and its objectives. From their point of view, negotiations with the government and participation in the steering committee constitute consent with the Belo Monte project. In contrast, the monitoring SMOs claim that their fight for mitigation measures and the fulfillment of the conditions proves their sense of reality and responsibility. Despite the conflict, intermittent cooperation across SMOs remains generally possible.

6 Evaluation, Conclusion and Outlook

The objective of this study was to analyze how collective identities and collective action frames have contributed to the persistence of the collective action and the maintenance of movement cohesion in the social movement against the Belo Monte Dam. To that end, the study was embedded in social movement research and adopted the collective identity approach and the framing approach as its theoretical perspectives. The empirical question required a research design that sought to uncover the deeper meanings that activists attribute to the conflict over Belo Monte and to their collective action. In order to obtain personal accounts of the individuals' identities, motives, and objectives, primary data was collected through semistructured interviews with activists in Altamira and Belém. Of the 28 activist interviews, 22 were transcribed and analyzed in detail by means of a combined top-down and bottom-up procedure based on the grounded theory methodology. Accordingly, concepts were developed from the empirical material and elaborated through constant comparison, first, with other concepts derived from the data and, second, with central theoretical concepts from the literature.

The in-depth analysis revealed that the election and coming into office of the Workers' Party, which is solidly based in grassroots organizations, altered the context conditions for civil society in Brazil. This had severe repercussions for the social movement against Belo Monte. Movement cohesion was challenged when the newly elected PT administration ordered the implementation of the Belo Monte project – hence, a change in context conditions. Eventually, the movement entered into a process of fragmentation. Throughout this study, I have advanced the following central argument:

> **The election and coming into office of the Workers' Party, which is solidly based in grassroots organizations, altered the context conditions for civil society in Brazil. It had severe repercussions for the social movement against Belo Monte in that it induced a divergence of the collective action frame and an identity crisis among activists, which in turn resulted in the fragmentation of the social movement.**

I argue that the factors promoting movement cohesion and fragmentation can be divided into internal factors (that is, factors arising from internal movement dynamics that can be instrumentalized by activists) and external factors (that is, factors arising outside the social movement). Inside the movement, the renegotiation of the collective action frame challenged movement cohesion. In terms of external factors, changing alliances, bribery, and discord contributed to the fragmentation of the social movement.

The analysis in Chapter 5 was deliberately done from the perspective of the interviewees. In contrast, this chapter takes the empirical findings to a higher level of abstraction and evaluates them in view of social movement theory and existing empirical research. Moreover, I assess my previous assumptions, which I disclosed in the sensitizing concepts (cf. Chapter 3), in terms of their relevance and adequateness, and discuss the applicability of Western theories and concepts in non-Western case studies. Finally, I evaluate the methods and procedures applied in this study and give an outlook for future research.

6.1 Evaluation of Empirical Findings

In the following, I present five findings (F1-F5) that I derived from the investigated case through an in-depth analysis that focused on the development of concepts and categories and the analysis of the relationships between them. These findings abstract from the empirical data and contribute to several theoretical debates. More precisely, they improve our understanding of

1. the general dynamics in the processes of framing and identity construction,
2. the influence of the regional context on political mobilization, and
3. the applicability of Western theories in non-Western case studies.

The findings have been formulated as hypotheses because they are meant to inform future research and be tested in other empirical cases with a view to verifying their value as building blocks of social movement theory. Some of the findings are not news to social movement scholars; however, they substantiate and refine existing research. Other findings – most notably, the fragmentation of the social movement – are indeed unexpected and have implications for future research.

6.1.1 Identity

The development of a collective identity in the social movement against Belo Monte has been built largely upon local activists' long-term personal relationships, close cooperation, shared objectives, and mutual success in the fight for civil rights in Altamira in the 1980s and 1990s. The social movement deliberately developed a collective identity through processes of identity work in order to create a sense of we-ness among movement participants and to enable the local population to identify with the movement. I refer to this collective identity as the Amazonian Identity, thus using an existing term from cultural studies.[138] The Amazonian Identity builds upon the personal and social identities of the local population. These are characterized by a strong geographical and time component, and make reference to the unique region and to the centuries-old history of its indigenous and traditional inhabitants. Moreover, they are informed by a sense of neglect, depreciation, and discrimination relative to the Brazilian majority population. The purpose of the Amazonian Identity is to mobilize hitherto unmobilized segments of society by creating a sense of we-ness. It enables the population to share in with the beliefs and interests of the social movement and to identify with the affected people in Altamira and the adjacent municipalities. Moreover, it allows activists to reconcile the conflict between being from the forest but leading a modern lifestyle in the city. Hence, identities play an important role in the Belo Monte conflict, as proposed in the second sensitizing concept (cf. Chapter 3). The identity of native peoples in the Brazilian Amazon has also been discussed by Lúcio Flávio Pinto who emphasizes the population's close connection with their natural environment and their estrangement from the majority society – thus confirming the results of this study.[139]

In addition, the analysis of identities shows that the cleavages in the social movement do not necessarily follow organizational lines. Individuals who oppose the Belo Monte Dam and support the fight against the project are integrated into the social movement regardless of their institutional affiliation(s). This finding is consistent with recent research by Donatella della Porta (2005), Dieter Rucht (2011b), and Gregory Maney (2012), among others, who suggest that social movements are increasingly relying on "tolerant identities" (Della Porta 2005). While homogeneous movements used to build strong identities in the past, contemporary social movements are characterized by stronger heterogeneity and weaker identities. These movements offer a range of opportunities for participation, and value ideological plurality and internal autonomy (Della Porta 2005: 178; Rucht 2011b: 78; also see Maney 2012: 192). According to Rucht, tolerant identities are characterized by (1) vague slogans and objectives,

138 This strand of research analyzes, for example, the construction of an Amazonian regional identity by musicians, dancers, listeners, and culture brokers (Lamen 2013), the influence of audiovisual media on the construction of an Amazonian Identity (Cordovil 2012), or the construction and display of Amazonian Identity through theatrical productions (Castro 2012).

139 Pinto is a sociologist and journalist born in Pará state who reports relentlessly on the notorious disregard of social and environmental rights in Amazonia.

(2) a lack of representative bodies and steering committees, (3) the avoiding of majority decisions, and (4) a preference for flexible collective action frames (Rucht 2011b: 82). In the social movement against Belo Monte the following factors enable the participation of diverse people and organizations:

1. the deliberate creation of an inclusive collective identity;
2. the development of a mechanism for unanimous decision making;
3. working principles that guarantee openness, respect for otherness, and internal autonomy; and
4. a comprehensive collective action frame.

As suggested by Rucht, these factors are an asset rather than a deficit in view of the movement's context conditions. However, in line with della Porta's research, this movement structure requires a significant level of trust among activists and efforts towards maintaining their commitment over the long term (cf. Della Porta 2005: 178).

The analysis of the social movement against Belo Monte also confirms research by Cristina Flesher Fominaya who suggests that shared emotional experiences are one central mechanism among others in the process of collective identity formation (Flesher Fominaya 2010b: 380). Building on her argument, I propose that the definition of a founding myth could be one example of a shared emotional experience that contributes to the development of a collective identity. As the analysis demonstrated, the incident of the indigenous female warrior Tuíra raising her machete against the former director of Eletronorte in 1989 became an important point of reference for the social movement. It is repeatedly framed as a significant event and created a sense of belonging that is effective over time and across generations. Abstracting from the specific case, I formulate the following finding that should be verified in future research:

> ***Finding (F1):*** *If an incident of collective action is deliberately framed as the beginning of a social movement, it can turn into a founding myth and contribute to collective identity formation based on its shared emotional value.*

6.1.2 Framing

The collective action frame of the social movement against Belo Monte deliberately builds upon shared understandings of persistent problems in the region while at the same time identifying a large array of topics that resonate with different segments of society. One central aspect is the identification of the hydropower project as representative of the prevalent economic model and a symbol of the persistent exploitation and domination of Amazonia. As the frame addresses people's grievances and alludes to their personal and social identities, it provides a rationale for the local population's participation in the social movement. Thus, the social movement communicates a consistent and credible collective action frame that achieves salience through its centrality, experiential commensurability, and narrative fidelity (cf. Chapter 2). At the same time, the interaction and mutual influence between the collective action frame, the regional dynamics, and the identities of the local population make the collective action frame unique.

As the analysis of movement dynamics shows, framing processes have a number of material and immaterial requirements. They demand people to (1) become aware of their problems, (2) abstract from specific problems to broader problems, and (3) articulate them to others. The fulfillment of these conditions is not self-evident in Amazonia; however, Xingu Vivo and the Metropolitan Committee consider themselves platforms for dialog and interaction that have been able to meet the requirements and thus foster collective action. On the other hand, the study shows that framing processes play an important role in the fragmentation of the social movement thus contributing to the literature on demobilization processes. Robert Benford (1997) and Lisa Kowalchuk (2005) criticize that too little attention has been paid to the dynamics of framing processes; for example, how they "can spark or sustain collective action, or conversely, contribute to its collapse" (Kowalchuk 2005: 241). The analysis of the fragmentation of the social movement against Belo Monte contributes to filling this research gap. I propose that after the election of the PT and with the advancement of the infrastructure project, activists came to argue about (1) the status of Belo Monte, (2) the social movement's role and influence in the conflict, and (3) the advantages and disadvantages of the mitigation measures. The protest and monitoring SMOs provided diverging interpretations of these issues and developed different strategies, tactics, attitudes, and forms of dealing with third parties.

6.1.3 Cohesion

The objective of this study was to analyze how collective identities and collective action frames contribute to the persistence of the collective action and to the maintenance of movement cohesion in the social movement against the Belo Monte Dam. I argue that both dynamics promote movement cohesion by establishing a strong and multidimensional link between existing regional dynamics and the planned implementation of a hydropower plant. The social movement starts from the predisposition of some local individuals for collective action, the foundations of which lie in the educational work of the Catholic Church. The movement alludes to existing identities and creates a new collective identity by acknowledging and promoting the beliefs, values, rights, and claims of the local population. It further establishes a link between the existing regional dynamics and the Belo Monte project by demonstrating how the project intensifies existing threats and needs. In doing so, the social movement motivates local people to participate in the collective action against Belo Monte. The cohesion of the social movement was promoted by internal factors (namely, identity work, working principles, leadership, framing process, and a founding myth) and external factors (namely, a common destiny and a common enemy).

Pearlman proposes that leadership and a collective purpose are among the most important factors that facilitate cooperation between SMOs (Pearlman 2011: 9). However, local activists disagree about the role of leadership and the content of a common purpose in the social movement against Belo Monte. Their concepts of leadership and their understandings of a common purpose are discussed in more detail in the following sections.

6.1.3.1 Leadership

The analysis shows that local activists disagree about the existence and the role of leaders in the social movement against Belo Monte. Leadership as such is disputed, first, because the public appearance of leaders may put these individuals at risk, and, second, because leadership may counteract pluralism in a social movement. In contrast, Pearlman suggests that pluralism needs to be governed in order to generate cooperative behavior. She implies that for a movement to persist in the long term, there need to be leaders who exercise internal command and control (cf. Pearlman 2011: 11). Indeed, the social movement against Belo Monte has created rules and mechanisms in order to use the pluralism and diversity in a constructive way; however, many interviewees refuse to attribute this to leadership and speak of collective efforts instead.

The skepticism of some movement participants does, however, not imply the absence of leadership in the social movement against Belo Monte. Interviewees agree on a small number of individuals that enjoy authority across SMOs based on their exceptional dedication, leadership skills, symbolic meaning, experience and historic legitimacy, integrity and courage, and their intellectual capacity. Interestingly, the individuals that are identified by others as leaders do not claim leadership nor sole responsibility for the collective action. They rather speak of themselves as fulfilling certain roles within the movement in cooperation with other movement participants.

This understanding is consistent with Dieter Rucht's (2013) concept of key figures (*Schlüsselfiguren*) in social movements. According to Rucht, the term leader implies power over and dependence of followers and subordinate people, while at the same time it remains imprecise with respect to people's functions in a social movement (Rucht 2013: 32). He proposes to evaluate leadership on the basis of two dimensions: the sphere of influence (internal vs. external) and the logic of action (instrumental vs. expressive). Based on these two dimensions of leadership, Rucht differentiates four types of key figures with different functions (Rucht 2012: 110, 2013: 34):

1. Organizer (internal focus, instrumental function)
2. Motivator (internal focus, expressive function)
3. Strategist (external focus, instrumental function)
4. President (external focus, expressive function)

Rucht's typology is suitable for describing leadership in the social movement against Belo Monte because most of the people who are identified as leaders act first and foremost internally. They are very modest and focus on organizing the collective action and empowering the local population to express their demands. In terms of Rucht's typology, these people act as organizers and motivators within the social movement. Moreover, analyzing leaders along these dimensions provides an insight into the self-perception of leaders in the movement and the relationship between leaders and followers. In view of the specific context conditions in the Belo Monte case and the interviewees' perception of leadership in the social movement, I propose the following argument that should be tested in other case studies:

> ***Finding (F2):*** *If the participants in a social movement are threatened with repression and prosecution, they are likely to share leadership among several people by focusing on key functions (cf. Rucht 2013) rather than formal leadership in a social movement.*

6.1.3.2 Common Purpose?

The existence of a common purpose in the social movement against Belo Monte is questionable. According to Pearlman, the absence of common purpose poses a threat to movement cohesion, as a "[c]ollective purpose is the ultimate guarantor of a movement's cohesion" (Pearlman 2011: 10). In contrast to Pearlman,

I argue that it is necessary to differentiate between a movement's instrumental goals and ultimate objectives when assessing movement cohesion.

The social movement against Belo Monte split into two factions as the result of a renegotiation of the collective action frame. Despite their shared opposition to the Belo Monte project, they follow different strategies for confronting it. This raises the question as to whether the fragmentation resulted in two factions within one movement or in two separate movements. I argue that an evaluation of this question ultimately depends on whether the two factions pursue a common long-term objective. The daily work of the monitoring SMOs focuses on the implementation of small-scale development projects in Altamira and the adjacent municipalities. By taking advantage of the increased government attention and allocation of resources, they seek to promote the development of the region – knowing that both the attention and the resources will decrease after Belo Monte is completed. In contrast, the protest SMOs were established for the purpose of uniting, coordinating, and expanding the collective action against Belo Monte. While the Xingu Vivo Movement emerged from the MDTX, Xingu Vivo does not carry out their own development projects – their daily work is the fight against Belo Monte. As a consequence of their focus on the prevention of Belo Monte, these organizations refuse to cooperate or negotiate with the authorities.

The question remains whether preventing Belo Monte is the ultimate objective of the protest SMOs – their raison d'être – or merely an instrumental goal that is supposed to contribute to the achievement of the ultimate objective. When considering the interviewee's definition of Plan A, one could easily get the impression that the objective of preventing Belo Monte has become an independent objective, detached from the MDTX's initial struggle for a differentiated development along the Trans-Amazon Highway and the Xingu. Nonetheless, most interviewees integrate the Belo Monte project into a much larger context that comprises historic and current experiences of exploitation and domination. Moreover, local activists in Altamira and Belém derive their identities as activists as well as their objectives and strategies for collective action from the context conditions of the Belo Monte project. Therefore, a differentiated development – based on respect and dignity, rights and justice, and the preservation of nature and traditional cultures – remains the single most important objective for activists in the region. While the instrumental goal of preventing Belo Monte has temporarily assumed a central position within the collective action frame of the protest SMOs, I still consider it an instrumental goal. It is supposed to contribute to the achievement of the ultimate objective, which is a differentiated development of the region. Given that the protest SMOs and the monitoring

SMOs still work towards the same long-term objective, I argue that the two factions still constitute a common movement for development – despite their separation in the course of the collective action against Belo Monte. The existence of one social movement against Belo Monte, which fulfills the criteria established in Chapter 2, confirms the first sensitizing concept (cf. Chapter 3).

6.1.4 Fragmentation

The cohesion of the social movement against Belo Monte was challenged when the newly elected PT administration ordered the implementation of the Belo Monte project. The factors that promoted its fragmentation can be divided into internal factors (namely, an internal divergence of the collective action frame) and external factors (namely, changing alliances, bribery, and discord). In terms of the internal factors, the advancement of the constructions and the firm stance of the PT government induced the renegotiation of the collective action frame among social movement participants. Regarding the external factors, the fact that a supposedly left-wing government authorized and initiated the implementation of the project severely strained the collective identity of the social movement and the institutional and personal relationships therein. Moreover, local activists claim that the government adopted a strategy of bribery and discord in order to silence the opponents of Belo Monte and disperse the collective action. Based on the analysis, I propose the following relationship between deprivation and willingness to participate in collective action that should be verified in future research:

> ***Finding (F3):*** *If a local population has experienced neglect and deprivation over a long period of time, it becomes susceptible to manipulation and bribery and more difficult to mobilize for collective action.*

The analysis further provides insights into the relationships between existing theoretical concepts and the core categories that emerged from the primary data. It shows that the collective identity and the collective action frame are closely interlinked with the regional dynamics that form the context conditions for the Belo Monte project. Activists of the monitoring SMOs claim to have reconsidered the meaning and implications of the project against the background of the region's socioeconomic deprivation and their own responsibilities towards the local population. Their self-perception and motivation for collective action (identity) coupled with their understanding of the conflict and their development concept for the region (framing) induced them to negotiate with the authorities for the purpose of securing regional development. In contrast, activists of the protest SMOs seek to retain internal consistency in terms of their self-perception and motivation for collective action (identity) and refuse to reconsider their understanding of the conflict (framing). The interaction between movement dynamics and regional dynamics also becomes apparent in the behavior of the local population. Interviewees claim that people conceded to the government because of the historic exploitation and underdevelopment of the region, and their experiences of dependence and lack of self-efficacy. These regional dynamics have an impact on the activists' personal identities, their motivation for collective action, and the framing of the Belo Monte conflict.

In this sense, the Belo Monte study contributes to the existing literature about factions and factionalism. I agree with Balser (1997) that "conflict leading to schism is a dynamic process that develops over time in response to multiple factors" (Balser 1997: 212). The authorities' strategy of bribing opponents and creating discord among the local population had a direct effect on the social movement against Belo Monte in that it challenged its cohesion. The political U-turn of the Workers' Party had an indirect effect on the movement in that it influenced identity work and framing processes – thus contributing substantially to the fragmentation of the movement. However, the emergence of two factions also shows that changes in context conditions require interpretation and framing. This insight strengthens my argument that framing plays an important role in the Belo Monte conflict, and it contributes to verifying the second sensitizing concept (cf. Chapter 3).

Kretschmer (2013) further argues that movements split into factions when a subgroup develops a distinct collective identity that distinguishes it from the rest of the movement (Kretschmer 2013: 443). I propose that a divergence of the collective action frame plays an equally important role in the fragmentation process. While movement participants from both factions share a collective identity and continue to fight for a common ultimate objective, they have developed different instrumental goals with respect to the Belo Monte conflict. I argue that the divergence of the collective action frame was an important driver of fragmentation in the social movement against Belo Monte.

6.1.5 *Social Movements in Brazil*

Beyond the investigation of the social movement against Belo Monte, this study contributes to our understanding of regional dynamics and their effects on political mobilization. It provides an insight into movement dynamics that occur under specific context conditions such as strong heterogeneity, complex socioeconomic conditions, and a sensitive ecosystem. Hence, the results are informative for the analysis of similar occurrences of collective action in other Latin American countries.

As the analysis shows, the demand for human and civil rights is a central issue in the collective action against the Belo Monte Dam. This finding is consistent with existing research (see, for example, Alvarez et al. 1998: 12). Some local people believe that they are not entitled to claim their rights vis-à-vis the government. The vast majority of interviewees report that they were educated about their rights and mobilized into collective action in the realm of the CEBs. Based on this grassroots activism a vivid civil society developed, and was already well organized when the fist plans about hydropower projects at the Xingu River became public. This finding can be generalized as follows in order to inform future research:

> ***Finding (F4):*** *Collective action against large infrastructure projects in Amazonia is more likely if a functioning civil society – that is, a general awareness of rights and demands, civil society organizations, and existing relationships between activists and CSOs – is already present and comparable experiences from nearby places, such as a comparable infrastructure project in the same region, exist.*

Another issue that is important in the context of collective action in Latin America and with respect to the applicability of Western concepts in non-Western case studies, is the relationship between civil society organizations and the state. Local activists in Altamira tend to talk about former President Lula as if he was an acquaintance of theirs. Against this background, local activists consider the licensing of the Belo Monte Dam and the start of the construction works as a stab in the back. They feel betrayed on a personal level and ask how Lula could do this to them. Hence, I argue that the PT's political U-turn does not only constitute a change in context conditions. Rather, the new positioning of the PT impacts upon the identities and the self-conceptions of PT members who participate(d) in the social movement against Belo Monte. The ideological divide that emerged between Brazil's civil society and the PT during its first administration has also been identified and analyzed by Kathryn Hochstetler (2008) and Harry Vanden (2014). The present study takes the analyses further by emphasizing the dynamics of identity work and the changing relationship between CSOs and the PT in the years of the first Lula administration.

A central aspect in the Belo Monte diagnostic frame is the controversial implementation of the project. Local activists criticize the attitude and behavior of the authorities and Norte Energía towards the social movement and the local population. They are particularly concerned about the persecution of the movement and the violation of law. Interviewees explicitly question whether it is possible to implement such a large infrastructure project in a democratic way. Based on this argument, I propose the following relationship between a project's characteristics and the authorities' strategy:

> ***Finding (F5):*** *The greater the social and environmental consequences of an infrastructure project and the weaker the enforcement of human and civil rights in the affected region, the more likely it is that the authorities will resort to authoritarian measures to counteract public protest and accomplish the infrastructure project.*

The analysis of the social movement against Belo Monte also sheds light on the consultation of indigenous communities regarding infrastructure projects that impact their territories. Participants in the social movement against Belo Monte claim that the lack of consultations constitutes an infringement of the Brazilian Constitution and the ILO Convention 169. However, the national and international regulations regarding the proper conduct of consultations with indigenous communities about infrastructure projects that affect their territories are vague. The conflict over the Belo Monte Dam confirms empirical studies on other cases demonstrating that opinions about the adequacy of participatory rights differ (see, for example, Flemmer and Schilling-Vacaflor 2016; Schilling-Vacaflor and Flemmer 2015).

6.2 Traveling of Concepts

Many of the theoretical concepts developed in North America and Europe turned out to be applicable in the analysis of the social movement against Belo Monte, although they sometimes seemed inappropriate at first sight. The study showed that researchers should reflect upon their expectations and assumptions before conducting social movement research in the global South; thus confirming the third sensitizing concept (cf. Chapter 3). The sensitizing concepts, which form an integral part of the grounded theory methodology, were particularly helpful in explicating my expectations and pointing out the differences between Western and non-Western social movements.

In the following, I discuss the applicability of social movement theory in cases characterized by specific context conditions as given in the Belo Monte conflict. I elaborate on the empirical differences between Western and non-Western social movements and discuss the methodological implications of doing original research on the latter. Then I draw a conclusion about the applicability of the identity approach and the framing approach in case studies from Amazonia – admittedly from the perspective of a western researcher, yet under careful consideration of the interviewees' perceptions.

6.2.1 Cleavages and Power Asymmetries

As the analysis of collective identities and collective action frames in the social movement against the Belo Monte Dam shows, activists are deeply rooted in their natural and social environment. Their historic and current experiences interact with visions of future development and form a unique local setting for the Belo Monte project. The natural environment shapes people's characters and constitutes an important point of reference for their personal and social identities. Moreover, the social movement's collective action frame draws on the region's centuries-old history and its physical characteristics – for example, its diversity in terms of ethnicities and cultures, and its vast natural resources. More specifically, the frame alludes to the region's colonial past and status as a development frontier, it makes reference to political neglect, power asymmetries, underdevelopment, and deprivation. These characteristics have originated a vulnerable society that is difficult to mobilize for fear of harassment and repression. These findings confirm the relevance and adequateness of the fourth sensitizing concept, which suggests that Amazonia constitutes a specific setting for social movements (cf. Chapter 3). Moreover, they specify the conditions under which collective action evolves in the region and to what extend it can be studied using Western theories and concepts.

Raising interviewee's statements to a higher level of abstraction, it becomes apparent that many interviewees allude to traditional cleavages and to questions of power asymmetry. According to Kriesi and colleagues, political cleavages are “social and cultural dividing lines” (Kriesi et al. 1995: 3) between social groups that are politicized by social actors and thus produce political conflicts. Traditional cleavages include conflicts between center and periphery, urban and rural, working class and bourgeoisie, as well as religious divides (Kriesi et al. 1995: 10; Rokkan 1970). While cleavage structures are generally country specific (Kriesi et al. 1995: xiv), scholars agree that modernization has caused profound social and cultural changes across Western societies that have resulted in stronger individualization and more personal freedom from social control mechanisms like class, religion, and family. At the same time new cleavages have emerged that replace, complement or otherwise alter the extant cleavage structures of a given society (Kriesi et al. 1995: xviii; Stekelenburg 2013: 223). In their analysis of four Western European countries, Kriesi and colleagues claim that modern societies suffer from new kinds of structurally determined conflicts that "have replaced the dependence on traditional bonds and the deprivation stemming from the inequality of resource distribution" (Kriesi et al. 1995: xix). By contrast, many people in Altamira and the adjacent municipalities still depend on traditional bonds in political and economic affairs. Inequality and poverty hamper the change towards a modern society that Kriesi and colleagues identify in Western societies. Consequently, I propose that traditional cleavages continue to be central determinants of mobilization in non-Western social movements.[140]

Another difference between Western and non-Western social movements is the degree to which people are aware of and willing to demand individual and collective rights. In Altamira and the adjacent municipalities, traditional cleavages tend to impede the development of political awareness and consciousness of civil rights in some segments of society. The Catholic Church played an important role in educating and empowering the local population in Altamira throughout the 1970s and 1980s, thus fostering the development of an active civil society. This empirical finding confirms the fifth sensitizing concept, which states that the Catholic Church, and more specifically the former Bishop of Xingu, Erwin Kräutler, have had a significant influence on Altamira's civil society (cf. Chapter 3). Most of the activists interviewed for this study started their activist careers in the realm of the CEBs and still maintain relationships with other church members. A Church Newsletter from 1992 confirms that education and the formation of conscience led to an awakening of the population and to the founding of groups that raise their voice and demand civil rights (Provinzialat der Missionare vom Kostbaren Blut 1992: 9). Hence, collective action in Altamira, and to a lesser degree in Belém, is characterized by the particularly influential role of the Catholic Church.

I propose that the limited awareness of civil rights in some parts of Brazil and in some segments of society is a structural difference between Western and non-Western social movements that should be verified empirically for other countries of the global South. Boudreau (1996) suggests that economically secure people have more freedom than impoverished people to choose if they want to participate in political activism, as for the latter "collective action may of

140 It should be noted that the applicability of the cleavage concept in non-Western countries has been questioned in general, as many of these countries have experienced a different social, political, and economic development than Western Europe (Bornschier 2009). However, this finding actually supports my argument (put forward further below) that the zero-sum game between traditional and new cleavages that has been confirmed for Western societies is questionable for non-Western societies, as the distinction between traditional and new cleavages seems to follow a eurocentric logic that is not universally applicable.

necessity be a more constant pheonomenon" (Boudreau 1996: 178). By contrast, this study shows that deprived people are especially difficult to mobilize, for at least two reasons. First, they often lack awareness of their own rights and/or feel incapable of influencing their destiny. Second, they are often socially and economically dependent upon powerful actors, who tend to be the ones that they would have to oppose if they chose to take action. Therefore, I suggest that Boudreau's assumption that "comprehensive constituent need, sweeping poverty, and oppression make individualistic life impossible and drive recruits with multifaceted demands into collective undertakings" (Boudreau 1996: 179) is actually a matter for empirical investigation.[141]

Moreover, I propose that the degree to which traditional cleavage structures have been replaced by new cleavages contributes to the differentiation between Western and non-Western social movements and to their conceptualization. In this regard, Brazil is a particularly interesting case, as the industrialized South of the country is likely to have performed the aforementioned social and cultural changes associated with modernization, while the underdeveloped North of the country seems to be lagging behind. This implies that even within one country (at least within emerging economies) and within the same time period different social movements may be facing different political conflict structures. Accordingly, cleavage structures are not only country specific as proposed by epistemological nationalism (cf. Kriesi et al. 1995). At least in developing countries they may even vary within a country.[142]

An interesting observation that is counterintuitive at first sight to the above argument – stating that traditional cleavages continue to be central determinants of mobilization in non-Western social movements – is that the participants in the social movement against Belo Monte express beliefs and values resembling those that have been classified as postmaterialist in a Western context. While local activists continue to suffer from historic social, political, and economic structures that manifest themselves in traditional cleavages, they ad-

141 At the same time I agree with Boudreau that poverty and its effects on collective action should be a central variable in the study of movement dynamics, especially in the global South (Boudreau 1996: 179).

142 Christopher Chase-Dunn and colleagues (2008) have studied North–South differences and complementarities among the participants of the World Social Forum (WSF) meeting in Porto Alegre, Brazil in 2005. While "political differences between WSF participants from the global South and those from the global North seem to be fairly modest", according to the authors, a focus on the participants' provenance produces interesting results (although some of them do not attain statistical significance). Their study shows that more attention should be paid to the core–semi-periphery–periphery distinction in the political views of activists.

vocate personal and collective rights, effective representation and participation, acknowledgment of traditional cultures and lifestyles, and environmental protection. The latter are often referred to as postmaterialist values in Western societies. As opposed to the finding of Kriesi and colleagues that "there exists a zero-sum relationship between the strength of traditional political cleavages and the possibility of new social movements to articulate a new societal cleavage" (Kriesi et al. 1995: 4), the case study suggests that the social movement against Belo Monte is able to integrate traditional and new cleavages. I propose that this integration is rendered possible by a different understanding of what Western societies have termed postmaterialist values. The Volta Grande has traditionally been populated by indigenous peoples and early settlers who came to the region in search of land and other resources to sustain a livelihood. They integrated into their natural environment and developed cultures and lifestyles that are closely connected to the characteristics of their habitat. Over time they acquired a profound knowledge of the flora and fauna; however, they claim that their expertise is generally ignored or even rejected by the Brazilian majority society. Interestingly, the local population takes a critical view of the concept of sustainable development, which promotes a balance between the economic, social, and environmental elements of development.[143] While it is reasonable to expect that this concept resonates with the population, it is actually perceived as a strategy of the economy to greenwash its activities and justify the centuries-old domination of the region. I propose that the local populations' understanding and the Western conceptualization can both be termed sustainable development according to the internationally shared definition. Both forms of development seek to balance economic, social, and environmental interests. However, they are based on different ideas of how to actually follow a sustainable lifestyle. As the traditional inhabitants of the Volta Grande see themselves as an integral part of the environment, they consider the integration of economic, social, and environmental interests as a matter of course.[144] By contrast,

143 The concept of sustainable development was significantly shaped by the so-called Brundtland Report of the World Commission on Environment and Development, published in 1987. The report criticized that development was commonly equated with economic progress at that time, and established relationships between poverty, environmental degradation, and the economy. Emphasizing the need for intra- and inter-generational equity, the commission called for the equal consideration of economic, social, and environmental elements of development, which became known as the "three pillars of sustainability" (von Hauff and Kleine 2009; Hauff 1987).

144 The impact of people on the environment is disputed. While the Brundtland report identifies poverty as a cause of environmental degradation (Hauff 1987), indigenous communities are said to follow a sustainable lifestyle. Research shows that legally designated indigenous terri-

Western societies took intellectual efforts in the 1980s to develop (or rather re-activate) a link to their natural environment. I argue that this led to a rather technical conceptualization of sustainable development that demands implementation and is prone to hypocrisy; moreover, it is perceived as a postmaterialist value. Questions arise as to whether societies of the global South that have retained closer relationships to nature and that promote environmental and social rights are able to set an example for industrialized countries.[145] In this regard, it has to be acknowledged that the Amazon rainforest is internationally valued for its biodiversity and influence on the global climate. This particular frame provides regional activists with strong arguments to promote their cause.

Summing up, I suggest that the concept of cleavages is useful in understanding the difference between Western and non-Western social movements. However, Western scholars should reconsider the meaning of traditional cleavages. When and why did these cleavages come to be considered traditional – thus implying that they have decreased in salience – and is this assessment valid for social conflict across societies? Moreover, what do the terms Western and non-Western really imply? Brazil as an emerging economy is internally divided into the developed South and the developing North of the country, between urban and rural areas, along the lines of class, race, and gender. The degree to which traditional cleavages dominate political and social conflicts – that is, their salience – may vary across the country. It is possible that traditional cleavages have been institutionalized, and thus pacified, to a larger extend in the developed South of Brazil than in the less developed North and the rural areas of the

tories are very effective in forest protection (Nelson and Chomitz 2011: 9). While an empirical verification of the impact of indigenous and traditional people on their natural environment is beyond the scope of this study, I suggest that on the whole they have a different understanding of and relationship towards their natural environment than Western societies tend to have. This argument is supported by ISA's perspective of development. The institute argues that, "if something is social, it can only be environmental. Because there is no 'environmental dimension' of economic growth, of social development, of progress in general: the environment is the name of the whole thing, of the entire problem. [...] Environment is a question of public health and of social justice, not only for those who live today but also for future generations. [...] Let us remember that environment is only another word for the necessary conditions for life. The mistake of separating the social from the environmental becomes even more serious once we imagine – as we imagine very frequently – that we can only develop when we pay an environmental price – that is, damaging something. This is not true. [...] Development is either sustainable, or it is no development" (Instituto Socioambiental 2003, author's translation).

145 For example, consider the concept of good life (*buen vivir*) and the rights of Mother Earth (*Derechos de la Madre Tierra*) that have shaped the legislation in Bolivia (see, for example, Fatheuer 2011).

country.[146] At least in the Amazon state of Pará, where the distribution of property and power is still largely influenced by historic structures, traditional cleavages seem to be salient until the present day, as the collective action frame of the social movement against Belo Monte indicates. At the same time, many activists perceive of so-called postmodern values like sustainable development as a matter of course. Consequently, concepts like traditional and new cleavages, postmaterialist values, etc. reveal a eurocentric perspective and should be applied carefully when studying social movements in the global South.

6.2.2 Implications for the Research Design

The Belo Monte study provided a number of challenges in terms of research design and methodology that are quite informative for future projects investigating collective action in the global South.

The first insight regards the relationship between organizations and individuals. I had planned to collect data about organizations by interviewing their members, thinking that they would be able and willing to represent their organizations and speak on behalf of their colleagues if asked to do so. However, this assumption turned out to be inadequate for the people I interviewed, as the entities were less relevant to at least some of the activists than I had assumed. The concept of an organization having contacts and partners in its own right seemed strange to some interviewees; thus raising the question if my assumption was a Western one and if the relationship between organizations and activists is generally different in non-Western social movements. Many interviewees did not seem to identify strongly with and represent a particular entity. Instead they were affiliated with several organizations at a time and sought to self-actualize and live out their personalities in several contexts. This reveals a different understanding of the relationship between organizations and activists than I had expected. However, does this finding imply that the relationship between organizations and activists is substantially different in Western and non-Western social movements? Interestingly, activists affiliated with the Catholic Church had a stronger sense of representation. They attributed an influential role to organizations based on their continuity and alluded to the unsteadiness of individual commitment. Hence, I conclude that the role of organizations and the relationship between organizations and activist are more likely to depend on the organizational structure of an entity than on its location in the global North or the global South. Yet, scholars should reflect upon their – probably unconscious –

146 On the salience and institutionalization of cleavages see Kriesi et al. (1995: 6–7).

expectations and assumptions about the organizational structure and relationships of SMOs and individual actors in social movements from the global South in order to avoid the development of unfounded expectations and assumptions.

The second insight results from the first insight, and regards the network structure of the social movement. As the interviews showed, the affiliation of movement participants with SMOs and the social movement at large varies significantly. Some activists participate continuously in a social movement organization whereas others participate on an ad hoc basis. Organizations affiliated with the Catholic Church tend to have hierarchical structures, while other SMOs merely provide platforms for the exchange of experiences, interests, and ideas among individual movement participants. While interviewees were unable (or unwilling) to provide information about institutional partners, the qualitative research design based on GTM enabled me to reveal underlying network dynamics and demonstrate that ties exist not only on the individual level (between activists) but also on the institutional level (between organizations). Hence, the social movement against Belo Monte fulfills the criteria established in Chapter 2, which confirms the first sensitizing concept (cf. Chapter 3).

A third insight regards the classification of social movements according to the purpose(s) and objective(s) of their collective action. The framing approach, which was largely developed in North America, implies that such a classification is generally possible and desirable. Consequently, social movements are frequently classified as environmental movements, justice movements, indigenous movements, etc. However, the analysis of the Belo Monte conflict shows that the movement developed a broad and inclusive frame that enables the participation of diverse actors. Movement participants emphasize the value of unity in diversity. They are particularly proud of having created a comprehensive diagnostic frame that resonates with the most diverse organizations and individuals. Questions arise about whether attempts to classify social movements are typical of Western social movement theory and research. Further empirical re-search could show if non-Western social movements have a higher tolerance and appreciation for diversity among activists and a higher willingness to open their collective action frames for other aspects of the contentious issue.

6.3 Evaluation of Method and Procedures

By its very nature, qualitative research cannot be representative in the strict statistical sense, let alone provide proof of causal mechanisms. The collection, treatment, and interpretation of qualitative data are inevitably influenced by the researcher, who has to decide how to handle subjectivity in her research. A key challenge of this study was the fact that it involved three different languages. Moreover, the generation of a comprehensive data set was hampered by the fact that I was unable to identify all of the organizations that I had sampled, and to interview all of the people that I considered relevant. Ultimately, the members of the Xingu Vivo Movement were overrepresented in the sample. This became a disadvantage when the data analysis revealed the fragmentation of the social movement. The strict application of GTM would have required another round of data collection with a focus on the underrepresented faction of the movement. This was not feasible due to limited resources. Nonetheless, the in-depth analysis of the available data produced consistent findings that adequately describe the internal logic of the phenomenon. Therefore, I argue that the available data was sufficient for the purpose of this study. However, future research could focus on the underrepresented faction of the movement in order to improve the theoretical saturation of the concepts.

Beyond data collection, the interpretation of qualitative data is another procedure that is prone to bias. In order to achieve intersubject comprehensibility, qualitative researchers prefer to discuss their interpretations in groups. The application of this approach was hampered by the multilingual character of this research. However, I sought to compensate for this shortcoming by writing lengthy memos about alternative interpretations of the data and by discussing my conceptual considerations with different colleagues. While coding requires the researcher to abstract from the data, it can be difficult to determine the underlying theoretical concept. Moreover, the separation of individual aspects – which is necessary to reduce the complexity of the empirical phenomenon – may seem artificial at times. I believe that the longsome and detailed examination of the data, which included the drafting of coding notes and conceptual memos, enabled me to make reasonable and comprehensible coding decisions and develop a comprehensive coding scheme.

Overall, the research design based on GTM was well suited to the analysis of collective identities and collective action frames in the social movement against the Belo Monte Dam because it produced results that would have been difficult to obtain with a deductive approach. The combined top-down and bottom-up procedure for the data analysis contributed to uncovering indexicality and reconstructing the meanings that local activists have attributed to the social conflict and to their collective action. GTM's inductive approach to data analysis enabled a context-sensitive and detailed analysis of latent structures. Thus, I was able to reconstruct the relationships between concepts and demonstrate how they interact in certain situations. Moreover, it was possible to reconstruct the meanings that local activists attribute to contentious concepts like sustainability and leadership and to compare them with existing theoretical conceptualizations. This enabled me to identify overlaps with existing research, to elaborate on their implications, and to contribute to ongoing theoretical debates. Moreover, the methodology was useful in revealing the origin and precise meaning of social categories. While I had based my research design and sampling strategy on actor categories that were frequently used in scholarly articles and in the media, field research revealed that these categories were artificially introduced to the region by outside agents and that their adequacy for conceptualizing the lifestyles and experiences of local people is limited. In this sense, GTM helped avoid conceptual stretching in the development of theoretical concepts, which is particularly relevant in the study of foreign countries.

6.4 Outlook

This study has shown that the conflict over Belo Monte is multifaceted and complex, reaching far beyond the hydropower project at the Xingu River. It offers explanations as to how collective identities and collective action frames influence movement cohesion and fragmentation. Moreover, its findings about central movement dynamics can inform future research and be verified empirically in other case studies.

Empirical research about social movements in Brazil and in other emerging countries could focus on various issues. Given the large number of infrastructure projects that are currently being implemented in the Brazilian Amazon in the realm of the growth acceleration program, comparative case studies could be used to investigate the preconditions for the emergence of social movements (cf. Finding F4). This research could be extended to include case studies from other Latin American countries that have experienced conflicts over the exploitation of natural resources and the implementation of large infrastructure projects. Moreover, cross-regional comparisons could improve our understanding of social movements in the global South. The analysis of social movements in authoritarian regimes and in underdeveloped regions of the world could contribute to our understanding of the regional context's influence on political mobilization and specific movement dynamics (cf. findings F2, F3, and F5). With regard to the applicability of Western theories in non-Western case studies, Brazil is a particularly interesting case. A comparison of social movements from different regions of the country would improve our understanding of the influence that these regional contexts and the prevalent "social and cultural dividing lines" (Kriesi et al. 1995: 3) have on political mobilization. It is possible that traditional cleavages have been pacified in the developed South of the country but not in its less developed North and in rural areas. Knowledge about regional context conditions and prevalent cleavage structures seems highly relevant from a policy point of view, given the recent mobilization in a variety of issue areas throughout the county.

Finally, this study raises theoretical questions that could be addressed in future research in order to advance our knowledge of general movement dynamics. I have advanced the concept of a founding myth that is deliberately framed by the social movement to instrumentalize a shared emotional experience in the process of collective identity formation. Further research is needed to confirm and substantiate this concept (cf. Finding F1). Moreover, I have argued that – despite its fragmentation – the two factions in the social movement against Belo Monte continue to form a common social movement because they share a common long-term objective. In order to substantiate this argument and advance the literature on cohesion and fragmentation in social movements, additional cases of movement fragmentation should be analyzed and compared in order to define criteria that determine whether two groups form factions of a common movement or two separate movements. Moreover, future research could focus on the causes of fragmentation – beyond the "normal fragmentation" as part of the social movement life cycle (cf. Mauss 1975) – and on the typical progression of fragmentation. It would be interesting to see if fragmentation involves different phases, how it is perceived by movement participants, and whether it can be stopped with identity work or framing processes.

Bibliography

Abers, Rebecca, and Marisa von Bülow (2011): Movimentos sociais na teoria e na prática: como estudar o ativismo através da fronteira entre Estado e sociedade? In: *Sociologias*, 13, p. 52–84.

Abranches, Sérgio (2013): Grüner Riese. In: *Kulturaustausch. Zeitschrift für internationale Perspektiven*, 63(1), p. 56–57.

Adler, Emanuel (1997): Seizing the Middle Ground: Constructivism in World Politics. In: *European Journal of International Relations*, 3(3), p. 319–363.

Alvarez, Sonia E., Evelina Dagnino and Arturo Escobar (1998): Introduction: The Cultural and the Political in Latin American Social Movements. In: Sonia E. Alvarez, Evelina Dagnino and Arturo Escobar (eds), *Cultures of Politics. Politics of Cultures. Re-visioning Latin American Social Movements*. Boulder: Westview Press, p. 1–29.

Avritzer, Leonardo (2009): *Participatory Institutions in Democratic Brazil*. Baltimore: Johns Hopkins University Press.

Balser, Deborah B. (1997): The Impact of Environmental Factors on Factionalism and Schism in Social Movement Organizations. In: *Social Forces*, 76(1), p. 199–228.

Basedau, Matthias, and Patrick Köllner (2007): Area Studies, Comparative Area Studies, and the Study of Politics: Context, Substance, and Methodological Challenges. In: *Zeitschrift für Vergleichende Politikwissenschaft*, 1(1), p. 105–124.

Behnke, Joachim, Nina Baur and Nathalie Behnke (2006): *Empirische Methoden der Politikwissenschaft*. 1st edition. Paderborn: Schöningh/UTB.

Benford, Robert D., and David A. Snow (2000): Framing Processes and Social Movements: An Overview and Assessment. In: *Annual Review of Sociology*, 26, p. 611–639.

Benford, Robert D. (1997): An Insider's Critique of the Social Movement Framing Perspective. In: *Sociological Inquiry*, 67(4), p. 409–430.

Berg, Bruce L. (2009): *Qualitative Research Methods for the Social Sciences*. 7th edition. Boston: Allyn & Bacon.

Bergman, Manfred M., and Anthony P. M. Coxon (2005): The Quality in Qualitative Methods. In: *Forum: Qualitative Social Research*, 6(2), Article 34. Online: http://www.qualitative-research.net/index.php/fqs/article/view/457, accessed on: 22.05.2017.

Bermann, Célio (2013): A resistência às obras hidrelétricas na Amazônia e a fragilização do Ministério Público Federal. In: *Novos Cadernos NAEA*, 16(2), p. 97–120.

Bitencourt, Rafael (2010): Norte Energia assina contrato de concessão de Belo Monte (26.08.2010). In: *Valor Econômico*. Online: http://www.valor.com.br/arquivo/675925/norte-energia-assina-contrato-de-concessao-de-belo-monte, accessed on: 22.05.2017.

Blanke, Svenja (2013): *Ein neues Eldorado? Rohstoffpolitik in Lateinamerika heute*. Friedrich-Ebert-Stiftung: Perspektive. Berlin. Online: http://library.fes.de/pdf-files/iez/10213.pdf, accessed on: 22.05.2017.

Bornschier, Simon (2009): Cleavage Politics in Old and New Democracies. In: *Living Reviews in Democracy*, 1.

Boudreau, Vincent (1996): Northern Theory, Southern Protest: Opportunity Structure Analysis in Cross-National Perspective. In: *Mobilization*, 1(2), p. 175–189.

Bratman, Eve Z. (2014): Contradictions of Green Development: Human Rights and Environmental Norms in Light of Belo Monte Dam Activism. In: *Journal of Latin American Studies*, 46(2), p. 261–289.

Breines, Winifred (2006): *The Trouble Between Us: An Uneasy History of White and Black Women in the Feminist Movement*. New York: Oxford University Press.

Bryant, Antony and Kathy Charmaz (eds) (2007): *The SAGE Handbook of Grounded Theory*. London: SAGE.

Buechler, Steven M. (1995): New Social Movement Theories. In: *The Sociological Quarterly*, 36(3), p. 441–464.

Cable, Sherry, and Thomas E. Shriver (2010): Wounded by Friendly Fire: Policy Palliatives and Internal Conflict in the Gulf War Illness Movement. In: *Current Sociology*, 58(1), p. 45–66.

Campanerut, Camila (2010): Lula fecha governo com 80% de aprovação e bate novo recorde, diz CNI/Ibope (16.12.2010). In: *UOL Notícias Política*. Online: http://noticias.uol.com.br/politica/ultimas-noticias/2010/12/16/aprovacao-a-governo-lula-e-de-80-e-bate-novo-recorde-diz-cniibope.htm, accessed on: 22.05.2017.

Cappai, Gabriele (2005): Der interkulturelle Vergleich. Herausforderungen und Strategien einer sozialwissenschaftlichen Methode. In: Ilja Srubar, Joachim Renn and Urlich Wenzel (eds), *Kulturen vergleichen. Sozial- und kulturwissenschaftliche Grundlagen und Kontroversen*. Wiesbaden: VS Verlag für Sozialwissenschaften, p. 48–78.

Carter, Miguel (2009): The Landless Rural Workers' Movement and the Struggle for Social Justice in Brazil. In: Carmen Diana Deere and Frederick S. Royce (eds), *Rural Social Movements in Latin America. Organizing for Sustainable Livelihoods*. Gainesville et al.: University Press of Florida, p. 87–115.

Castro, Fábio Fonseca de (2012): A identidade encenada. A produção artística de Belém como laboratório e teatro da identidade amazônica. In: *Contemporânea*, 10(2), p. 137–149.

CCBM (2014): O Consórcio. In: *Consórcio Construtor Belo Monte*. Online: https://www.consorciobelomonte.com.br/Publico.aspx?id=2, accessed on: 22.05.2017.

Charmaz, Kathy (2003): Grounded theory: Objectivist and constructivist methods. In: Norman K. Denzin and Yvonna S. Lincoln (eds), *Strategies for qualitative inquiry*. 2nd edition. Thousand Oaks: SAGE, p. 249–291.

Chase-Dunn, Christopher, Ellen Reese, Mark Herkenrath, Rebecca Giem, Erika Gutierrez, Linda Kim and Christine Petit (2008): North–South Contradictions and Bridges at the World Social Forum. In: *North and South in the World Political Economy*. Malden: Blackwell Publishing, p. 341–366.

Christopoulos, Dimitrios C. (2008): The Governance of Networks: Heuristic or Formal Analysis? A Reply to Rachel Parker. In: *Political Studies*, 56(2), p. 475–481.

Coe, Michael T., Marcos H. Costa, and Britaldo S. Soares-Filho (2009): The influence of historical and potential future deforestation on the stream flow of the Amazon River – Land surface processes and atmospheric feedbacks. In: *Journal of Hydrology*, 369(1–2), p. 165–174.

Cole, John C., and Diana M. Liverman (2011): Brazil's Clean Development Mechanism governance in the context of Brazil's historical environment–development discourses. In: *Carbon Management*, 2(2), p. 145–160.

Controladoria-Geral da União (n.d.): Seguro Defeso - Pescador Artesanal. In: *Portal da Transparência*. Online: http://www.portaldatransparencia.gov.br/defeso/download.asp, accessed on: 22.05.2017.

Cooper, Andrew F. (2008): *Celebrity diplomacy*. Paradigm Publishers.

Corbin, Juliet and Anselm L. Strauss (2008): *Basics of Qualitative Research. Techniques and Procedures for Developing Grounded Theory*. 3rd edition. Thousand Oaks: SAGE.

Cordovil, Daniela (2012): Afro-Brazilian religions and audiovisual narratives in Amazonia: research tools. In: *Vibrant: Virtual Brazilian Anthropology*, 9(2), p. 513–534.

Coy, Martin, and Michael Klingler (2011): Pionierfronten im brasilianischen Amazonien zwischen alten Problemen und neuen Dynamiken. Das Beispiel des "Entwicklungskorridors" Cuiabá (Mato Grosso) – Santarém (Pará). In: *Innsbrucker Jahresbericht 2008-2010. Innsbruck: Innsbrucker Geographische Gesellschaft*, p. 109–129.

Coy, Martin (2012): Sozioökonomische und regionale Ausgangsbedingungen in Brasilien. In: Dana De la Fontaine and Thomas Stehnken (eds), *Das politische System Brasiliens*. Wiesbaden: VS Verlag für Sozialwissenschaften, p. 52–61.

Coy, Patrick G. (2013): Co-optation. In: David A. Snow, Donatella Della Porta, Bert Klandermans and Doug McAdam (eds), *The Wiley-Blackwell Encyclopedia of Social and Political Movements*. Chichester: Blackwell Publishing, p. 280–282.

Daphi, Priska, and Dieter Rucht (2011): Wir und die Anderen. Klärungen und Anwendungen des Konzepts kollektiver Identität. In: *Forschungsjournal Soziale Bewegungen*, 24(4), p. 2–3.

Daphi, Priska (2011): Soziale Bewegungen und kollektive Identität. Forschungsstand und Forschungslücken. In: *Forschungsjournal Soziale Bewegungen*, 24(4), p. 13–26.

Davies, Noel and Martin Conway (2008): *World Christianity in the 20th Century*. London: SCM Press.

De la Fontaine, Dana and Thomas Stehnken (eds) (2012a): *Das politische System Brasiliens*. Wiesbaden: VS Verlag für Sozialwissenschaften.

De la Fontaine, Dana and Thomas Stehnken (2012b): Einleitung. In: Dana De la Fontaine and Thomas Stehnken (eds), *Das politische System Brasiliens*. Wiesbaden: VS Verlag für Sozialwissenschaften, p. 13–22.

Deaux, Kay and Anne Reid (2000): Contemplating Collectivism. In: Sheldon Stryker, Timothy J. Owens and Robert W. White (eds), *Self, Identity, and Social Movements*, p. 172–190.

Della Cava, Ralph (1989): The "People's Church," the Vatican, and Abertura. In: Alfred Stepan (ed), *Democratizing Brazil. Problems of Transition and Consolidation*. New York: Oxford University Press, p. 143–167.

Della Porta, Donatella and Mario Diani (2006): *Social Movements. An Introduction*. 2nd edition. Malden: Blackwell.

Della Porta, Donatella (2005): Multiple Belongings, Tolerant Identities, and the Construction of "Another Politics": Between the European Social Forum and the Local Social Fora. In: Donatella Della Porta and Sidney Tarrow (eds), *Transnational Protest and Global Activism*. Lanham: Rowman & Littlefield, p. 175–202.

Deutsche Welle (2011): Ibama autoriza a construção da polêmica usina de Belo Monte (01.06.2011). In: *Deutsche Welle*. Online: http://p.dw.com/p/11Sfm, accessed on: 22.05.2017.

Diani, Mario, and Ivano Bison (2004): Organizations, coalitions, and movements. In: *Theory and Society*, 33(3–4), p. 281–309.

Diani, Mario (1992): The concept of social movement. In: *The Sociological Review*, 40(1), p. 1–25.

Diani, Mario (2002): Network Analysis. In: Bert Klandermans and Suzanne Staggenborg (eds), *Methods of Social Movement Research. Social Movements, Protest, and Contention. Vol. 16*. Minneapolis: University of Minnesota Press, p. 173–200.

Diani, Mario (2003): Networks and Social Movements: A Research Programme. In: Mario Diani and Doug McAdam (eds), *Social Movements and Networks. Relational Approaches to Collective Action*. Oxford/New York: Oxford University Press, p. 299–319.

Diani, Mario (2009): The Structural Bases of Protest Events. Multiple Memberships and Civil Society Networks in the 15 February 2003 Anti-War Demonstrations. In: *Acta Sociologica*, 52(1), p. 63–83.

Dyck, Bruno, and Frederick A. Starke (1999): The Formation of Breakaway Organizations: Observations and a Process Model. In: *Administrative Science Quarterly*, 44(4), p. 792–822.

EIA (2014): Brazil (as of 29.12.2014). In: *U.S. Energy Information Administration (EIA)*. Online: http://www.eia.gov/countries/cab.cfm?fips=br, accessed on: 22.05.2017.

Eletrobras (n.d.): Sobre a Eletrobras. In: *Portal da Eletrobras*. Online: http://eletrobras.com/pt/Paginas/Sobre-a-Eletrobras.aspx, accessed on: 22.05.2017.

Encarnación, Omar G. (2003): *The Myth of Civil Society: Social Capital and Democratic Consolidation in Spain and Brazil*. New York/Houndsmill: Palgrave Macmillan.

EPE (2014): *Balanço Energético Nacional 2014: Ano base 2013*. Rio de Janeiro: Empresa de Pesquisa Energética. Online: http://www.epe.gov.br, accessed on: 22.05.2017.

Fatheuer, Thomas (2011): *Buen Vivir: A brief introduction to Latin America's new concepts for the good life and the rights of nature*. Heinrich Böll Stiftung: Publication Series on Ecology, No. 17. Berlin. Online: http://www.boell.de/sites/default/files/endf_buen_vivir_engl.pdf, accessed on: 22.05.2017.

Fearnside, Philip M. (1999): Social Impacts of Brazil's Tucuruí Dam. In: *Environmental Management*, 24(4), p. 483–495.

Fearnside, Philip M. (2006): Dams in the Amazon: Belo Monte and Brazil's Hydroelectric Development of the Xingu River Basin. In: *Environmental Management*, 38(1), p. 16–27.

Fearnside, Philip M. (2008): The roles and movements of actors in the deforestation of Brazilian Amazonia. In: *Ecology and Society*, 13(1), Article 23.

Fearnside, Philip M. (2009): Brazil's environmental policies for the Amazon: Lessons from the last 20 years. Paper presented at the conference "Environmental Policy, Social Movements, and Science for the Brazilian Amazon", 5.-6.11.2009, University of Chicago. Online: http://www.unicentro.br/redemc/2011/conteudo/mc_artigos/Midia_Cidada_Silva.pdf, accessed on: 22.05.2017.

Fearnside, Philip M. (2012): *Belo Monte Dam: A spearhead for Brazil's dam-building attack on Amazonia?* GWF Discussion Paper 1210. Canberra: Global Water Forum. Online: http://www.globalwaterforum.org/2012/03/19/belo-monte-dam-a-spearhead-for-brazils-dam-building-attack-on-amazonia, accessed on: 22.05.2017.

Figueira, Ádna (2011): Máquinas pesadas chegam à Região do Xingu para obras de Belo Monte (06.07.2011). In: *Central de Notícias do Portal do Governo do*

Estado do Pará. Online: http://www.pa.gov.br/noticia_interna.asp?id_ver=798 13, accessed on: 22.05.2017.

Filho, A. Oswaldo Sevá (ed) (2005): *TENOTÃ-MÕ. Alertas sobre as conseqüências dos projetos hidrelétricos no rio Xingu*. São Paulo: International Rivers Network.

Finnemore, Martha, and Kathryn Sikkink (2001): Taking Stock: The Constructivist Research Program in International Relations and Comparative Politics. In: *Annual Review of Political Science*, 4, p. 391–416.

Flemmer, Riccarda, and Almut Schilling-Vacaflor (2016): Unfulfilled promises of the consultation approach: the limits to effective indigenous participation in Bolivia's and Peru's extractive industries. In: *Third World Quarterly*, 37(1), p. 172–188.

Flesher Fominaya, Cristina (2010a): Collective Identity in Social Movements: Central Concepts and Debates. In: *Sociology Compass*, 4(6), p. 393–404.

Flesher Fominaya, Cristina (2010b): Creating Cohesion from Diversity: The Challenge of Collective Identity Formation in the Global Justice Movement. In: *Sociological Inquiry*, 80(3), p. 377–404.

Fleury, Lorena Cândido, and Jalcione Almeida (2013): The construction of the Belo Monte hydroelectric power plant: environmental conflict and the development dilemma. In: *Ambiente & Sociedade*, 16(4), p. 141–156.

Flick, Uwe (2005): Qualitative Research in Sociology in Germany and the US – State of the Art, Differences and Developments. In: *Forum: Qualitative Social Research*, 6(3), Article 23. Online: http://www.qualitative-research.net/index.php/fqs/article/view/17, accessed on: 22.05.2017.

Folha de São Paulo (2013): Altamira invadida. In: *A Batalha de Belo Monte*. Online: http://arte.folha.uol.com.br/especiais/2013/12/16/belo-monte/capitulo-3-sociedade.html, accessed on: 22.05.2017.

Forline, Louis, and Eneida Assis (2004): Dams and Social Movements in Brazil: Quiet Victories on the Xingu. In: *Practicing Anthropology*, 26(3), p. 21–25.

Foweraker, Joe (1981): *The struggle for land: a political economy of the pioneer frontier in Brazil from 1930 to the present day*. Cambridge: Cambridge University Press.

Foweraker, Joe (1995): *Theorizing social movements*. London: Pluto Press.

Franco, Luiza Mello (2010): Brazil – The Environment, Lula and Marina Silva. "There is nothing as powerful as an idea whose time has come": Marina Silva's Unwinnable But Noble Bid for the Brazilian Presidency, and Why it Matters (25.08.2010). In: *Council on Hemispheric Affairs*. Online: http://www.coha.org/brazil-%E2%80%93-the-environment-lula-and-marina-silva-%E2%80%9Cthere-is-nothing-as-powerful-as-an-idea-whose-time-has-come%E2%80%9D-marina-silva%E2%80%99s-unwinnable-but-noble-bid-for-the-brazilia, accessed on: 22.05.2017.

FUNAI (n.d.): Quem Somos. In: *Fundação Nacional do Índio*. Online: http://www.funai.gov.br/index.php/quem-somos, accessed on: 22.05.2017.

FVPP (2008): Apresentação. In: *Fundação Viver Produzir e Preservar*. Online: http://www.fvpp.org.br/index.php/conheca/apresentacao, accessed on: 22.05.2017.

Gamson, William A., Bruce Fireman and Steven Rytina (1982): *Encounters with Unjust Authority*. Homewood: The Dorsey Press.

Gamson, William A. (1975): *The Strategy of Social Protest*. Homewood: Dorsey Press.

Gamson, William A. (1992): The Social Psychology of Collective Action. In: Aldon D. Morris and Carol McClurg Mueller (eds), *Frontiers in Social Movement Theory*. New Haven: Yale University Press, p. 53–76.

Gardner, John W. (1993): *On Leadership*. New York: Simon and Schuster.

Garfinkel, Harold (1981): Das Alltagswissen über Soziale und Innerhalb Sozialer Strukturen. In: Arbeitsgruppe Bielefelder Soziologen (ed), *Alltagswissen, Interaktion und gesellschaftliche Wirklichkeit*. 5th edition. Opladen: Westdeutscher Verlag, p. 189–262.

Gerhards, Jürgen, and Dieter Rucht (1992): Mesomobilization: Organizing and Framing in Two Protest Campaigns in West Germany. In: *American Journal of Sociology*, 98(3), p. 555–596.

Gerlach, Luther P. and Virginia H. Hine (1970): *People, Power, Change: Movements of Social Transformation*. Indianapolis: Bobbs-Merrill.

GfbV (n.d.): Brasilien: Kein Bau des Belo Monte-Staudamms ohne Mitbestimmung der Indigenen. In: *Gesellschaft für bedrohte Völker*. Online: http://gfbv.ch/de/kampagnen___projekte/belo_monte.cfm, accessed on: 22.05.2017.

globo.com (2010): Eleições 2010. Eleição presidencial. Apuração 1° turno. In: *G1*. Online: http://g1.globo.com/especiais/eleicoes-2010/apuracao-1-turno/index.html, accessed on: 22.05.2017.

globo.com (2014): Eleições 2014. Apuração de votos para Presidente. 1° turno. In: *G1*. Online: http://g1.globo.com/politica/eleicoes/2014/apuracao-votos-presidente.html, accessed on: 22.05.2017.

Goffman, Erving (1974): *Frame Analysis: An Essay on the Organization of the Experience*. New York: Harper Colophon.

Gohn, Maria da Glória (2000): 500 anos de lutas sociais no Brasil: movimentos sociais, ONGs e terceiro setor. In: *Mediações - Revista de Ciências Sociais*, 5(1), p. 11–40.

Gohn, Maria da Glória (2008): Abordagens teóricas no estudo dos movimentos sociais na américa latina. In: *Caderno CRH*, 21(54), p. 439–455.

Graeff, Bibiana (2012): Should We Adopt a Specific Regulation to Protect People That Are Displaced by Hydroelectric Projects: Reflections Based on Brazilian Law and the Belo Monte Case. In: *Florida A & M University Law Review*, 7(2), p. 261–289.

Gramacho, Maiesse (2010): Ibama concede licença ambiental prévia para a usina hidrelétrica de Belo Monte (01.02.2010). In: *Ministério do Meio Ambiente*. Online: http://www.mma.gov.br/informma/item/6071-ibama-concede-licenca-ambiental-previa-para-a-usina-hidreletrica-de-belo-monte, accessed on: 22.05.2017.

Gramsci, Antonio (1971): *Selections from the prison notebooks of Antonio Gramsci*. London: Lawrence & Wishart.

Hafner-Burton, Emilie M., Miles Kahler, and Alexander H. Montgomery (2009): Network Analysis for International Relations. In: *International Organization*, 63(3), p. 559–592.

Hage, Jerald (1972): *Techniques and Problems of Theory Construction in Sociology*. New York: Wiley.

Halai, Nelofer (2007): Making Use of Bilingual Interview Data: Some Experiences from the Field. In: *The Qualitative Report*, 12(3), p. 344–355.

Hall, Anthony L., and Sue Branford (2012): Development, Dams and Dilma: The Saga of Belo Monte. In: *Critical Sociology*, 38(6), p. 851–862.

Hammond, John L. (2014): Mística, meaning and popular education in the Brazilian Landless Workers Movement. In: *Interface*, 6(1), p. 372–391.

Hart, Claire M., and Mark Van Vugt (2006): From Fault Line to Group Fission: Understanding Membership Changes in Small Groups. In: *Personality and Social Psychology Bulletin*, 32(3), p. 392–404.

von Hauff, Michael and Alexandro Kleine (2009): *Nachhaltige Entwicklung: Grundlagen und Umsetzung*. München: Oldenbourg.

Hauff, Volker (1987): *Unsere gemeinsame Zukunft. Der Brundtland-Bericht der Weltkommission für Umwelt und Entwicklung*. Greven: Eggenkamp Verlag.

Haunss, Sebastian (2004): *Identität in Bewegung. Prozesse kollektiver Identität bei den Autonomen und in der Schwulenbewegung*. Wiesbaden: VS Verlag für Sozialwissenschaften.

Haunss, Sebastian (2011): Was ist der beste methodische Zugang? Bewegungsdiskurse und Prozesse kollektiver Identität. In: *Forschungsjournal Soziale Bewegungen*, 24(4), p. 36–38.

Helfferich, Cornelia (2009): *Die Qualität qualitativer Daten. Manual für die Durchführung qualitativer Interviews*. 3rd edition. Wiebaden: VS Verlag für Sozialwissenschaften.

Hellmann, Kai-Uwe (1998): Paradigmen der Bewegungsforschung. Forschungs- und Erklärungsansätze – ein Überblick. In: Kai-Uwe Hellmann and Ruud Koopmans (eds), *Paradigmen der Bewegungsforschung. Entstehung und Entwicklung von Neuen sozialen Bewegungen und Rechtsextremismus*. Opladen and Wiesbaden: Westdeutscher Verlag, p. 9–30.

Herkenrath, Mark (2011): *Die Globalisierung der sozialen Bewegungen. Transnationale Zivilgesellschaft und die Suche nach einer gerechten Weltordnung*. Wiesbaden: VS Verlag für Sozialwissenschaften.

Hernández, Francisco del Moral, and Sonia Barbosa Magalhães (2011): Ciência, cientistas e democracia desfigurada: o caso Belo Monte. In: *Novos Cadernos NAEA*, 14(1), p. 79–96.

Hjelmar, Ulf (1996): Constructivist Analysis and Movement Organizations: Conceptual Clarifications. In: *Acta Sociologica*, 39(2), p. 169–186.

Hochstetler, Kathryn (2008): Organized Civil Society in Lula's Brazil. In: Peter R. Kingstone and Timothy J. Power (eds), *Democratic Brazil Revisited*. Pittsburgh: University of Pittsburgh Press, p. 33–53.

Hochstetler, Kathryn (2011): The Politics of Environmental Licensing: Energy Projects of the Past and Future in Brazil. In: *Studies in Comparative International Development*, 46(4), p. 349–371.

Hoffman French, Jan (2006): *A Tale of Two Priests: Three Decades of Liberation Theology in the Brazilian Northeast*. Working Paper, No. 328. Notre Dame: Kellogg Institute for International Studies. Online: http://kellogg.nd.edu/publications/workingpapers/WPS/328.pdf, accessed on: 22.05.2017.

Hollstein, Betina, and Carsten G. Ullrich (2003): Einheit trotz Vielfalt? Zum konstitutiven Kern qualitativer Forschung. In: *Soziologie*, 32(4), p. 29–43.

Htun, Mala (2004): From 'Racial Democracy' to Affirmative Action: Changing State Policy on Race in Brazil. In: *Latin American Research Review*, 39(1), p. 60–89.

Hunt, Scott A., Robert D. Benford and David A. Snow (1994): Identity fields: Framing Processes and the Social Construction of Movement Identities. In: Enrique Laraña, Johnston Hank and Joseph R. Gusfield (eds), *New Social Movements: From Ideology to Identity*. Philadelphia: Temple University Press, p. 185–208.

Hunt, Scott A. and Robert D. Benford (2004): Collective Identity, Solidarity, and Commitment. In: David A. Snow, Sarah A. Soule and Hanspeter Kriesi (eds), *The Blackwell Companion to Social Movements*. Oxford: Blackwell, p. 433–457.

Hunt, Scott A. and Robert D. Benford (2008): Collective Identity, Solidarity, and Commitment. In: David A. Snow, Sarah A. Soule and Hanspeter Kriesi (eds), *The Blackwell Companion to Social Movements*. 2nd edition. Malden et al.: Blackwell, p. 433–457.

Hurwitz, Zachary, Brent Millikan, Telma Monteiro and Roland Widmer (2011): *Mega-Projeto, Mega-Riscos. Análise de Riscos para Investidores no Complexo Hidrelétrico Belo Monte*. São Paulo: International Rivers, Amigos da Terra – Amazônia Brasileira.

IACHR (2011): *Annual Report of the Inter-American Commission on Human Rights 2011*. Washington: Organization of American States, Inter-American Commission on Human Rights. Online: http://www.oas.org/en/iachr/docs/annual/2011/TOC.asp, accessed on: 22.05.2017.

IBAMA (n.d.): Processo de licenciamento. In: *Instituto Brasileiro do Meio Ambiente e dos Recursos Naturais Renováveis*. Online: http://www.ibama.gov.br/licenciamento-ambiental-processo-de-licenciamento, accessed on: 22.05.2017.

IBAMA (2010): Sobre o Ibama. In: *Instituto Brasileiro do Meio Ambiente e dos Recursos Naturais Renováveis*. Online: http://www.ibama.gov.br/institucional/quem-somos, accessed on: 22.05.2017.

IBGE (2014): Cidades : Pará : Altamira. In: *Instituto Brasileiro de Geografia e Estatística*. Online: http://cidades.ibge.gov.br/xtras/perfil.php?codmun=150060, accessed on: 22.05.2017.

ILO (1989): C169 - Indigenous and Tribal Peoples Convention, 1989 (No. 169). In: *International Labour Organization*. Online: http://www.ilo.org/dyn/normlex/en/f?p=NORMLEXPUB:12100:0::NO::P12100_ILO_CODE:C169, accessed on: 22.05.2017.

ILO (2012): Ratifications of C169 - Indigenous and Tribal Peoples Convention, 1989 (No. 169). In: *International Labour Organization*. Online: http:// www.ilo.org/dyn/normlex/en/f?p=1000:11300:0::NO:11300:P11300_INSTRUMENT_ID:312314, accessed on: 22.05.2017.

Instituto Socioambiental (n.d.a): Cronologia do projeto. In: *Especial Belo Monte*. Online: https://site-antigo.socioambiental.org/esp/bm/hist.asp, accessed on: 22.05.2017.

Instituto Socioambiental (n.d.b): A Fundação Nacional do Índio (FUNAI). In: *Povos Indígenas no Brasil*. Online: http://pib.socioambiental.org/pt/c/politicas-indigenistas/orgao-indigenista-oficial/funai, accessed on: 22.05.2017.

Instituto Socioambiental (n.d.c): Mebêngôkre (Kayapó). In: *Povos Indígenas no Brasil*. Online: https://pib.socioambiental.org/pt/povo/mebengokre-kayapo, accessed on: 22.05.2017.

Instituto Socioambiental (n.d.d): Reserva Extrativista. In: *Unidades de Conservação*. Online: https://uc.socioambiental.org/uso-sustent%C3%A1vel/reservaextrativista, accessed on: 22.05.2017.

Instituto Socioambiental (n.d.e): Munduruku. In: *Povos Indígenas no Brasil*. Online: https://pib.socioambiental.org/pt/povo/munduruku, accessed on: 22.05.2017.

Instituto Socioambiental (2003): Amansa Brasil. Convite a uma colaboração (10.10.2003). In: *Notícias Socioambientais*. Online: http://site-antigo.socioambiental.org/nsa/detalhe?id=1439, accessed on: 22.05.2017.

Instituto Socioambiental (2014a): o ISA. In: *Instituto Socioambiental*. Online: http://www.socioambiental.org/pt-br/o-isa, accessed on: 22.05.2017.

Instituto Socioambiental (2014b): Xingu. In: *Instituto Socioambiental*. Online: http://www.socioambiental.org/pt-br/o-isa/programas/xingu, accessed on: 22.05.2017.

International Rivers, Fundación Proteger and ECOA (n.d.): Dams in Amazonia. In: *Dams in Amazonia*. Online: http://dams-info.org/en, accessed on: 22.05.2017.

International Rivers (n.d.): Xingu River. In: *International Rivers*. Online: http://www.internationalrivers.org/campaigns/xingu-river, accessed on: 22.05.2017.

International Rivers (2010): *Belo Monte. Massive dam project strikes at the heart of the Amazon*. Berkeley: International Rivers. Online: https://www.internationalrivers.org/resources/belo-monte-fact-sheet-2637, accessed on: 22.05.2017.

IPAM (n.d.): Povos da Floresta. In: *Instituto de Pesquisa Ambiental da Amazônia*. Online: http://ipam.org.br/glossario/#P, accessed on: 22.05.2017.

Irigaray, Maira (2014): Voices of the Xingu: Antonia Melo, Amazon Warrior (13.02.2014). In: *Amazon Watch*. Online: http://amazonwatch.org/news/2014/0213-voices-of-the-xingu-antonia-melo-amazon-warrior, accessed on: 22.05.2017.

Jagger, Bianca (2012): The Belo Monte Dam: An Environmental Crime (21.06.2012). In: *The Huffington Post*. Online: http://social.huffingtonpost.com/bianca-jagger/the-belo-monte-dam-an-env_b_1614057.html, accessed on: 22.05.2017.

Jary, David and Julia Jary (eds) (1991): *Collins Dictionary of Sociology*. Glasgow: Harper Collins.

Jones, Rhidian (2011): *The Canon Law of the Roman Catholic Church and the Church of England. A Handbook*. 2nd edition. London and New York: T&T Clark International.

Jungmann, Mariana (2010): Dilma destaca importância do projeto da Usina de Belo Monte durante balanço do PAC (04.02.2010). In: *Agência Brasil*. Online: http://memoria.ebc.com.br/agenciabrasil/noticia/2010-02-04/dilma-destaca-importancia-do-projeto-da-usina-de-belo-monte-durante-balanco-do-pac, accessed on: 22.05.2017.

Kelle, Udo (1997): *Empirisch begründete Theoriebildung. Zur Logik und Methodologie interpretativer Sozialforschung*. 2nd edition. Weinheim: Deutscher Studien Verlag.

Kelle, Udo (2011): "Emergence" oder "Forcing"? Einige methodologische Überlegungen zu einem zentralen Problem der Grounded-Theory. In: Günter Mey and Katja Mruck (eds), *Grounded Theory Reader*. 2nd edition. Wiesbaden: VS Verlag für Sozialwissenschaften, p. 235–260.

Keller, Reiner (2005): Analysing Discourse. An Approach From the Sociology of Knowledge. In: *Forum: Qualitative Social Research*, 6(3), Article 32. Online: http://www.qualitative-research.net/index.php/fqs/article/view/19, accessed on: 22.05.2017.

Klandermans, Bert, Hanspeter Kriesi and Sidney Tarrow (1988): *From Structure to Action: Comparing Social Movement Research Across Cultures*. Greenwich: JAI Press.

Klandermans, Bert (1997): *The Social Psychology of Protest*. Oxford: Blackwell.

Kleiber, Tina and Christian Russau (2014): *Der Belo-Monte-Staudamm und die Rolle europäischer Konzerne*. Köln: GegenStrömung. Online: http://www.GegenstroemungOrg/web/wp-content/uploads/2014/07/GegenStr%C3%B6mung_Belo-Monte-und-Europ-Konzerne_2014.pdf, accessed on: 22.05.2017.

Kocka, Jürgen (2004): Civil society from a historical perspective. In: *European Review*, 12(1), p. 65–79.

Kowalchuk, Lisa (2005): The Discourse of Demobilization: Shifts in Activist Priorities and the Framing of Political Opportunities in a Peasant Land Struggle. In: *Sociological Quarterly*, 46(2), p. 237–261.

Kräutler, Erwin and Josef Bruckmoser (2014): *Mein Leben für Amazonien: An der Seite der unterdrückten Völker*. Innsbruck: Tyrolia.

Kräutler, Erwin (2006): *Lebenswelten und Problemfelder in Amazonien heute*. Wien: Picus.

Kräutler, Erwin (2011): *Kämpfen, glauben, hoffen: Mein Leben als Bischof am Amazonas*. 2nd edition. Münsterschwarzach: Vier Türme Verlag.

Kräutler, Erwin (2012): *Rot wie Blut die Blumen: Ein Bischof zwischen Tod und Leben*. Innsbruck: Topos plus.

Kretschmer, Kelsy (2013): Factions/Factionalism. In: David A. Snow, Donatella Della Porta, Bert Klandermans and Doug McAdam (eds), *The Wiley-Blackwell Encyclopedia of Social and Political Movements*. Malden: Blackwell Publishing, p. 443–446.

Kriesi, Hanspeter, Ruud Koopmans, Jan Willem Duyvendak and Marco G. Giugni (1995): *New Social Movements in Western Europe: A Comparative Analysis*. Minneapolis: University of Minnesota Press.

Kruse, Jan, Stephanie Bethmann, Judith Eckert, Debora Niermann and Christian Schmieder (2012a): In und mit fremden Sprachen forschen. Eine empirische Bestandsaufnahme zu Erfahrungs- und Handlungswissen von Forschenden. In: Jan Kruse, Stephanie Bethmann, Debora Niermann and Christian Schmieder (eds), *Qualitative Interviewforschung in und mit fremden Sprachen. Eine Einführung in Theorie und Praxis*. Weinheim and Basel: Beltz Juventa, p. 27–68.

Kruse, Jan, Stephanie Bethmann, Debora Niermann and Christian Schmieder (2012b): Qualitative Interviewforschung im Kontext fremder Sprachen. Eine Einleitung. In: Jan Kruse, Stephanie Bethmann, Debora Niermann and Christian Schmieder (eds), *Qualitative Interviewforschung in und mit fremden Sprachen. Eine Einführung in Theorie und Praxis*. Weinheim and Basel: Beltz Juventa, p. 9–26.

Kruse, Jan and Christian Schmieder (2012): In fremden Gewässern. Ein integratives Basisverfahren als sensibilisierendes Programm für rekonstruktive Analyseprozesse im Kontext fremder Sprachen. In: Jan Kruse, Stephanie Bethmann, Debora Niermann and Christian Schmieder (eds), *Qualitative Interviewforschung in und mit fremden Sprachen. Eine Einführung in Theorie und Praxis*. Weinheim and Basel: Beltz Juventa, p. 248–295.

Kruse, Jan (2015): *Qualitative Interviewforschung: Ein integrativer Ansatz*. Beltz Juventa.

Kuckartz, Udo (2010): *Einführung in die computergestützte Analyse qualitativer Daten*. 3rd edition. Wiesbaden: VS Verlag für Sozialwissenschaften.

Lamen, Darien (2013): Claiming Caribbeanness in the Brazilian Amazon: Lambada, Critical Cosmopolitanism, and the Creation of an Alternative Amazon. In: *Latin American Music Review*, 34(2), p. 131–161.

Landman, Todd (2008): *Issues and Methods in Comparative Politics. An Introduction*. 3rd edition. London et al.: Routledge.

Lapadat, Judith C. (2000): Problematizing transcription: Purpose, paradigm and quality. In: *International Journal of Social Research Methodology*, 3(3), p. 203–219.

Lau, Dora C., and J. Keith Murnighan (1998): Demographic Diversity and Faultlines: The Compositional Dynamics of Organizational Groups. In: *The Academy of Management Review*, 23(2), p. 325–340.

Leme (2009): *Aproveitamento Hidrelétrico Belo Monte. Relatório de Impacto Ambiental - Rima*. Report elaborated by Leme Engenharia for Eletrobrás and the Ministry of Mines and Energy. Online: http://norteenergiasa.com.br/site/wp-content/uploads/2011/04/NE.Rima_.pdf, accessed on: 08.06.2017.

Lima, Maria Regina Soares de, and Monica Hirst (2006): Brazil as an intermediate state and regional power: action, choice and responsibilities. In: *International Affairs*, 82(1), p. 21–40.

Lourenço, Luana (2014): Dilma diz que governo lança PAC 3 em agosto (04.04.2014). In: *Agência Brasil*. Online: http://agenciabrasil.ebc.com.br/politica/noticia/2014-04/dilma-diz-que-governo-lancara-pac-3-em-agosto, accessed on: 25.06.2017.

MAB (2011a): História do MAB: 20 anos de organização, lutas e conquistas. In: *Movimento dos Atingidos por Barragens*. Online: http://www.mabnacional.org.br/historia, accessed on: 08.06.2017.

MAB (2011b): Organização. In: *Movimento dos Atingidos por Barragens*. Online: http://www.mabnacional.org.br/organizacao, accessed on: 08.06.2017.

Macedo, Danilo (2013): Dilma: cumprir prazos de obras do PAC é uma das maiores preocupações do governo (26.11.2013). In: *Agência Brasil*. Online: http://memoria.ebc.com.br/agenciabrasil/noticia/2013-11-26/dilma-cumprir-prazos-de-obras-do-pac-e-uma-das-maiores-preocupacoes-do-governo, accessed on: 08.06.2017.

Machado, Christina (2010): Decreto autoriza a exploração da Usina de Belo Monte pela empresa Norte Energia (27.08.2010). In: *Agência Brasil*. Online: http://memoria.ebc.com.br/agenciabrasil/noticia/2010-08-27/decreto-autoriza-exploracao-da-usina-de-belo-monte-pela-empresa-norte-energia, accessed on: 08.06.2017.

Maihold, Günther and Sebastian A. Müller (2012): Energiepolitik – zentrale Stellschaube für die Entwicklung Brasiliens. In: Dana De la Fontaine and Thomas Stehnken (eds), *Das politische System Brasiliens*. Wiesbaden: VS Verlag für Sozialwissenschaften, p. 300–324.

Mainwaring, Scott (1986): *The Catholic Church and Politics in Brazil, 1916-1985*. Stanford: Stanford University Press.

Maney, Gregory M. (2012): Agreeing for Different Reasons: Ideology, Strategic Differences, and Coalition Dynamics in the Northern Ireland Civil Rights Movement. In: Gregory M. Maney, Rachel V. Kutz-Flamenbaum, Deana A. Rohlinger and Jeff Goodwin (eds), *Strategies for Social Change*. Minneapolis: University of Minnesota Press, p. 170–196.

Marra, Ana Paula (2007): Dilma destaca importância do PAC no atendimento a demandas dos menos favorecidos (27.06.2007). In: *Agência Brasil*. Online: http://memoria.ebc.com.br/agenciabrasil/noticia/2007-06-27/dilma-destaca-importancia-do-pac-no-atendimento-demandas-dos-menos-favorecidos, accessed on: 08.06.2017.

Mauss, Armand L. (1975): *Social Problems as Social Movements*. Philadelphia: Lippincott.

Mayring, Philipp (2010): *Qualitative Inhaltsanalyse. Grundlagen und Techniken*. 11th edition. Weinheim and Basel: Beltz.

McAdam, Doug, John D. McCarthy and Mayer N. Zald (1996): Introduction: Opportunities, mobilizing structures, and framing processes – toward a synthetic, comparative perspective on social movements. In: Doug McAdam, John D. McCarthy and Mayer N. Zald (eds), *Comparative Perspectives on Social Movements. Political Opportunities, Mobilizing Structures, and Cultural Framings*. Cambridge: Cambridge University Press, p. 1–20.

McAllister, Lesley K. (2008): *Making Law Matter: Environmental Protection and Legal Institutions in Brazil*. Stanford: Stanford Law Books.

McCarthy, John D., and Mayer N. Zald (1977): Resource Mobilization and Social Movements: A Partial Theory. In: *American Journal of Sociology*, 82(6), p. 1212–1241.

McCormick, Sabrina (2006): The Brazilian Anti-Dam Movement: Knowledge Contestation as Communicative Action. In: *Organization Environment*, 19(3), p. 321–346.

McCormick, Sabrina (2007a): The Governance of Hydroelectric Dams in Brazil. In: *Journal of Latin American Studies*, 39(2), p. 227–261.

McCormick, Sabrina (2007b): Democratizing Science Movements: A New Framework for Mobilization and Contestation. In: *Social Studies of Science*, 37(4), p. 609–623.

McCormick, Sabrina (2009): *Mobilizing Science: Movements, Participation, and the Remaking of Knowledge*. Philadelphia: Temple University Press.

McCormick, Sabrina (2011): Damming the Amazon: Local Movements and Transnational Struggles Over Water. In: *Society and Natural Resources*, 24(1), p. 34–48.

McCully, Patrick (1996): *Silenced Rivers. The Ecology and Politics of Large Dams*. London: Zed Books.

MCTI (2012): Amazônia: Apresentação. In: *Ministério da Ciência, Tecnologia e Inovação*. Online: http://www.mct.gov.br/index.php/content/view/8116/Apresentacao.html, accessed on: 08.06.2017.

MDS (2016): Povos e Comunidades Tradicionais. In: *Ministério do Desenvolvimento Social*. Online: http://mds.gov.br/acesso-a-informacao/povos-e-comuni dades-tradicionais/povos-e-comunidades-tradicionais, accessed on: 08.06.2017.

Melucci, Alberto (1988): Getting Involved: Identity and Mobilization in Social Movements. In: Bert Klandermans, Hanspeter Kiesi and Sidney Tarrow (eds), *From Structure to Action: Comparing Social Movement Research Across Cultures (International Social Movement Research, Vol. 1)*. Greenwich: JAI Press, p. 329–348.

Melucci, Alberto (1996): *Challenging codes. Collective action in the information age.* Cambridge: Cambridge University Press.

Mercer, Claire (2002): NGOs, civil society and democratization: a critical review of the literature. In: *Progress in Development Studies*, 2(1), p. 5–22.

Merriam Webster (2015): Dictionary. In: *Merriam Webster.* Online: http://www.merriam-webster.com, accessed on: 06.05.2015.

Mey, Günter and Katja Mruck (2009): Methodologie und Methodik der Grounded Theory. In: Wilhelm Kempf and Markus Kiefer (eds), *Forschungsmethoden der Psychologie. Zwischen naturwissenschaftlichem Experient und sozialwissenschaftlicher Hermeneutik. Band 3: Natur und Kultur.* Berlin: Regener, p. 100–152.

Miles, Matthew B. and Michael A. Huberman (1994): *Qualitative Data Analysis: An Expanded Sourcebook*. 2nd edition. Thousand Oaks: SAGE.

Mizruchi, Mark S. (1992): *The Structure of Corporate Political Action: Interfirm Relations and Their Consequences*. Cambridge, MA: Harvard University Press.

MMA (2006): *FVPP – A história do movimento pelo desenvolvimento da Transamazônica e Xingu*. Brasília: Ministério do Meio Ambiente. Online: http://www.mma.gov.br/estruturas/pda/_publicacao/51_publicacao12012011110058.pdf, accessed on: 08.06.2017.

MME and EPE (2011): *Projeto da Usina Hidrelétrica de Belo Monte. Fatos e Dados*. Ministério de Minas e Energia (MME), Empresa de Pesquisa Energética (EPE). Online: http://www.epe.gov.br/leiloes/Documents/Leil%C3%A3o%20Belo%20Monte/Belo%20Monte%20-%20Fatos%20e%20Dados%20-%20POR.pdf, accessed on: 08.06.2017.

MME (2011): *Projeto da Usina Hidrelétrica de Belo Monte. Perguntas mais Frequentes*. Ministério de Minas e Energia. Online: http://www.mme.gov.br/documents/10584/1590364/BELO_MONTE_-_Perguntas_mais_Frequentes.pdf/20edbaee-c096-49a8-b117-22bf0262c80a, accessed on: 08.06.2017.

MP (n.d.): PAC. In: *Ministério do Planejamento, Orçamento e Gestão*. Online: http://www.pac.gov.br, accessed on: 08.06.2017.

Münch, Richard (2004): *Soziologische Theorie. Band 2: Handlungstheorie*. Frankfurt a. M.: Campus Verlag.

MXVPS (n.d.): Quem somos. In: *Movimento Xingu Vivo para Sempre*. Online: http://www.xinguvivo.org.br/quem-somos, accessed on: 25.06.2017.

Nelson, Andrew, and Kenneth M. Chomitz (2011): Effectiveness of Strict vs. Multiple Use Protected Areas in Reducing Tropical Forest Fires: A Global Analysis Using Matching Methods. In: *PLoS ONE*, 6(8), p. e22722.

Norte Energia (2017a): Getting to know Norte Energia S.A. In: *Norte Energia S.A Usina Hidrelétrica Belo Monte*. Online: http://norteenergiasa.com.br/site/ingles/norte-energia, accessed on: 08.06.2017.

Norte Energia (2017b): Shareholding Structure of Norte Energia. In: *Norte Energia S.A Usina Hidrelétrica Belo Monte*. Online: http://norteenergiasa.com.br/site/ingles/shareholding-structure, accessed on: 08.06.2017.

Oberschall, Anthony (1973): *Social Conflict and Social Movements*. Englewood Cliffs: Prentice-Hall.

Oertzen, Jürgen von (2006): Grounded Theory. In: Joachim Behnke, Thomas Gschwend, Delia Schindler and Kai-Uwe Schnapp (eds), *Methoden der Politikwissenschaft. Neuere qualitative und quantitative Analyseverfahren*. Baden-Baden: Nomos.

Oliveira, Mariana (2010): Obra nem começou, mas já atrai migrantes e investimento para Altamira (06.04.2010). In: *G1*. Online: http://g1.globo.com/Noticias/Economia_Negocios/0,,MUL1547975-9356,00-OBRA+NEM+COMECOU+MAS+JA+ATRAI+MIGRANTES+E+INVESTIMENTO+PARA+ALTAMIRA.html, accessed on: 08.06.2017.

Oliveira, Nielmar de (2014): EPE: demanda de energia crescerá 4,3% por ano até 2023 (23.01.2014). In: *Agência Brasil*. Online: http://agenciabrasil.ebc.com.br/economia/noticia/2014-01/epe-demanda-de-energia-crescera-43-por-ano-ate-2023, accessed on: 08.06.2017.

Opp, Karl-Dieter (2009): *Theories of Political Protest and Social Movements. A multidisciplinary introduction, critique, and synthesis*. London et al.: Routledge.

Ordoñez, Ramona and Danilo Fariello (2017): Consórcio de Belo Monte busca comprador para usina (11.02.2017). Online: http://oglobo.globo.com/economia/consorcio-de-belo-monte-busca-comprador-para-usina-20910492, accessed on: 23.03.2017.

Painel de Especialistas (2009): *Análise Crítica do Estudo de Impacto Ambiental do Aproveitamento Hidrelétrico de Belo Monte*. Edited by Sônia Maria Simões Barbosa Magalhães Santos and Francisco del Moral Hernandez. Belém. Online: http://www.socioambiental.org/banco_imagens/pdfs/Belo_Monte_Painel_especialistas_EIA.pdf, accessed on: 08.06.2017.

Palmares (2017): Comunidades Remanescentes de Quilombos (CRQ's). In: *Fundação Cultural Palmares*. Online: http://www.palmares.gov.br/?page_id=37551, accessed on: 08.06.2017.

Pearlman, Wendy (2011): *Violence, Nonviolence, and the Palestinian National Movement*. Cambridge: Cambridge University Press.

Peduzzi, Pedro (2015): Aneel nega pedido de alteração no cronograma das obras de Belo Monte (07.05.2015). In: *Agência Brasil*. Online: http://agenciabrasil.ebc.com.br/geral/noticia/2015-04/aneel-nega-pedido-de-alteracao-no-cronograma-da-usina-de-belo-monte, accessed on: 09.06.2017.

Peters, Ina (May 2014): *Too Abstract to Be Feasible? Applying the Grounded Theory Method in Social Movement Research*. GIGA Working Paper, No. 247. Hamburg: GIGA German Institute of Global and Area Studies. Online: http://www.giga-hamburg.de/de/publication/too-abstract-to-be-feasible-applying-the-grounded-theory-method-in-social-movement, accessed on: 09.06.2017.

Polletta, Francesca, and James M. Jasper (2001): Collective Identity and Social Movements. In: *Annual Review of Sociology*, 27, p. 283–305.

Pondy, Louis R. (1967): Organizational Conflict: Concepts and Models. In: *Administrative Science Quarterly*, 12(2), p. 296–320.

Portal Amazônia (2017): População da Amazônia. In: *Amazônia de A a Z*. Online: http://portalamazonia.com.br/secao/amazoniadeaz/interna.php?id=266, accessed on: 09.06.2017.

Portal Brasil (2014a): Saiba mais sobre o Ministério Público do Brasil (28.07.2014). In: *Portal Brasil*. Online: http://www.brasil.gov.br/governo/2010/01/ministerio-publico, accessed on: 24.06.2017.

Portal Brasil (2014b): População (28.07.2014). In: *Portal Brasil*. Online: http://www.brasil.gov.br/governo/2009/11/populacao, accessed on: 24.06.2017.

Portal Brasil (2015): Dilma inaugura parque eólico e ressalta importância de diversificar a matriz energética (27.02.2015). In: *Portal Brasil*. Online: http://www.brasil.gov.br/infraestrutura/2015/02/dilma-inaugura-parque-eolico-e-resalta-importancia-de-diversificar-a-matriz-energetica, accessed on: 24.06.2017.

Portal Brasil (May 2016): Dilma inaugura usina hidrelétrica de Belo Monte (05.05.2016). In: *Portal Brasil*. Online: http://www.brasil.gov.br/governo/2016/05/dilma-inaugura-usina-hidreletrica-de-belo-monte, accessed on: 23.03.2017.

Prelazia do Xingu (2010): Lebenslauf. In: *Dom Erwin Kräutler unterwegs mit dem Volk Gottes am Xingu*. Online: http://www.domerwin.com/lebensweg/cv-dom-erwin.html, accessed on: 09.06.2017.

Programa de Comunicação Indígena – UHE Belo Monte (2011): *UHE Belo Monte e as Comunidades Indigenas - Acompanhamento*. Fundação Nacional do Índio. Online: http://www.funai.gov.br/arquivos/conteudo/cogedi/pdf/Outras_Publicacoes/UHE_BeloMonte/Cartilha_UHE_Belo_Monte_e_Comunidades_Web.pdf, accessed on: 09.06.2017.

Provinzialat der Missionare vom Kostbaren Blut (ed) (1992): *Xingu Briefe 92*. Salzburg/Traunstein.

Przyborski, Aglaja and Monika Wohlrab-Sahr (2010): *Qualitative Sozialforschung. Ein Arbeitsbuch*. 3rd edition. München: Oldenbourg.

Ragin, Charles C. (1992): "Casing" and the process of social inquiry. In: Charles C. Ragin and Howard S. Becker (eds), *What is a Case? Exploring the Foundations of Social Inquiry*. Cambridge: Cambridge University Press.

Ramos, Alcida Rita (n.d.): *Belo Monte: A crônica de um desastre anunciado*. Brasília: Associação Brasileira de Antropologia. Online: www.abant.org.br/file?id=171, accessed on: 09.06.2017.

Reinhold, Gerd, Siegfried Lamnek and Helga Recker (1997): *Soziologie-Lexikon*. 3rd edition. München et al.: Oldenbourg.

Reis, Claudio (2012): Belo Monte e o Progresso. In: *Sociologia*, 4(40), p. 24–31.

Rokkan, Stein (1970): *Citizens, elections, parties: approaches to the comparative study of the processes of development*. Scandinavian university books. Oslo: Universitetsforlaget.

Rothman, Franklin D., and Pamela Oliver (1999): From Local to Global: The Anti-Dam Movement in Southern Brazil, 1979-1992. In: *Mobilization*, 4(1), p. 41–57.

Rothman, Franklin D. (2001): A Comparative Study of Dam-Resistance Campaigns and Environmental Policy in Brazil. In: *The Journal of Environment Development*, 10(4), p. 317–344.

Rucht, Dieter (1995): Kollektive Identität: Konzeptionelle Überlegungen zu einem Desiderat der Bewegungsforschung. In: *Forschungsjournal Neue Soziale Bewegungen*, 8(1), p. 9–23.

Rucht, Dieter (2002): Transnationale Öffentlichkeiten und Identitäten in neuen sozialen Bewegungen. In: Hartmut Kaelble, Martin Kirsch and Alexander Schmidt-Gernig (eds), *Transnationale Öffentlichkeiten und Identitäten im 20. Jahrhundert*. Frankfurt a. M.: Campus Verlag, p. 327–351.

Rucht, Dieter (2011a): Lassen sich personale, soziale und kollektive Identität sinnvoll voneinander abgrenzen? In: *Forschungsjournal Soziale Bewegungen*, 24(4), p. 26–29.

Rucht, Dieter (2011b): The Strength of Weak Identities. In: *Forschungsjournal Soziale Bewegungen*, 24(4), p. 73–84.

Rucht, Dieter (2012): Leadership in Social and Political Movements: A Comparative Exploration. In: Ludger Helms (ed), *Comparative Political Leadership*. Houndmills: Palgrave Macmillan, p. 99–118.

Rucht, Dieter (2013): Schlüsselfiguren statt Führer: Zur (Selbst-)Steuerung sozialer Bewegungen. In: *Forschungsjournal Soziale Bewegungen*, 26(4), p. 32–43.

Salazar-Lopez, Leila (2011): Sheyla Juruna Shares the Truth About Belo Monte at Events in NY, DC and SF (23.09.2011). In: *Amazon Watch*. Online: http://amazonwatch.org/news/2011/0923-sheyla-juruna-shares-the-truth-about-belo-monte-at-events-in-ny-dc-and-sf, accessed on: 09.06.2017.

Sandstrom, Kent L., Daniel D. Martin and Gary A. Fine (2010): *Symbols, Selves, and Social Reality. A symbolic interactionist approach to social psychology and sociology*. 3rd edition. New York / Oxford: Oxford University Press.

Sartori, Giovanni (1970): Concept Misformation in Comparative Politics. In: *The American Political Science Review*, 64(4), p. 1033–1053.

Scaramuzzo, Mônica and Renée Pereira (2017): Controle da usina de Belo Monte é colocado à venda por R$ 10 bilhões (10.02.2017). In: *O Estado de S. Paulo*. Online: http://economia.estadao.com.br/noticias/negocios,controle-da-usina-de-belo-monte-e-colocado-a-venda-por-r-10-bilhoes,70001660269, accessed on: 23.03.2017.

Scherer-Warren, Ilse, and Ligia Helena Hahn Lüchmann (2004): Situando o debate sobre movimentos sociais e sociedade civil no Brasil – Introdução. In: *Política & Sociedade*, 3(5), p. 13–36.

Scherer-Warren, Ilse (2015): Desafios para uma sociologia política brasileira: os elos entre movimentos e instituições. In: *Sociologias*, 17(38), p. 44–62.

Schilling-Vacaflor, Almut, and Riccarda Flemmer (2015): Conflict Transformation through Prior Consultation? Lessons from Peru. In: *Journal of Latin American Studies*, 47(4), p. 811–839.

Schmalz, Stefan (2012): Die brasilianische Wirtschaftspolitik seit dem Ende der Militärdiktatur: Von der Krise der Importsubstitution zum Programa de Aceleração de Crescimento. In: Dana De la Fontaine and Thomas Stehnken (eds), *Das politische System Brasiliens*. Wiesbaden: VS Verlag für Sozialwissenschaften, p. 365–280.

Scholz, Imme, Daniel Dräger, Isabelle Floer, Constanze Neher and Julia Unger (2003): *Handlungsspielräume zivilgesellschaftlicher Gruppen und Chancen für kooperative Umweltpolitik in Amazonien. Darstellung anhand des Staudamms von Belo Monte und der Bundesstraße BR-163*. Berichte und Gutachten 12/2003. Bonn: Deutsches Institut für Entwicklungspolitik.

Schulz, Ole (2013): Wie die brasilianische Justiz für und gegen den Megastaudamm Belo Monte kämpft (02.05.2013). In: *Heinrich-Böll-Stiftung*.

Online: http://www.boell.de/de/2013/05/02/wie-die-brasilianische-justiz-fuer-und-gegen-den-megastaudamm-belo-monte-kaempft, accessed on: 09.06.2017.

Schütz, Alfred and Thomas Luckmann (2003): *Strukturen der Lebenswelt*. 1st edition. UTB. Stuttgart: UVK.

Schwartzman, Luisa Farah (2008): Who are the Blacks? In: *Cahiers de la recherche sur l'éducation et les saviors*, 7, p. 27–47.

Scott, John (2000): *Social Network Analysis. A Handbook*. 2nd edition. London: SAGE.

Secretaria Executiva do CGDEX (n.d.): O PDRS Xingu. In: *Plano de Desenvolvimento Regional Sustentável do Xingu*. Online: http://www.pdrsxingu.org.br/apresentacao.aspx, accessed on: 09.06.2017.

Shoemaker, Pamela J., James W. Tankard Jr. and Dominic L. Lasorsa (2004): *How to Build Social Science Theories*. Thousand Oaks: SAGE.

Shriver, Thomas E., and Chris Messer (2009): Ideological Cleavages and Schism in the Czech Environmental Movement. In: *Human Ecology Review*, 16(2), p. 161–171.

Sikkink, Kathryn (1991): *Ideas and Institutions. Developmentalism in Brazil and Argentina*. Ithaca: Cornell University Press.

Silva, Josiele Sousa da (2011): Movimento Xingu Vivo para Sempre e o Discurso da Contestação contra Belo Monte. Paper presented at the conference "Conferência de Mídia Cidadã. Amazônia e o direito de comunicar", 20.-22.10.2011, Belém, Brazil. Online: http://www.unicentro.br/redemc/2011/conteudo/mc_artigos/Midia_Cidada_Silva.pdf, accessed on: 09.06.2017.

Silva, Lindomar de Jesus de Sousa and Tânia Nazarena de Oliveira Miranda (2010): Resistencia e articulação de atores sociais contra a construção da hidrelétrica de Belo Monte: A contribuição da Igeja Católica. Paper presented at the conference "III Encontro Latinoamericano Ciências Sociais e Barragens", 30.11.-03.12.2010, Belém, Brazil. Online: https://caritasnorte2.files.wordpress.com/2010/12/iii-encontro-latino-americano.pdf, accessed on: 09.06.2017.

Simmel, Georg (1955): *Conflict and the Web of Group Affiliations*. Glencoe: Free Press.

Simmel, George (1950): *The Sociology of Georg Simmel*. Glencoe: Free Press.

Simon, Bernd (2011): Was ist der beste methodische Zugang? Nicht über unsere Köpfe hinweg! Kollektive Identität als sozialpsychologisches Konzept. In: *Forschungsjournal Soziale Bewegungen*, 24(4), p. 39–41.

Simon, Roger (1991): *Gramsci's political thought: an introduction*. London: Lawrence & Wishart.

Skvoretz, John, and Katherine Faust (1999): Logit Models for Affiliation Networks. In: *Sociological Methodology*, 29, p. 253–280.

Smelser, Neil J. (1962): *Theory of Collective Behavior.* New York: The Free Press.

Snow, David A. and Robert D. Benford (1988): Ideology, frame resonance, and participant mobilization. In: Bert Klandermans, Hanspeter Kiesi and Sidney Tarrow (eds), *From Structure to Action: Comparing Social Movement Research Across Cultures (International Social Movement Research, Vol. 1)*. Greenwich: JAI Press, p. 197–217.

Snow, David A. and Robert D. Benford (1992): Master Frames and Cycles of Protest. In: Aldon D. Morris and Carol McClurg Mueller (eds), *Frontiers in Social Movement Theory.* New Haven: Yale University Press, p. 133–155.

Snow, David A. and Pamela E. Oliver (1995): Social Movements and Collective Behavior: Social Psychological Dimensions and Considerations. In: Karen S. Cook, Gary A. Fine and James S. House (eds), *Sociological Perspectives on Social Psychology.* Boston et al.: Allyn and Bacon, p. 571–599.

Snow, David A., Burke E. Jr. Rochford, Steven K. Worden, and Robert D. Benford (1986): Frame Alignment Processes, Micromobilization and Movement Participation. In: *American Sociological Review*, 51(4), p. 456–581.

Snow, David A., Sarah A. Soule and Hanspeter Kriesi (2008): Mapping the Terrain. In: David A. Snow, Sarah A. Soule and Hanspeter Kriesi (eds), *The Blackwell Companion to Social Movements*. Malden: Blackwell Publishing, p. 3–16.

Snow, David A. (2001): Collective Identity and Expressive Forms. In: Neil J. Smelser and Paul B. Baltes (eds), *International Encyclopedia of the Social & Behavioral Sciences. Vol. 4*. London: Elsevier, p. 2212–2219.

Snow, David A. (2008): Framing Processes, Ideologies, and Discursive Fields. In: David A. Snow, Sarah A. Soule and Hanspeter Kriesi (eds), *The Blackwell Companion to Social Movements*. 2nd edition. Malden: Blackwell Publishing, p. 380–412.

Snow, David and Doug McAdam (2000): Identity Work Processes in the Context of Social Movements: Clarifying the Identity/Movement Nexus. In: Sheldon Stryker, Timothy J. Owens and Robert W. White (eds), *Self, Identity, and Social Movements*, p. 41–67.

Sousa Júnior, Wilson Cabral de, John Reid and Neidja Cristine Silvestre Leitão (2006): *Custos e benefícios do complexo hidrelétrico Belo Monte: Uma abordagem econômico-ambiental*. Online: http://www.iieb.org.br/index.php/download_file/866/1086, accessed on: 09.06.2017.

Sousa Júnior, Wilson Cabral de, and John Reid (2010): Uncertainties in Amazon hydropower development: Risk scenarios and environmental issues around the Belo Monte dam. In: *Water Alternatives*, 3(2), p. 249–268.

Staggenborg, Suzanne (2008): *Social Movements*. Oxford: Oxford University Press.

Stark, Rodney and William S. Bainbridge (1985): *The Future of Religion: Secularization, Revival, and Cult Formation*. Berkeley and Los Angeles: University of California Press.

Steinke, Ines (2005): Gütekriterien qualitativer Forschung. In: Uwe Flick, Ernst von Kardorff and Ines Steinke (eds), *Qualitative Forschung. Ein Handbuch*. 4th edition. Reinbek: Rowohlt, p. 319–331.

Stekelenburg, Jacquelien van (2013): Collective Identity. In: David A. Snow, Donatella Della Porta, Bert Klandermans and Doug McAdam (eds), *The Wiley-Blackwell Encyclopedia of Social and Political Movements*. Chichester: Blackwell Publishing.

Stickler, Claudia M., Michael T. Coe, Marcos H. Costa, Daniel C. Nepstad, David G. McGrath, Livia C. P. Dias, Hermann O. Rodrigues, and Britaldo S. Soares-Filho (2013): Dependence of hydropower energy generation on forests in the Amazon Basin at local and regional scales. In: *Proceedings of the National Academy of Sciences*, 110(23), p. 9601–9606.

Stock, Jonathan (2013): Der Rest vom Paradies (28.01.2013). In: *Der Spiegel*. Online: http://www.spiegel.de/spiegel/print/d-90750480.html, accessed on: 09.06.2017.

Storm, Peter (2013): In Brazil, a dual struggle against neoliberalism (17.06.2013). In: *ROARMAG.org reflections on a revolution*. Online: http://roarmag.org/2013/06/brazil-sao-paulo-protests-bus-fares/, accessed on: 09.06.2017.

Strauss, Anselm L. (1998): *Grundlagen qualitativer Sozialforschung. Datenanalyse und Theoriebildung in der empirischen soziologischen Forschung*. 2nd edition. München: Wilhelm Fink Verlag.

Stryker, Sheldon, Timothy J. Owens and Robert W. White (2000a): Introduction. Social Psychology and Social Movements: Cloudy Past and Bright Future. In: Sheldon Stryker, Timothy J. Owens and Robert W. White (eds), *Self, Identity, and Social Movements*, p. 1–17.

Stryker, Sheldon, Timothy J. Owens and Robert W. White (eds) (2000b): *Self, Identity, and Social Movements*. Minneapolis and London: University of Minnesota Press.

Stryker, Sheldon (2000): Identity Competition: Key to Differential Social Movement Participation? In: Sheldon Stryker, Timothy J. Owens and Robert W. White (eds), *Self, Identity, and Social Movements*. Minneapolis and London: University of Minnesota Press, p. 21–40.

Survival International (n.d.): Belo Monte-Staudamm. In: *Survival*. Online: http://www.survivalinternational.de/ueber/belo-monte, accessed on: 09.06.2017.

Szanton, David L. (2004): Introduction. The Origin, Nature, and Challenges of Area Studies in the United States. In: David L. Szanton (ed), *The Politics of Knowledge: Area Studies and the Disciplines*. Berkeley, Los Angeles and London: University of California Press, p. 1–33.

Telles, Edward Eric (2004): *Race in Another America: The Significance of Skin Color in Brazil*. Princeton: Princeton University Press.

Teune, Simon (2008): "Gibt es so etwas überhaupt noch?" Forschung zu Protest und sozialen Bewegungen. In: *Politische Vierteljahresschrift*, 49(3), p. 528–547.

The Economist (2013): Dams in the Amazon. The rights and wrongs of Belo Monte (04.05.2013). In: *The Economist*. Online: http://www.economist.com/news/americas/21577073-having-spent-heavily-make-worlds-third-biggest-hydroelectric-project-greener-brazil, accessed on: 09.06.2017.

Tilly, Charles (1978): *From Mobilization to Revolution*. Reading: Addison-Wesley Publishing Company.

Toni, Fabiano (2007): *Party Politics, Social Movements, and Local Democracy: Institutional Choices in the Brazilian Amazon*. Working Paper, No. 32. Online: http://pdf.wri.org/wp32_ftoni.pdf, accessed on: 09.06.2017.

Touraine, Alain (1973): *Production de la société*. Paris: Edition du Seuil.

Turner, Ralph H. and Lewis M. Killian (1987): *Collective Behavior.* 3rd edition. Englewood Cliffs: Prentice Hall.

Turner, Terence, and Vanessa Fajans-Turner (2006): Political innovation and inter-ethnic alliance. Kayapo resistance to the developmentalist state. In: *Anthropology Today*, 22(5), p. 3–10.

Umbuzeiro, Antônio Ubirajara Bogea and Ubirajara Marques Umbuzeiro (2012): *Altamira e sua História*. 4th edition. Belém: Ponto Press.

UOL (2009a): Michaelis Moderno Dicionário Inglês & Português. In: *Dicionários Michaelis*. Online: http://michaelis.uol.com.br/moderno/ingles/index.php, accessed on: 09.06.2017.

UOL (2009b): Michaelis Moderno Dicionário da Língua Portuguesa. In: *Dicionários Michaelis*. Online: http://michaelis.uol.com.br/moderno/portugues/index.php, accessed on: 09.06.2017.

Vanden, Harry E. (2014): Brazil: Taking the Streets, Swaming Public Spaces: The 2013 Popular Protests. In: Richard Stahler-Sholk, Harry E. Vanden and Marc Becker (eds), *Rethinking Latin American Social Movements: Radical Action from Below.* Lanham: Rowman & Littlefield, p. 233–250.

Verdum, Ricardo (2011): *Belo Monte e seus impactos sobre os povos indígenas*. Interview with Ricardo Verdum, conducted by IHU On-Line on 23.02.2011. Portal EcoDebate. Online: http://www.ecodebate.com.br/2011/02/23/belo-monte-e-seus-impactos-sobre-os-povos-indigenas-entrevista-com-ricardo-verdum, accessed on: 09.06.2017.

Wasserman, Stanley and Katherine Faust (1994): *Social Network Analysis: Methods and Applications*. Cambridge: Cambridge University Press.

Wellman, Barry (1988): Structural analysis: from method and metaphor to theory and substance. In: Barry Wellman and S. D. Berkowitz (eds), *Social structures: a network approach*. Cambridge: Cambridge University Press, p. 19–61.

Westle, Bettina (2005): „Identität und Äquivalenz". Der Vergleich in der internationalen Survey-Forschung. In: Sabine Kropp and Michael Minkenberg (eds), *Vergleichen in der Politikwissenschaft*. Wiesbaden: VS Verlag für Sozialwissenschaften, p. 140–167.

Worchel, Stephen, Dawna Coutant-Sassic and Michele Grossman (1992): A Developmental Approach to Group Dynamics: A Model and Illustrative

Reserach. In: Stephen Worchel, Wendy Wood and Jeffry A. Simpson (eds), *Group Process and Productivity*. London: SAGE, p. 181–202.

World Bank (2013): Brazil Protects the Amazon (09.10.2013). In: *The World Bank*. Online: http://www.worldbank.org/en/results/2013/10/09/Brazil-protects-Amazon-increasing-size-protected-areas, accessed on: 09.06.2017.

Zald, Mayer N., and Roberta Ash (March 1966): Social Movement Organizations: Growth, Decay and Change. In: *Social Forces*, 44(3), p. 327.

Zellhuber, Andrea (2012): Umweltpolitik in Brasilien. Spannungsfeld zwischen Umweltschutz und Wachstumsideologie. In: Dana De la Fontaine and Thomas Stehnken (eds), *Das politische System Brasiliens*. Wiesbaden: VS Verlag für Sozialwissenschaften, p. 347–366.

Zinecker, Heidrun (2011): Civil Society in Developing Countries. Conceptual Considerations. In: *Journal of Conflictology*, 2(1), p. 1–18.

Annex

Annex 1: List of Expert Interviews

Interviews conducted in São Paulo, Brazil

Date	Affiliation of interviewee/ Area of expertise	Language
14.10.2011	University of São Paulo (Universidade de São Paulo, USP) / Brazilian Center for Analysis and Planning (Centro Brasileiro de Análise e Planejamento, CEBRAP)	English
15.10.2011	Activist	Portuguese
15.10.2011	Activist	Portuguese
15.10.2011	Activist	English
19.10.2011	University of São Paulo (Universidade de São Paulo, USP)	English
19.10.2011	University of São Paulo (Universidade de São Paulo, USP)	English
20.10.2011	Friedrich Ebert Foundation (Friedrich Ebert Stiftung, FES)	English
21.10.2011	Brazilian Association of Non-Governmental Organizations (Associação Brasileira de Organizações não Governamentais, ABONG)	English
21.10.2011	Movement of Dam Affected People (Movimento dos Atingidos por Barragens, MAB)	Portuguese

Date	Affiliation of interviewee/ Area of expertise	Language
24.10.2011	Friedrich Ebert Foundation (Friedrich Ebert Stiftung, FES)	German

Interviews conducted in Brasília, Brazil

Date	Affiliation of interviewee/ Area of expertise	Language
26.10.2011	National Foundation for Indians (Fundação Nacional do Índio, FUNAI)	Portuguese
26.10.2011	Intellectual and activist	Portuguese
27.10.2011	Amazon Working Group (Grupo de Trabalho Amazônico, GTA)	Portuguese
27.10.2011	World Wide Fund For Nature (WWF)	English
28.10.2011	Protected Forest Association (Associação Floresta Protegida, AFP)	English
28.10.2011	Greenpeace	Portuguese
31.10.2011	Articulation of the Indigenous Peoples of Brazil (Articulação dos Povos Indígenas do Brasil, APIB) / Coordination of the Indigenous Organizations of the Brazilian Amazon (Coordenação das Organizações Indígenas da Amazônia Brasileira, COIAB)	Portuguese
31.10.2011	Xingu Indigenous Land Association (Associação Terra Indígena Xingu, ATIX)	Portuguese
31.10.2011	Indigenous Missionary Council (Conselho Indigenista Missionário, CIMI)	Portuguese

Date	Affiliation of interviewee/ Area of expertise	Language
31.10.2011	International Institute of Education of Brasil (Instituto Internacional de Educação do Brasil, IEB)	English
01.11.2011	Institute for Socioeconomic Studies (Insituto de Estudos Socioeconômicos, Inesc)	Portuguese
01.11.2011	The Nature Conservancy (TNC)	English
02.11.2011	Federal Public Ministry (Ministério Público Federal, MPF)	German
03.11.2011	University of Brasília (Universidade de Brasília, UnB)	English
04.11.2011	Socio-Environmental Institute (Instituto Socioambiental, ISA)	Portuguese
04.11.2011	International Rivers	English

Interviews conducted in Rio de Janeiro, Brazil

Date	Affiliation of interviewee/ Area of expertise	Language
07.11.2011	Ford Foundation	English
07.11.2011	Brazilian Center for International Relations (Centro Brasileiro de Relações Internacionais, CEBRI)	Portuguese
09.11.2011	Global Justice (Justiça Global)	English
10.11.2011	Federal University of Rio de Janeiro (Universidade Federal do Rio de Janeiro, UFRJ)	English

Date	Affiliation of interviewee/ Area of expertise	Language
11.11.2017	Federation of Organs for Social and Educational Assistance (Federação de Órgãos para Assistência Social e Educacional, FASE) / Brazilian Network of Environmental Justice (Rede Brasileira de Justiça Ambiental, RBJA)	Portuguese

Annex 2: List of Activist Interview

Document ID[1]	Date	Affiliation of interviewee/ Area of expertise	Language
*	07.05.2012	Attorney of the Republic for the State of Pará (Procurador da República no Pará)	English
P1	07.05.2012	Forum of the Eastern Amazon (Fórum da Amazônia Oriental, FAOR)	Portuguese
P3	08.05.2012	Metropolitan Committee (Comitê Metropolitano)	Portuguese
P51	09.05.2012	Pastoral Land Commission (Comissão Pastoral da Terra, CPT)	Portuguese
P16	11.05.2012	National Conference of Bishops of Brazil (Conferência Nacional dos Bispos do Brasil, CNBB)	Portuguese
P53	11.05.2012	Brazilian Caritas (Cáritas Brasileira)	Portuguese
P21	11.05.2012	Institute for a Solidary and Sustainable Amazonia (Instituto Amazônia Solidária e Sustentável, IAMAS) / Metropolitan Committee (Comitê Metropolitano)	Portuguese
P55	14.05.2012	Society for the Defense of Human Rights of Pará (Sociedade Paraense de Defesa dos Direitos Humanos, SDDH)	Portuguese
P41	17.05.2012/ 18.05.2012	Foundation Live, Produce, Preserve (Fundação Viver Produzir e Preservar, FVPP)	Portuguese

1 Interviews marked with an asterisk were not included in the analysis. All other interviews were transcribed by the research assistant and revised and analyzed by the author of this study.

Document ID	Date	Affiliation of interviewee/ Area of expertise	Language
P37	18.05.2012/ 19.05.2012	Socio-Environmental Institute (Instituto Socioambiental, ISA)	Portuguese
P49	21.05.2012	Cleric	Portuguese
P23	23.05.2012	Movement of Dam Affected People (Movimento dos Atingidos por Barragens, MAB)	Portuguese
*	23.05.2012	Union of Workers in Public Education of Pará (Sindicato dos Trabalhadores em Educação Pública do Pará, SINTEPP)	Portuguese
*	24.05.2012	Cacao farmer	Portuguese
*	24.05.2012	Cacao farmer	Portuguese
P25	25.05.2012	Association of Urban and Rural Women (Associação de Mulheres Urbanas e Rurais)	Portuguese
*	26.05.2012	Women's Movement (Movimento de Mulheres) / Health Council (Conselho de Saúde)	Portuguese
P27	28.05.2012	Black Movement (Movimento Negro)	Portuguese
P39	29.05.2012	Federation of Agricultural Workers (Federação dos Trabalhadores e Trabalhadoras na Agricultura, FETAGRI)	Portuguese
P29	30.05.2012	Indigenous activist	Portuguese
*	30.05.2012	Santafé Ideias, enterprise commissioned with the external communication of Norte Energia	Portuguese
P13	31.05.2012	Cleric	Portuguese
P31	31.05.2012	S.O.S. Life (S.O.S. Vida)	Portuguese

Document ID	Date	Affiliation of interviewee/ Area of expertise	Language
P19	01.06.2012	Indigenous Missionary Council (Conselho Indigenista Missionário, CIMI)	Portuguese
P47	01.06.2012	Cleric	Portuguese
P9	03.06.2012	Xingu Forever Alive Movement (Movimento Xingu Vivo Para Sempre, MXVPS)	Portuguese
P35	06.06.2012	Foundation Live, Produce, Preserve (Fundação Viver Produzir e Preservar, FVPP)	Portuguese
P43	07.06.2012	Cleric	Portuguese

Secondary Source

Document ID	Type	Language
P45	Interview with Erwin Kräutler conducted by Eliane Brum and published in the magazin Época (Brum 2012)	Portugues

MIX
Papier aus verantwortungsvollen Quellen
Paper from responsible sources
FSC® C105338

If you have any concerns about our products,
you can contact us on
ProductSafety@springernature.com

In case Publisher is established outside the EU,
the EU authorized representative is:
Springer Nature Customer Service Center GmbH
Europaplatz 3, 69115 Heidelberg, Germany

Printed by Libri Plureos GmbH
in Hamburg, Germany